The Sub-national Dimension of the EU

Carlo Panara

The Sub-national Dimension of the EU

A Legal Study of Multilevel Governance

 Springer

Carlo Panara
School of Law
Liverpool John Moores University
Liverpool
United Kingdom

ISBN 978-3-319-14588-4   ISBN 978-3-319-14589-1   (eBook)
DOI 10.1007/978-3-319-14589-1

Library of Congress Control Number: 2015932774

Springer Cham Heidelberg New York Dordrecht London

Printed on acid-free paper

Springer International Publishing AG Switzerland is part of Springer Science+Business Media
(www.springer.com)

Ad Alessandra Maria, Ali, mia figlia,
Carlo, il tuo papà

Foreword

I would like to express my gratitude to Prof. Dr. Martin Nettesheim for a very valuable discussion on this project and for hosting me so wonderfully at Tübingen University during its execution. I am also indebted to the Alexander von Humboldt Foundation for supporting this research with a Fellowship for Experienced Researchers and to Springer, particularly in the person of Dr. Brigitte Reschke, for publishing this monograph. I would also like to thank Erin O'Leary, research assistant at Liverpool John Moores University, for her precious help during the initial stage of the research and my friend Dr. Michael Varney, from Hull University, for revising the final manuscript. Finally and most importantly, I would like to declare my unconditional love and gratitude to my parents in Italy for all they have done and still do for me.

Tübingen, Germany   Carlo Panara
October 2014

Friends, Romans, countrymen, lend me your ears;
I come to bury Caesar, not to praise him.
The evil that men do lives after them;
The good is oft interred with their bones;
So let it be with Caesar.

[From Mark Anthony's speech
in *Julius Caesar*, Act 3, Scene 2
by William Shakespeare]

List of Principal Abbreviations

AER	Assembly of European Regions
AG	Advocate General
BGBl	Bundesgesetzblatt (Germany)
BOE	Boletín Oficial del Estado (Spain)
BVerfGE	Entscheidungen des Bundesverfassungsgericht (Germany)
B-VG	Bundes-Verfassungsgesetz (Austria)
CALRE	Conference of European Regional Legislative Assemblies
CARCE	Conferencia para Asuntos Relacionados con las Comunidades Europeas (Spain)
CdR	Comité des régions
CDU	Christlich Demokratische Union Deutschlands
CEMR	Council of European Municipalities and Regions
CFI	Court of First Instance
CFSP	Common Foreign and Security Policy
CJEU	Court of Justice of the European Union
CoR	Committee of the Regions
CUP	Cambridge University Press
EC	European Community
ECHR	European Convention on Human Rights
ECI	European Citizens' Initiative
ECJ	European Court of Justice
ECR	European Court Reports
EEC	European Economic Community
EMK	Europaministerkonferenz
EP	European Parliament
ERDF	European Regional Development Fund
EU	European Union
EULG	Gesetz über die Beteiligung des Landtags in Angelegenheiten der Europäischen Union

EUV	Vertrag über die Europäische Union
EUZBLG	Gesetz über die Zusammenarbeit von Bund und Ländern in Angelegenheiten der Europäischen Union (Germany)
EWS	Early Warning System
FAG	Finanzausgleichsgesetz (Germany)
GC	General Court
GG	Grundgesetz (Germany)
LEP	Local enterprise partnership
LJMU	Liverpool John Moores University
MBO	Merseyside Brussels Office
MEP	Member of the European Parliament
MLG	Multilevel governance
MoU	Memorandum of Understanding (UK)
MP	Member of Parliament
OJ	Official Journal of the European Union
OUP	Oxford University Press
P	Pourvoi
REGLEG	Conference of European Regions with Legislative Power
Rn	Randnummer
Rz	Randzahl (or Randziffer)
SMN	Subsidiarity Monitoring Network
SPD	Sozialdemokratische Partei Deutschlands
TEC	Treaty establishing the European Community
TEU	Treaty on the European Union
TFEU	Treaty on the Functioning of the European Union
TUEL	Testo Unico degli Enti Locali (Italy)
UKRep	United Kingdom Permanent Representation to the European Union
VfSlg	Sammlung der Erkentnisse und wichtigsten Beschlüsse des Verfassungsgerichtshofes (Austria)

Contents

Chapter 1
Introduction: A Legal Study of Multilevel Governance

A. Why a Legal Study of Multilevel Governance?

The notion of 'governance' is typically used to indicate a new mode of governing that is distinct from the hierarchical model of the past. It is a cooperative mode of governing where non-state players are involved in authoritative decision-making in the public sphere through public or private networks. Significantly, Schmitter and Kim write that 'MLG can be defined as an arrangement for making binding decisions that engages a multiplicity of politically independent but otherwise interdependent actors – *private and public* – at different levels of territorial aggregation in more-or-less continuous negotiation/deliberation/implementation' (emphasis added).[1] Accordingly, in the phrase 'multilevel governance', the adjective 'multilevel' refers to the increased interdependence between different political arenas (national, sub-national, supranational), whilst the term 'governance' signals the growing interdependence between public authorities and nongovernmental actors at various territorial levels.[2] Aligned with the Committee of the Regions' 2009 *White Paper on Multilevel Governance*, this study focuses on the role of public authorities that are expression of a territorial community (territorial authorities),[3] that is, according to the terminology used by the Italian legal scholar Massimo Severo Giannini, those public authorities (including the state) that are 'enti esponenziali di collettività' ('exponential entities', or better 'representative institutions', of territorial communities).[4]

---

[1] Schmitter and Kim (2005), p. 5. The involvement in governance of nongovernmental actors is highlighted also by Piattoni (2010), p. 250. A clear explanation of the concept of 'governance' and of the difference between 'governance' and 'political steering' ('politische Steuerung', 'Steuerungstheorie') can be found in Mayntz (1998), passim.

[2] Cf. Bache and Flinders (2004), p. 3.

[3] Cf. Committee of the Regions (2009b). A similar focus on the regional and local levels in the EU can be found in Benz and Eberlein (1999), pp. 329 ff.

[4] Cf. Giannini (1993), pp. 104 ff.

© Springer International Publishing Switzerland 2015
C. Panara, *The Sub-national Dimension of the EU*,
DOI 10.1007/978-3-319-14589-1_1

The notion of multilevel governance that emerges from the literature is mainly descriptive and does not offer prescriptive guidance as to how the EU ought to function. This submission is confirmed by an analysis of the most influential studies on multilevel governance. For example, Hooghe and Marks clearly illustrate the descriptive nature of the concept when they write that 'Multi-level governance [...] describes the dispersion of authoritative decision making across multiple territorial levels'.[5] Also, Piattoni, whose work is partly concerned with the normative value of multilevel governance, adopts a descriptive approach: 'MLG indicates interrelated changes in political mobilization, policy-making, and polity restructuring; in particular, it indicates: (a) the participation of subnational authorities in policy-making at levels and through the procedures that defy existing hierarchies and may further upset their stability; (b) the mobilization of societal actors at all territorial and governmental levels and their contribution to policy-making, implementation and monitoring; (c) the creation and institutionalization of governance arrangements that see the simultaneous involvement of institutional and non-institutional actors and that, by accretion, reconfigure the supranational level as a fundamental level of government'.[6] George does not depart fundamentally from the same descriptive pattern when he writes that 'As a distinct perspective on the European Union, multi-level governance offers not a description, but a theory of what sort of organization the European Union is. It is hypothesized to be an organization in which the central executives of states do not do all the governing but share and contest responsibility and authority with other actors, both supranational and subnational'.[7] Even if this hypothesis proved valid, it would only help one to understand the nature and functioning of the Union. However, we would know nothing or very little in relation to how the EU ought to be organised to comply with multilevel governance. In particular, we would not know *if* or *why* the EU ought to be organised, and the decision-making structured, in a certain way.

Why study multilevel governance, rather than analysing or further developing another notion, such as the more traditional concepts of 'federalism' or 'multilevel polity'? The concept of federalism appears too specific and not fit for purpose. By requiring a central authority with sovereign power (the federation), that notion could be confusing in the European context. Indeed, there is no doubt that the Union, despite many similarities with federal states, is not a fully fledged federation.[8] On the other hand, the notion of 'multilevel polity' appears too generic and all

---

[5] Hooghe and Marks (2001), p. xi.

[6] Piattoni (2010), p. 250. On Piattoni's interesting notion of multilevel governance, see also Piattoni (2009), pp. 163 ff.

[7] George (2004), p. 125.

[8] On the EU as a 'federation of states', cf. Schütze (2012), pp. 47 ff. Albeit very elegant and thoughtful, Schütze's analysis brings us back to the old debate between those who think that sovereignty is indivisible and those (like Schütze) who think that sovereignty can be divided. That debate is culturally interesting but no longer crucial. On the lack of importance of that discussion, cf. the sharp notes of the Italian legal scholar Massimo Severo Giannini. Cf. Giannini (1986), pp. 87 ff.

purpose to be really useful. *Any* multilevel entity, from a federal state to an atypical organisation like the EU, could be correctly described as a 'multilevel polity' or 'system'. By contrast, the concept of multilevel governance emerging from scholarly works on EU integration and the Committee of the Regions' *White Paper on Multilevel Governance*[9] is becoming a key concept specifically for the EU. Accordingly, rather than focusing on other notions or creating an alternative conceptuality, it appears more promising to study multilevel governance from a different and as yet unexplored angle: that of legal scholarship.

There are some fundamental reasons for studying this topic from a legal perspective. Until now, the concept of multilevel governance has remained the almost exclusive domain of political science and of some official documents outlining the future strategy and development of the EU.[10] The phrase 'multilevel governance' is often used by legal scholars as an evocative formula pointing to the multilayered and polycentric structure of the EU, without attaching to it a specific legal meaning. Single aspects of multilevel governance in the EU have been the subject of legal studies, especially those dealing with the involvement of regional and local authorities in the EU lawmaking process.[11] However, to date, no legal study has analysed multilevel governance as such, on its own, using the criteria that are typical of the legal discipline. The absence of substantial legal research on this fundamental theme is the first justification for an analysis of multilevel governance from a legal perspective.

Another important reason for studying multilevel governance from a legal perspective is that there is a clear and still ongoing shift towards a 'prescriptive' notion of multilevel governance. The Commission's *White Paper* of 2001 and especially the 2009 Committee of the Regions' *White Paper on Multilevel Governance* refer to multilevel governance not only in descriptive terms (what multilevel governance is) but also in 'prescriptive' terms (which model of multilevel governance, what has to be done to establish multilevel governance). Recently, this approach has culminated into the adoption by the Committee of the Regions of the *Charter for Multilevel Governance* (April 2014).[12] This is a first attempt to 'codify' multilevel governance, even though in the form of 'soft law'.[13] At the same

---

[9] Cf. Committee of the Regions (CoR) (2009b), p. 3. See also the CoR (2009a).

[10] Cf. especially Commission of the European Union (2001) and Committee of the Regions (2009b). See also the Opinion of the Committee of the Regions (2012).

[11] Cf., for example, Toniatti et al. (2004), Weatherill and Bernitz (2005), Panara and De Becker (2011a) and Panara and Varney (2013).

[12] Cf. Committee of the Regions (2014).

[13] The Charter is a political document embodied in a resolution of the CoR. As such, it does not have a legally binding effect. It is open to signature by the local and regional authorities of the EU, as well as by the representatives of the other levels of governance (national, EU, international). Cf. Point 2 of the CoR Resolution of 2/3 April 2014. The CoR's aspiration is to create a 'soft law' arrangement as a first step to implement multilevel governance in the EU. At the time of writing (10 September 2014), the Charter has been signed by 154 local/regional authorities (including 13 associations of sub-national authorities).

time, multilevel governance became an important subject of EU (hard) secondary law. For example, Regulation (EU) No 1303/2013 on EU funding for economic, social and territorial cohesion indicates multilevel governance as a 'principle' to be respected by the Member States when creating partnerships with the sub-national authorities for the implementation of the EU economic, social and territorial cohesion policy.[14] Legal scholarship is obviously equipped to study prescriptive phenomena and legal frameworks. Accordingly, the legal perspective permits a more enhanced understanding of the concept and the logical and legal implications of multilevel governance in the EU.

The most important contribution of the legal perspective, however, comes from the approach typical of legal discipline. Lawyers investigate the rationale for a legal framework or regulation. This is the underlying raison d'être of a specific legal arrangement. Multilevel governance is reflected in legal arrangements at EU and national levels, and the raison d'être of these arrangements can be understood best through legal analysis.

B. Overview of the Work

In the second chapter, I will construe the Union as a multilevel system that includes a 'sub-national' dimension. In contrast with the mainstream legal literature on European integration, which focuses on the Union-Member States dichotomy and sees the sub-national authorities as components of the state, I will argue that the sub-national authorities are an integral part of the EU atypical multilevel system and have the status of 'full subjects' within that system, i.e., they enjoy 'rights' and 'duties' stemming from the European constitutional composite.

In Chap. 3, I will argue that multilevel governance is a legal principle commanding the involvement of the sub-national authorities in the EU decision-making process and in the implementation of EU law and policy. In this way, multilevel governance emerges as a 'procedural' principle, i.e., as a principle commanding a certain decisional 'procedure'. Such involvement is required for the protection of the constitutional identity of the Member States [cf. Art. 4(2) TEU] and, accordingly, for the legitimacy of the Member States' participation in the EU and of the EU decision-making process.

In Chap. 4, I will discuss the principle of subsidiarity, which is considered a cornerstone of the multilevel architecture of the EU. I will argue that, like the principle of multilevel governance, subsidiarity too is a 'procedural' principle, i.e.,

---

[14] Regulation (EU) No 1303/2013 of the European Parliament and of the Council of 17 December 2013 laying down common provisions on the European Regional Development Fund, the European Social Fund, the Cohesion Fund, the European Agricultural Fund for Rural Development and the European Maritime and Fisheries Fund and laying down general provisions on the European Regional Development Fund, the European Social Fund, the Cohesion Fund and the European Maritime and Fisheries fund and repealing Council Regulation (EC) No 1083/2006.

a principle that can only exceptionally be judicially enforced and that should normally be implemented through multilevel participation and cooperation.

In Chap. 5, I will deal with the responsibility of the sub-national level for European integration. Indeed, regional/local participation is not only a responsibility of the EU and of the Member States. Sub-national authorities must also take their European role seriously and engage in the making and implementation of EU law/policy. I will analyse three case studies representative of three different constitutional patterns: (1) Baden-Württemberg (Germany, component of a typical federal state), (2) Lombardia (region of a typical regional state), (3) Merseyside (region of England, now incorporated by Liverpool City Region Combined Authority).

In Chap. 6, I will deal with the constitutional dimension of multilevel governance. I will argue that the concept of multilevel governance is not limited to soft law and it is embedded in the constitutional structure of the EU. I will also examine the role played by multilevel governance in constitutionalism and democracy in the EU.

C. A Required Post-Scriptum on the Heterogeneity of the 'Sub-national Level'

A crucial element to take into account is that the 'sub-national level' is not a homogeneous level of government.[15] This is a large category containing many different types of entities, from regional (e.g., the Spanish Self-Governing Communities or the Italian Regions) to local (e.g., municipalities), to even regional entities claiming to be states in their own right within a federal framework (German *Länder*[16]). Accordingly, multilevel governance too will have a different application for the different types of regional or local authorities existing within the EU.

The summa divisio among sub-national authorities is between 'regional' and 'local'. Both are self-governed authorities enjoying a degree of autonomy from the

---

[15] On the heterogeneity of the regional level, cf., for example, Bullmann (1997), pp. 4 ff. ('Against this backdrop it would be misleading to think of any homogeneously constructed "Europe of the regions" within the near future'). Cf. also Sturm (2009), pp. 16 ff.

[16] The typical arguments used to uphold the 'Staatsqualität' (state quality) of the German *Länder* are their participation in the exercise of all three traditional state functions (legislative, executive, judicial); their right to approve their own constitution (cf. the Ruling of the Second Senate of the Federal Constitutional Court of 23 October 1951, published in *BVerfGE* 1, 14 [34]); their limited right to sign agreements with foreign states [cf. Federal Constitutional Court, rulings published in *BVerfGE* 2, 347 [379] and 6, 309 [362]; cf. also Erbguth 2003, pp. 1089–1090 (Rn. 5)]; their right to have and maintain an armamentarium of competences as an asset ('Hausgut', 'family possessions') that cannot be taken away from them, not even through a constitutional amendment (cf. Ruling of the Federal Constitutional Court of 26 July 1972, published in *BVerfGE* 34, 9 [19]); their right to exercise all the responsibilities not reserved by the Basic Law to the Federation. Cf. Art. 30 GG. Cf. also Isensee (1999), p. 552 (Rn. 64).

centre in the context of a nation-state. The notion of 'sub-national level' includes any sub-national, territorial, self-governed authority whose territory and population are a fraction of the overall territory and population of a nation-state. The most common example of local authority is the municipality, which may coincide with a city or a town. By contrast, the regional level of government is an intermediate tier of government situated between local authorities and the national government. The term 'region' itself may refer to very different legal entities, for example, the German *Länder* (which are constitutive parts of a federation), the Spanish Autonomous Communities, the UK administrations with devolved powers, the Belgian Regions and Communities, to name but a few.[17]

The territory of regional authorities usually includes a number of local authorities. Despite some notable exceptions (for example, the *Land* Hamburg in Germany, which coincides with the city of Hamburg), normally regions have a larger territory and population than one city. Also, whilst local authorities are typically vested only with administrative powers, including the power to pass hybrid forms of legislation (e.g., bylaws and ordinances), regional authorities may have the power to pass acts having the same force of the statutes passed by the national parliament.[18] Often the regions have powers of coordination and control over the local authorities situated within their territory, and in some Member States (Austria, Belgium, Germany, UK) they have important regulatory powers concerning the structure and organisation of local government.[19]

Since the sub-national authorities belonging to the same level (regional or local) have different status, structure and powers across the EU, or even in the same Member State, also the areas of overlap between the powers of the sub-national authorities and the EU vary from Member State to Member State. They may also vary across the same level of government within one Member State (e.g., from region to region). For example, in Belgium, the position of the Communities is different from that of the Regions. Whilst the responsibilities of the Communities are linked to personal matters (such as education, culture, healthcare, youth and social policy), the Regions have responsibilities linked to territory (e.g., environment, fisheries, woods, agriculture, economy, natural resources, energy).[20] In the

---

[17] On the concept of 'region', cf. Panara and De Becker (2011b), p. 298 (fn. 3).

[18] The European regions with legislative powers are grouped in the Conference of the European Regions with Legislative Power (REGLEG). Currently, this political network includes representatives of 73 regions spread across 8 Member States: the 9 Austrian *Länder*, the 5 Belgian Regions and Communities, the 16 German *Länder*, the 20 Italian Regions, the 17 Spanish Self-Governing Communities, the 2 Portuguese Autonomous Regions (Azores and Madeira), the Aland Islands in Finland and the 3 UK authorities with devolved power (Northern Ireland, Scotland and Wales).

[19] The French Regions have the same status as any other French territorial authority. In particular, they have no hierarchical power over communes and departments. This demonstrates that the development of a notion of local or regional government that aspires to be valid beyond the borders of a single state is always approximate to an extent.

[20] See Articles 4, 5 and 6 of the Belgian Special Act of 8 August 1980, as last modified by the Special Act of 12 August 2003.

UK, there is large asymmetry between the powers of the devolved administrations in Scotland, Wales and Northern Ireland,[21] and in Portugal the competences of Azores and Madeira are separately defined in their own statutes of autonomy.[22] Asymmetries exist also in Spain and Italy. Such twofold asymmetry (*between* and *within* the Member States) explains why only with considerable approximation regional and local authorities can be considered as a clear-cut tier of government within the EU.

A number of other elements (economic, cultural, historical, demographic, etc.) contribute to increase the heterogeneity of the 'sub-national level'. For example, some regions are well developed economically, whilst the development of others lags significantly behind (a striking example could be the difference between the North and the South of Italy and also between Flanders and Wallonia in Belgium).[23] Cultural and historical influences play a major role. Some regions have a defined identity. This is, for example, the case of Scotland or of the Basque Country. Other regions protect certain ethnolinguistic groups (e.g., the Belgian Communities and Aland). In other cases, the regions have a past as independent states; this is the case of Bavaria in Germany or, again, of Scotland. By contrast, some regions were created by force of law without being anchored to any historical identity; this is the case of most Italian regions and also of some German *Länder*. Regions also differ significantly in terms of size and population; for example, in Germany the *Land* Bremen counts around 660,000 inhabitants, and its territory is limited to the city of Bremen, whereas the *Land* Nord-Rhine Westphalia counts nearly 18 million inhabitants, and its territory is about 83 times bigger than Bremen (in terms of population and territory, Nord-Rhine Westphalia is comparable to a medium-size EU Member State like the Netherlands).

Another important element is the geographical location of a region, for example, its insularity (Sicily, Sardinia, etc.). The geographical location has an enormous impact on the economic activities and, as a result, on the interest of the regions in certain areas of EU policy. Among the regions, there are the ultra-peripheral regions of the EU: Guadeloupe, French Guiana, Martinique, Réunion, Saint-Barthelemy, Saint-Martin (all belonging to France); the Azores and Madeira (belonging to Portugal); and the Canary Islands (belonging to Spain). The adoption of ad hoc measures for these regions is expressly provided by Article 349 TFEU. This is

---

[21] Cf. Scotland Act 1998, Government of Wales Act 1998 and 2006, Northern Ireland Act 1998. On this topic cf. Himsworth (2007), pp. 31 ff.

[22] Cf. *Estatuto político-administrativo da Região Autómoma dos Açores* (Law No. 2 of 12 January 2009); *Estatuto político-administrativo da Região Autónoma da Madeira* (Law No. 13 of 5 June 1991, later amended).

[23] The type of economy varies enormously from region to region, and so do the interests of the sub-national authorities in the European arena: for example, Scotland is a gas and oil producer; other regions have an industry-based economy (such as the *Land* Lower Saxony in Germany); other regions' economy is essentially based on agriculture and tourism (e.g., Puglia in Italy). Also, the type of industry and agriculture, the size of companies, etc., vary considerably from place to place.

justified by the specificity of the ultra-peripheral regions in consideration of their remoteness, insularity, small size, economic dependence on a few products, difficult topography and climate. In the case of Aland, the special status of this region within the EU is recognised by the Aland Protocol attached to the Accession Treaty, which brought Finland into the Union.[24]

References

I. Bache, M. Flinders, Themes and issues in multi-level governance, in *Multi-Level Governance*, ed. by I. Bache, M. Flinders (OUP, Oxford, 2004), pp. 1 ff

A. Benz, B. Eberlein, The Europeanization of regional policies: patterns of multilevel governance. J. Eur. Policy **6**(2), 329 f. (1999)

U. Bullmann, The politics of the third level, in *The Regional Dimension of the European Union. Towards a Third Level in Europe?* ed. by C. Jeffery (Cass, London, 1997), pp. 3 ff

Commission of the European Union, *European Governance – A White Paper*, COM (2001) 428, 25 July 2001

Committee of the Regions, *Charter for Multilevel Governance in Europe* (April 2014)

Committee of the Regions, *Mission Statement*, CdR 56/2009 fin, 21 April 2009a

Committee of the Regions, *White Paper on Multilevel Governance*, CdR 89/2009, 17–18 June 2009b

Committee of the Regions, Opinion, *Building a European Culture of Multilevel Governance: Follow-Up from the Committee of the Regions' White Paper*, 94th plenary session, 15–16 February 2012

Committee of the Regions, *Resolution on the Charter for Multilevel Governance in Europe*, 106th plenary session, 2 and 3 April 2014, RESOL-V-012

W. Erbguth, Commentary to Article 30 GG, in *Grundgesetz. Kommentar*, 3rd edn, ed. by M. Sachs (C.H. Beck, München, 2003), pp. 1087 ff

S. George, Multi-level governance and the European Union, in *Multi-Level Governance*, ed. by I. Bache, M. Flinders (OUP, Oxford, 2004), pp. 107 ff

M.S. Giannini, *Il pubblico potere Stati e amministrazioni pubbliche* (il Mulino, Bologna, 1986)

M.S. Giannini, *Diritto amministrativo*, vol. I, 3rd edn. (Giuffrè, Milano, 1993)

C. Himsworth, Devolution and its jurisdictional asymmetries. Mod. Law Rev. **70**(1), 31 f. (2007)

L. Hooghe, G. Marks, *Multi-Level Governance and European Integration* (Rowman & Littlefield, Lanham, 2001)

J. Isensee, Idee und Gestalt des Föderalismus im Grundgesetz, in *Handbuch des Staatsrechts*, vol. IV, 2nd edn. ed. by J. Isensee, P. Kirchhof (C.F. Müller, Heidelberg, 1999), pp. 517 ff

R. Mayntz, *New Challenges to Governance Theory*. Jean Monnet Chair Paper RSC No. 98/50, European University Institute (1998)

C. Panara, A. De Becker (eds.), *The Role of the Regions in EU Governance* (Springer, Berlin/ Heidelberg, 2011a)

C. Panara, A. De Becker, The role of the regions in the European Union: the "Regional Blindness" of both the EU and the Member States, in *The Role of the Regions in EU Governance*, ed. by C. Panara, A. De Becker (Springer, Berlin Heidelberg, 2011b), pp. 297 ff

C. Panara, M. Varney (eds.), *Local Government in Europe: The 'Fourth Level' in the EU Multi-Layered System of Governance* (Routledge, Oxford, 2013)

---

[24] Protocol No. 2 annexed to the Accession Treaty of 24 June 1994.

S. Piattoni, Multi-level governance: a historical and conceptual analysis. J. Eur Integr. **31**(2), 163 f. (2009)

S. Piattoni, *The Theory of Multi-Level Governance. Conceptual, Empirical, and Normative Challenges* (OUP, Oxford, 2010)

P. Schmitter, S. Kim, *The Experience of European Integration and the Potential for Northeast Asian Integration*, East–West Center Working Papers, No. 10, August 2005

R. Schütze, *European Constitutional Law* (CUP, Cambridge, 2012)

R. Sturm, Die Europafähigkeit der Regionen, in *Europapolitik und Europafähigkeit von Regionen*, ed. by K.-H. Lambertz, M. Große Hüttmann (Nomos, Baden-Baden, 2009), pp. 11 ff

R. Toniatti et al. (eds.), *An Ever More Complex Union: The Regional Variable as a Missing Link in the EU Constitution?* (Nomos, Baden-Baden, 2004)

S. Weatherill, U. Bernitz (eds.), *The Role of Regions and Sub-national Actors in Europe* (Hart, Oxford, 2005)

Chapter 2
The Sub-national Dimension of the EU

A. Introduction

The emergence of the 'Third Level', i.e. the sub-national dimension of the EU, raises the question of the status of the sub-state authorities in the EU. Are these authorities full European players in their own right (i.e., with their 'own' rights and duties in the EU multilevel system), or is the EU a 'union of states' in which only the Member States (and their citizens) are subjects of rights and duties stemming from the EU multilevel system? The Union is not a State, and as such it does not have a constitution comparable to a State constitution, even though the ECJ regards the Treaties as the 'constitutional charter' of the Union.[1] The creation of the Communities and later of the Union placed a further echelon of power above the Member States. One of the results of European integration is that the European citizen nowadays is subjected to the authority of the State and also to the authority of another entity, the Union, above the State, which is responsible for certain policy areas. Whilst until the 1950s (or maybe, more realistically, until the Single European Act of 1986) the exercise of public power had to abide fundamentally by only one constitution in each Member State (the State constitution), today the State constitution regulates only the State power. The authoritative decision-making of the Union is largely regulated by *another*, albeit coordinated with the former, 'tier' of constitutional law, i.e., EU primary law (the Treaties). This landscape suggests that there must be a degree of *homogeneity* between the State constitutional law and the EU primary law. Only States with a liberal-democratic setting, market economy, respectful of human rights, can join and remain members

---

[1] Cf. Judgment of the Court of Justice of 23 April 1986, *Parti écologiste "Les Verts" v European Parliament*, Case 294/83, ECR 1986-4, p. 1339: '[The EEC] is a Community based on the rule of law, inasmuch as neither its Member States nor its institutions can avoid a review of the question whether the measures adopted by them are in conformity with the basic constitutional charter, the Treaty' (p. 1365). See also Judgment of the Court of 23 March 1993, *Beate Weber v European Parliament*, Case C.314/91, ECR 1993-I, p. 1093, para. 8.

© Springer International Publishing Switzerland 2015
C. Panara, *The Sub-national Dimension of the EU*,
DOI 10.1007/978-3-319-14589-1_2

of the Union. The coexistence of multiple layers of authority (State and supranational) and of multiple constitutional levels corroborates the idea that the European constitutional space is a constitutional mosaic resulting from the EU and the Member States' constitutions.

The constitutional principles of the European constitutional space (i.e., of this composite of Member States' constitutions and EU constitution) have a national and a supranational dimension. For example, this is the case of the principle of supremacy of EU law. This principle has a supranational dimension (determined by the ECJ and rooted in the Treaty) and a national dimension. It is conjugated by each Member State in their own way, despite being fundamentally accepted by all the Member States as an integral part of the 'acquis communautaire'.[2] Another example is the doctrine of general principles of Community (now Union) law. According to this doctrine, fundamental human rights are part of a heritage that is common to the EU and to all the Member States. These rights are general principles of Union law, and their sources are essentially the ECHR (of which all the Member States are parties) and the common constitutional traditions of the Member States.[3] So it is apparent that these principles result from the coexistence and interaction, or better the combination, the 'fusion',[4] of different constitutional levels. Accordingly, the EU can be realistically defined as a 'constitutional composite' resulting from the own primary law and the constitutional laws of the Member States. The principles of this 'composite' (or 'compound of constitutions', *Verfassungsverbund*) have both national and supranational dimensions in the context of the European *Mehrebenensystem* (multilevel system).[5]

This chapter will test the hypothesis that the EU is a unique setting in which the sub-national authorities (the 'Third Level') are an integral part of the European architecture. Their position is the result not only of the EU law but also of the combination of the EU law and of the national laws ('compound of constitutions' theory). The rights and duties of the sub-national authorities *vis-à-vis* the EU stem both from the Treaties and the constitutions of the Member States. The position of the sub-national authorities in the EU context is characterised by a certain degree of strength and stability and also by significant asymmetry across the different Member States.

This hypothesis will be tested through the analysis of the EU primary lawmaking (Sect. B), of the involvement of the sub-national authorities in lawmaking in the Council (Sect. C), of the implementation of EU law by the sub-national authorities (Sect. D) and of the direct challenge of Union acts by the sub-national authorities (Sect. E).

---

[2] Cf. Weiler (1981), pp. 267 ff.

[3] Cf. Art. 6(3) TEU. On the general principles of EC/EU law, see Tridimas (2006).

[4] Often scholars describe European integration as a 'fusion' (Wessels) or an 'amalgamation' (*Amalgamierung*, Nettesheim) of the Member States in the EU. Cf. Wessels (1997), pp. 268 ff.; Nettesheim (2012), p. 324.

[5] Cf. Pernice (2010), pp. 102 ff. On Pernice's multilevel constitutionalism theory, cf. Pernice (2009), pp. 349 ff. Birkinshaw's notion of 'European Public Law' entails the very same idea that the national public law of the UK has been radically changed by the UK accession to the Union. Accordingly, the full understanding of the public law and, more in general, of the legal system in force in one Member State requires a consideration of both the national and the supranational dimensions. Cf. Birkinshaw (2003), pp. 361 ff.

B. Beyond the 'Masters of the Treaties' Dogma

The traditional and 'orthodox' EU law perspective is that the Member States are the 'masters of the Treaties'. This is confirmed by a prima facie reading of Article 48 TEU on the procedures for amending the Treaties. However, the transfer of powers from the national level to the EU could undermine the role of the local/regional authorities and alter the constitutional balance between central and sub-national government. This complexity of the EU multilevel system is addressed at Member State level through the involvement of the local/regional authorities in different ways in the decisions concerning the amendment of the Treaties. The following excursus corroborates the submission that the sub-national dimension, albeit to a varying degree in the different Member States, is an integral part of the EU multilevel system. At the same time it challenges the traditional/orthodox picture of the Member States as the sole 'masters of the Treaties'.

In Belgium, the rights of the regional entities in the European context are guaranteed in accordance with the constitutional principle 'in foro interno et in foro externo' (lit. in the domestic and in the external jurisdiction).[6] From this principle derives that the Belgian Regions and Communities are able to decide on the transfer to the EU of the exclusive powers they enjoy on the domestic level. A Treaty concerning these powers can only enter into force in Belgium if the parliaments of *all* the regional entities concerned consent to it.[7] As a result, every sub-state parliament has a right of veto regarding the ratification of the Treaty by Belgium.[8] This feature of the Belgian system is at odds with the conventional opinion that the Member States are the sole 'masters of the Treaties'. It shows how a more accurate analysis of the Member States' constitutional systems discloses a much more variegated reality.

In Germany, the *Länder* are involved *collectively*, as a level of government, in the approval of a Treaty. An individual *Land* does not have a right of veto. Every new Treaty would need to be approved by two-thirds majority in the *Bundesrat* (the

---

[6] Art. 167(3) Belgian Constitution: 'The Community and Regional Governments conclude, each one in so far as it is concerned, treaties regarding matters that fall within the competences of their Parliament. These treaties take effect only after they have received the approval from the Parliament'.

[7] In Belgium, there is a double divide of the sub-national entities. There are three Communities (Flemish, French speaking and German speaking), which are competent for person-bound matters (culture, education, etc.), and three Regions (Flemish, Walloon and Brussels-Capital). The Regions are competent for territorial matters, such as economy, fisheries, agriculture, labour market, etc.

[8] On the 'in foro interno et in foro externo' principle and its impact on the involvement of the Belgian Regions and Communities in the EU, cf. De Becker (2011), p. 256. Mutatis mutandis the Belgian position is similar to the Finnish position. According to Chapter 9 of the Act on the Autonomy of Åland (1991/1144), the government of Åland must be informed of negotiations on a treaty impacting on the autonomy of Åland and, if necessary, must be given the opportunity to participate in the negotiations (cf. Section 58). If a term of a treaty concerns a matter within the competence of Åland, the Åland Parliament must consent to the statute implementing that term in order to have it entering into force in Åland (Section 59).

legislative chamber representing the *Länder* on the federal level), as well as in the *Bundestag* (democratically elected chamber representing the German people).[9] The German pattern is similar to the solution adopted in Austria, where amendments to the founding Treaties require the approval by two-thirds majority in both the *Nationalrat* (chamber representing all the Austrian people) and the *Bundesrat* (chamber representing the *Länder* at federal level).[10] The main difference between the German and the Austrian patterns is that the representatives of the *Länder* in the German *Bundesrat* are appointed (and recalled) by the government of their *Land*, whereas those in the Austrian *Bundesrat* are elected by each regional parliament. Moreover, whilst in Germany the *Länder* representatives are bound by the instructions coming from the government of their *Land*, the *Länder* representatives in the Austrian *Bundesrat* enjoy a free mandate. These arrangements grant the German and Austrian *Länder* an indirect participation in the Treaty-making procedure and, again, show how a holistic assessment of the Treaty-amending process leads to a more inclusive concept of the European Union as a multilevel system that embraces the sub-national dimension.[11]

The participation of the Spanish Autonomous Communities in the Treaty-amendment processes is weak compared to that of the German and Austrian *Länder*.

---

[9] Art. 23(1) of the Basic Law (this is the German constitution of 1949; the name 'Basic Law' is the literal translation of *Grundgesetz*, hereafter also GG). The *Bundesrat* (meaning 'Federal Council') is a constitutional body where the governments of the 16 *Länder* are represented at federal level. The members of the *Bundesrat* are not elected but appointed by the various *Länder* cabinets. Each *Land* is allocated a number of votes (from a minimum of three to a maximum of six) according to the size of the respective population. The *Bundesrat* participates in federal legislation and administration and in matters relating to the EU. The *Bundestag* (meaning 'Federal Diet') is instead a democratically elected chamber representing the entire German people.

[10] According to Article 24 of the Federal Constitutional Law (*Bundes-Verfassungsgesetz*, hereafter also B-VG), the Federal Parliament in Austria comprises two chambers: the *Nationalrat* (meaning 'National Council') and the *Bundesrat* (meaning 'Federal Council'). The *Nationalrat* is directly elected by the people for a period of 5 years (Art. 26–27 B-VG). The members of the *Bundesrat* are elected by the *Landtage* (the regional parliaments). The *Länder* are represented in the *Bundesrat* in proportion to the number of nationals in each *Land* (Arts. 34 and 35 B-VG).

[11] In the wake of the 'Lisbon Ruling' of the Federal Constitutional Court of 30 June 2009, in Germany also the 'bridging clauses' became the subject of specific legislative attention. These clauses allow the introduction of a procedural change in the EU in a simplified way (shift from special to ordinary legislative procedure, shift from unanimity to qualified majority). A shift from unanimity to qualified majority may affect the position of the *Länder*, given that the Member States would lose their veto in the Council. Accordingly, the approval of a proposed procedural change by Germany would require the passage of a law with the consent of the *Bundesrat*. This rule applies to the general bridging clause of Article 48(7) TEU and to Article 81(3) TFEU concerning family law matters with cross-border implications. Cf. Section 4 of the Law on the Responsibility for [European] Integration (*Integrationsverantwortungsgesetz*, IntVG in acronym) of 22 September 2009. Sections 5 and 6 *IntVG* cover the 'special bridging clauses', that is, those whose scope is more limited. In relation to these clauses, the approval by the *Bundesrat* is needed if the Basic Law requires the consent of the *Bundesrat* for passing a law in that area or it is an area belonging to the legislative responsibility of the *Länder*. 'Special bridging clauses' can be found in a number of Treaty provisions: Art. 31(3) TEU (CFSP), Art. 312(2) TFEU (multiannual financial framework), Art. 153(2) TFEU (social policy), Art. 192(2) TFEU (environment), Art. 333 (1) TFEU (enhanced cooperation).

The Spanish Senate is not a real 'chamber of the regions'. The representation of the Autonomous Communities as a proportion of the membership of the Spanish Senate is not significant.[12] Furthermore, although the Senate is involved in the ratification of new Treaties, the Congress[13] (the chamber representing the totality of Spanish people) still retains the power to overcome the Senate's possible veto by absolute majority or even, but only after 2 months, by simple majority.[14] However, whilst not necessarily decisive in practice, the involvement of the Autonomous Communities in the decision on the transfer of powers to the EU is quite important from a constitutional perspective, insofar as it contributes to the legitimacy of the Treaty-amending process in Spain, i.e., insofar as it brings into line the EU and the Spanish constitutional systems by recognising the role of the Autonomous Communities.

In the UK, foreign relations are under the exclusive control of Westminster. The Concordat on Co-ordination of European Policy Issues, a political document binding in honour only, says that the UK government should share with the devolved administrations any information concerning the EU that is relevant to them, including any proposal for Treaty change.[15] It would be unthinkable for a Treaty amendment touching on devolved matters to take place without prior consultation with the devolved administrations. The constitutional standing of these administrations requires this type of involvement for the legitimacy of the EU primary lawmaking. In the absence of such involvement, there would be an obvious clash with the national constitutional framework. The same issue is addressed in a similar way also by the Portuguese Constitution. The two Autonomous Regions of Portugal (Azores and Madeira) are not directly involved in the negotiation of a new Treaty. However, if the Treaty touches on matters falling within their responsibility, they must be heard.[16]

In Italy, there is no specific basis for regional or local involvement in the EU primary lawmaking. The Italian Senate is elected in region-wide electoral constituencies, but it does not comprise representatives of the Regions. Still, political opportunity and legitimacy of the Italian participation in the EU would require that a proposed Treaty amendment, affecting significantly the constitutional role and responsibilities of the sub-national authorities, would have to be discussed by the central government with the sub-national stakeholders in the appropriate institutional loci (for example, in the State-Regions Conference or the State-Regions-Local Authorities' Conference).

In addition to the ex post involvement of the sub-national authorities in the ratification of a new European Treaty, the Member States may also involve the

---

[12] The Spanish Senate consists of 266 members. Two-hundred eight members are directly elected by popular vote. The other 58 are appointed by the regional legislatures.

[13] It is worth noting that in 2006 the Spanish Council of State (the Government's supreme advisory body) proposed to reshape the Spanish Senate in a way similar to the German and the Austrian *Bundesräte*. However this bid has not been translated into political initiative. Cf. Rubio Llorente and Alvarez Junco (2006).

[14] Art. 90 Spanish Constitution.

[15] Section B4.1 Concordat on Co-ordination of European Policy Issues (September 2012).

[16] Cf. Art. 227 *t)* and *u)* Portuguese Constitution.

sub-national level in the work of an Intergovernmental Conference (IGC) or Convention leading to a new Treaty. The German *Länder* obtained two representatives in the German delegation to the IGC, which led to the Treaty of Maastricht. These contributed to secure the introduction of the principle of subsidiarity, the establishment of the Committee of the Regions and the opening up of the Council to regional representatives 'at ministerial level'.[17] This type of involvement is very important, given that participating in the negotiation of a new Treaty could result more fruitful than the simple ex post approval (or threat of non-approval) of a Treaty already negotiated and signed by the Member States' national governments.

C. Sub-national Participation in Lawmaking in the Council and Through the Committee of the Regions (CoR)

Article 16(2) TEU stipulates that a Member State can be represented in the Council by a person 'at ministerial level' entitled to 'commit' the national government and to 'cast its vote'.[18] This Treaty provision makes it possible for the sub-national authorities to participate in Council meetings if/when the Member State allows their participation (external representation). However, participation of the sub-national authorities in Council meetings is not limited to the 'external representation' pattern outlined by Article 16(2) TEU. In the Member States, there are ad hoc arrangements for the involvement of sub-national authorities in the preparation of Council meetings when the Council agenda features topics of regional interest (internal cooperation). In the Member States, there are different patterns of external and internal involvement of the sub-national authorities in the Council lawmaking activity (cf. Table 2.1 for a summary of the different national positions). It emerges that the EU lawmaking process in the Council is not entirely 'State dominated'. The participation rights of the sub-national entities result from the combination of EU and national processes, which corroborates the hypothesis that the sub-national actors are an integral part of the EU 'multilevel system'.[19]

---

[17] Cf. Gunlicks (2003), p. 1238. The Committee of the Regions had the status of Observer in the European Convention that drafted the Treaty establishing a Constitution for Europe (2002–2003).

[18] Art. 16(2) TEU: 'The Council shall consist of a representative of each Member State at ministerial level, who may commit the government of the Member State in question and cast its vote'. The Conference of European Regions with Legislative Power (REGLEG in acronym) released the Declaration of Brussels of 4–5 December 2008. This document underlines the strong lobbying carried out by the regions during the negotiations leading to the Treaty of Lisbon for obtaining the strengthening of their position in the EU decision-making process. This document contains a specific request from REGLEG to the European Council to promote further involvement of the regions with legislative power in the preparatory, decision-making, and implementation phases of EU law.

[19] The sharing of authoritative decision-making across multiple levels of government within the EU is the basic assumption of the theory of 'multilevel governance'. Cf. Marks et al. (1996), pp. 341 ff. See also Hooghe and Marks (2001), p. xi. Cf. infra Chap. 3.

Table 2.1 Participation of sub-national authorities in lawmaking in the Council[a]

	Internal cooperation	External representation in the Council
Member State	Internal cooperation is the internal coordination of the positions of the central government and of the sub-national authorities prior to a Council meeting. The aim is to achieve a common position that is to be defended in the Council by either the central government or a representative 'at ministerial level' of a regional government.	External representation is the participation of regional representatives in Council meetings in accordance with Article 16(2) TEU.
Austria	When the *Länder* reach a common position in a matter falling within their responsibility, the Federal Government is bound to uphold this stance in the Council. The Federal Government can only depart from this common position on grounds of compelling issues of European integration policy and foreign policy ('*aus zwingenden integrations- und außenpolitischen Gründen*'; cf. Art. 23d (2) Federal Constitutional Law). The existence of such compelling issues is determined by the Federal Government and is not justiciable.	The Austrian Constitution (cf. Art. 23d (1) Federal Constitutional Law) provides that if a matter that belongs to the competence of the *Länder*, or which is of interest to them, is dealt with at European level, the Federal Government *may* allow a regional minister to represent Austria in the Council. The regional minister will have to collaborate with the representative of the Federation, and like a federal minister (when representation is withheld by the Federal Government), he will be bound to defend the common position of the *Länder*. The regional representative does not represent his *Land* but the entire Member State. To date, this participation opportunity has never been used by the *Länder*.
Belgium	Pursuant to the Cooperation Agreement of 17 November 1994, all Councils on matters falling within the responsibility of the Belgian Regions or Communities are preceded by a coordination meeting between the national government and the sub-national governments. The common position agreed at the meeting is binding and must be defended by the Belgian representative in the Council. In the event that no common position is achieved, it is mainly understood that the Belgian representative will have to abstain from voting.	The Cooperation Agreement of 8 March 1994 provides three possible forms of representation in the Council: (1) a representation by the national government for exclusive federal responsibilities; (2) an exclusive representation by the Communities and the Regions for those responsibilities that belong exclusively to the Communities or the Regions; (3) a mixed representation that finds application when there are matters on the Council agenda that belong partly to the exclusive responsibility of the national government and partly to the exclusive responsibility of the Regions or the Communities. In mixed representation, the head of the Belgian delegation to the Council may be a federal or a regional minister.

(continued)

Table 2.1 (continued)

	Internal cooperation	External representation in the Council
Member State	Internal cooperation is the internal coordination of the positions of the central government and of the sub-national authorities prior to a Council meeting. The aim is to achieve a common position that is to be defended in the Council by either the central government or a representative 'at ministerial level' of a regional government.	External representation is the participation of regional representatives in Council meetings in accordance with Article 16(2) TEU.
Germany	When an EU proposal focuses on a matter falling within the legislative competence of the *Länder*, the Basic Law establishes that in such a situation the Federal Government must pay 'the greatest possible respect' (*maßgeblich zu berücksichtigen*) to the *Bundesrat*'s position (cf. Art. 23(5) Basic Law). This expression presumably means that the Federal Government has to defend the position of the *Bundesrat* in the Council, unless this goes against the interest of Germany as a Member State or unless compelling reasons of foreign policy or European integration justify departure from that position.	The Basic Law provides for the representation of Germany in the Council by a regional minister when draft EU acts primarily concern the exclusive competences of the *Länder* in the areas of education, culture or radio/TV (cf. Art. 23(6) Basic Law). The right to represent Germany belongs to a representative of the *Länder* designated by the *Bundesrat*. The representative of the *Länder* (who becomes the representative of the entire Federal Republic and not only of a single *Land*) must act 'with the participation of and in coordination with' the Federal Government. 'Participation' implies that the representatives of the Federation have the right to participate in all meetings and official contacts, together with the *Länder* representative. 'Coordination' is more difficult to construe. According to the bicameral commission that drafted Article 23 of the Basic Law, 'coordination' is something less than an 'agreement' but something more than simple 'respect for the other's point of view'. It is arguable that the representative of the *Länder* should pay the greatest possible respect to the position of the Federal Government.
Spain	The Autonomous Communities have the right to express common positions in matters that fall within their responsibility. There are two possible scenarios depending on the type of competence of the Autonomous Communities. If an EU draft act falls within an area of exclusive autonomic responsibility, the common position of the Autonomous Communities 'will be taken into account [by the national government] in a decisive way'	A representative of the Autonomous Communities is admitted to the Spanish delegation to the Council for matters of regional interest. The Spanish Autonomous Communities are allowed to participate in five Council configurations: employment, social policy, health and consumer affairs; agriculture and fisheries; environment; education, youth and culture; competitiveness. The regional representative may be

(continued)

Table 2.1 (continued)

	Internal cooperation	External representation in the Council
Member State	Internal cooperation is the internal coordination of the positions of the central government and of the sub-national authorities prior to a Council meeting. The aim is to achieve a common position that is to be defended in the Council by either the central government or a representative 'at ministerial level' of a regional government.	External representation is the participation of regional representatives in Council meetings in accordance with Article 16(2) TEU.
	(*será tenida en cuenta de forma determinante*). If an EU proposal falls within an area of non-exclusive autonomic competence (i.e., an area where the legislative power is shared by the State and the Autonomous Communities), the Autonomous Communities need to reach a common position, and this position needs to be agreed with the national government. In both scenarios, the government will normally defend the regional position or the position agreed with the regional authorities. The government may *exceptionally* depart from the regional position, if this is necessary in Spain's best interest. Cf. Agreement of 30 November 1994.	authorised by the head of the Spanish delegation to speak during Council meetings, but in no case is he entitled to cast the vote on behalf of Spain. Cf. Agreement of 9 December 2004.
Italy	The Interdepartmental Committee for European Affairs (CIAE in acronym) is a body comprising the Italian prime minister and other ministers. CIAE discusses EU-related issues in order to decide the position of the Italian government on the EU level. This is an important forum for discussion and consultation. When issues relating to regional or local interests and/or responsibilities are on the agenda, regional and local delegates (4 in total) participate in the meetings and in this way can make a contribution to defining the Italian position (cf. Art. 2 Law No. 234 of 24 December 2012). The Italian Regions may also request the submission to the State-Regions Conference of any EU proposal touching on matters falling within their legislative responsibility. If no agreement is reached within the Conference, the government in the Council is free to depart from the	In theory, Italy offers a significant possibility that representatives of the Regions will be included in the external representation of Italy in the Council. Direct participation of Regions in EU decision-making process is based on Article 117(5) of the Constitution. This provision establishes that the Regions (as well as the Autonomous Provinces of Trento and Bolzano) have the right to participate in all the decisions about the formation of Union law in relation to matters that fall within their responsibility. Article 5 of Law No. 131 of 5 June 2003 specifies that regional participation in the Council takes place in the framework of the national government's delegation and that a president of a Region (that is, the head of a regional government) may even be appointed as head of the delegation. This may happen when a matter of exclusive legislative competence of the Regions is on the

(continued)

Table 2.1 (continued)

	Internal cooperation	External representation in the Council
Member State	Internal cooperation is the internal coordination of the positions of the central government and of the sub-national authorities prior to a Council meeting. The aim is to achieve a common position that is to be defended in the Council by either the central government or a representative 'at ministerial level' of a regional government.	External representation is the participation of regional representatives in Council meetings in accordance with Article 16(2) TEU.
	position of the Regions (cf. Art. 24 Law No. 234 of 24 December 2012).	agenda. The true and actual weight of such participation is limited, though, by the *indivisibility* of the Italian delegation before the EU. This is due to the need to guarantee the unitary position of the Italian Republic and to speak with a *single voice* in the international and supranational arena. This legal requirement is rooted in Article 5 of the Italian Constitution ('The Republic is one and indivisible'). So far, Italy has not yet been represented by a head of a regional government, nor has the Italian vote ever been cast by a regional representative. In fact, the role of the Italian Regions is limited to consultation by the national government.
UK	In the UK, there is no formal legal basis for consultation of the three devolved administrations (Northern Ireland, Scotland, Wales). In principle, the UK government and parliament are the sole authorities responsible for relations with the EU. There is a quasi-legal agreement in place (Memorandum of Understanding, which is 'binding in honour only') that requires the UK government to consult the devolved administrations when EU proposals have an impact on their responsibilities. The position of the devolved administrations is not legally binding on the national government.	In the UK, ministers and officials from the devolved administrations have to play a role in Council meetings. This has to happen when on the Council agenda there are matters likely to have a significant impact on devolved powers. Decisions on ministerial attendance at these meetings are taken on a case-by-case basis by the competent UK minister. It is the UK minister who is responsible for conducting the negotiations and who determines how each member of the team can best contribute to secure the agreed position. This implies that the UK minister may even allow a regional minister to act as the UK spokesperson in the Council, but there is no guarantee that this will be the case. The UK minister may decide that the regional minister should not have a particular role to play, even in a situation where the matter on the Council agenda has a

(continued)

Table 2.1 (continued)

	Internal cooperation	External representation in the Council
Member State	Internal cooperation is the internal coordination of the positions of the central government and of the sub-national authorities prior to a Council meeting. The aim is to achieve a common position that is to be defended in the Council by either the central government or a representative 'at ministerial level' of a regional government.	External representation is the participation of regional representatives in Council meetings in accordance with Article 16(2) TEU.
		significant impact on the devolved authorities. In any case, it will need to be ensured that the UK speaks with a single voice on the EU level. To this purpose, the regional minister who eventually represents the UK in the Council will need to agree his position with the UK government. Local authorities from England are not involved in the EU lawmaking process through national channels of participation. Local authorities are only involved through the Committee of the Regions. These authorities can also *lobby* the EU institutions through liaison offices in Brussels and/or through their participation in national and/or European associations.
France	The French sub-national authorities are not involved in the preparation of Council meetings. They perform a role only where the Committee of Local Financing (which comprises representatives of the Regions and Departments) needs to be consulted on EU legislative proposals having technical and financial impact on the territorial communities (cf. Art. L 1211-4 of the General Code of Territorial Communities).	French territorial communities cannot represent their Member State in the Council. They are not represented in the French delegation to the Council or in the COREPER or in Council working groups. The lack of involvement of the French territorial communities may explain why alternative forms of participation have been sought persistently by French regional and local authorities; for example, liaison offices and other lobbying initiatives directed to the EU institutions appear to have flourished significantly in France. It must be taken into account that the French territorial authorities do not have substantial legislative power. Accordingly, not being endowed with the power to shape policy through legislation comparable to that of the national parliament, they are not as heavily constitutionally affected by European integration as the regions with

(continued)

Table 2.1 (continued)

	Internal cooperation	External representation in the Council
Member State	Internal cooperation is the internal coordination of the positions of the central government and of the sub-national authorities prior to a Council meeting. The aim is to achieve a common position that is to be defended in the Council by either the central government or a representative 'at ministerial level' of a regional government.	External representation is the participation of regional representatives in Council meetings in accordance with Article 16(2) TEU.
		legislative power in federal or regional systems.
Finland	The Åland Islands are full participants in the preparation of Council meetings due to their special status. If the government of Åland and the government of Finland are not able to agree on a common position, the government of Åland can ask the Finnish government to declare the position of Åland in the Council.	The Åland government may request to participate in the work of the Finnish delegation to the Council when the issue on the agenda falls within the competence of Åland. In such a case, the Åland government may also request to become part of the Finnish delegation to the Council. The Finnish government and the government of Åland are under the duty to negotiate a common position; however, if no agreement is reached, the Finnish government has no duty to uphold the position of Åland. The Finnish representative has to declare that position upon request from the Åland government. Cf. Section 59a of the Act on the Autonomy of Åland (1991/1144) and Section 26 of the Government of Finland Act 175/2003 of 28 February 2003.
Portugal	The two Autonomous Regions (Azores and Madeira) are involved in the preparation of Council meetings. The Autonomous Regions have to be consulted by the national government if matters of regional interest are on the agenda of the Council. There is no legal obligation to uphold their position in the Council. Cf. Art. 227 No. 1 Lit. *v* Portuguese Constitution.	Azores and Madeira have the right to participate in the Portuguese delegations involved in EU decision-making processes when matters that concern them are on the agenda. There is no legal obligation for the Portuguese delegation to uphold the regional position in the Council. Cf. Art. 227 No. 1 Lit. *x* Portuguese Constitution.

[a]The table includes only the Member States whose sub-national authorities have legislative powers. The French sub-national authorities do not have substantial legislative powers; however, France too is included in the table due to the importance and influence of the French constitutional system in the EU and beyond Europe. This table is mainly based on Panara and De Becker (2011), pp. 297 ff

Another at least symbolically important form of sub-national participation in EU lawmaking and policymaking is the CoR. This body comprises regional/local representatives with an electoral mandate or politically accountable to an elected assembly. It has to be consulted (even though the resulting opinion is not binding) in those fields of intervention that are more closely linked to the interests of the sub-national authorities.[20] The CoR can be consulted also on any other topic *if* the political institutions consider it appropriate. It can submit opinions on its own initiative to the Council, the Commission and the European Parliament. In this way, the advisory activity of the CoR embraces potentially the whole spectrum of activity of the EU.[21]

D. The Implementation of EU Law and Policy by the Sub-national Authorities

1. Beyond the Doctrine of the Exclusive Responsibility of the Member States for the Fulfilment of EU Obligations: The Role of the Sub-national Authorities

A qualifying element of the EU multilevel system is that the Union shall respect the 'national identity' of the Member States, including regional/local self-government (cf. Art. 4(2) TEU). Accordingly, in conformity with the institutional and procedural autonomy principle, the Union cannot alter the allocation of responsibilities that is in place in a Member State.[22] In a number of Member States, the sub-national authorities have primary responsibility for the implementation of EU law/policy

---

[20] Article 300(3) TFEU stipulates that 'The CoR shall consist of regional and local representatives who either hold a regional or local authority electoral mandate or are politically accountable to an elected assembly'. In all the Member States, the regional and local authorities are involved in the choice of the members of the CoR directly or through their associations. Consultation of the CoR is mandatory for the following areas: transport (Art. 91(1) TFEU); employment (Arts. 148(2) and 149(1) TFEU); social policy (Art. 153(2) TFEU); education, vocational training, youth and sport (Arts. 165(4) and 166(4) TFEU); culture (Art. 167(5) TFEU); public health (Art. 168(4) TFEU); trans-European networks (Art. 172 TFEU); economic, social and territorial cohesion (Arts. 175(3), 177(1) and 178(1) TFEU); environment (Art. 175(1), (2) and (3) TFEU). All the aforementioned subjects were within the sphere of competence of the CoR before the entry into force of the Treaty of Lisbon. The Treaty of Lisbon increased the number and range of policies in which the opinion of the CoR is required. More specifically, the Treaty of Lisbon added the following areas to the aforementioned ones: sea and air transport (Art. 100(2) TFEU, within the framework of the transport policy), a number of measures aimed at protecting public health (Art. 168(5) TFEU, within the framework of the public health policy), extension of the ordinary legislative procedure to some areas of environmental protection (Art. 192(2) TFEU, within the framework of the environment policy), energy policy (Art. 194(2) TFEU).

[21] Cf. Art. 307 (1) and (4) TFEU. In the literature, cf. Ricci (2011), pp. 109 ff. See further Chap. 3.

[22] Cf. ECJ Joined Cases 51–54/71, *International Fruit Company NV and others v Produktschap voor Groenten en Fruit* [1971] ECR 1107. In the literature cf. Guillermin (1992), pp. 319 ff.

and to ensure compliance with EU requirements in the areas falling within their remit. Exceptions are possible exclusively in particular circumstances. For example, in Ruling No. 126 of 24 April 1996, the Italian Constitutional Court stated that an alteration of the normal distribution of competences between the State and Regions may *exceptionally* be justified if an EU regulation is such to require uniform implementation across the entire national territory.[23]

In addition to being entitled to implement EU law in their fields of competence, the sub-national authorities have a duty to comply with obligations stemming from the EU. Regardless of whether an infringement of EU obligations is due to the behaviour of a national or of a sub-national authority, from an 'orthodox' EU law perspective a Member State is the only entity liable *vis-à-vis* the Union for the non-compliance.[24] However, a holistic approach taking into account the national dimension, along with the European dimension, suggests that the constitutional laws of the Member States create a right and at the same time a duty of the sub-national authorities to comply with EU obligations.

This idea of a right/duty of the sub-national authorities to comply with/implement EU law emerges with particular strength and clarity in the context of the Austrian federation. The Austrian Constitutional Court created the concept of a 'double bond' (*doppelte Bindung*).[25] The domestic legislator is 'bound twice'; on the one hand, it has to comply with EU obligations and, on the other, with the norms of the national constitution, including those concerning the distribution of responsibilities between Federation and *Länder*. The consequence is that the *Länder* have the constitutional *right* and, at the same time, the *duty* to implement EU measures falling within their sphere of competence. Unlike the Italian *Corte costituzionale*, the Austrian Constitutional Court rejected the idea that a hypothetical requirement for uniform implementation of EU law could justify 'implied powers' of the

---

[23] Another example of this approach can be seen in Ruling No. 16 of 21 January 2010, where the Court held that the ongoing economic crisis required the creation, at State level, of a national fund for infrastructure. Additionally, the Court held that the need for uniform State action derived also from EC law. More specifically, it originated from the Community aim to reduce the social, economic and territorial disparities that have arisen particularly in countries and regions whose development is lagging behind. Cf. also the Ruling of the German Federal Constitutional Court of 14 October 2008 concerning the federal law implementing EC Regulation No. 1782/2003 of 29 September 2003 (common rules for direct support schemes under the common agricultural policy). Here, the Court held that the federal law is justified under Article 72(2) GG since it ensures the maintenance of legal unity in the national interest. Indeed, the adequate implementation of the regulation in question requires uniform legal provisions at federal level and in this way ensures the correct functioning of the single economic area of the Federal Republic (cf. §§ 88–89 of the judgment).

[24] Cf. ECJ Case 72/81, *Commission v Belgium* [1982] ECR 183, and Joined Cases 227–230/85 *Commission v Belgium* [1988] ECR 1. See also ECJ Case 8/88 *Germany v Commission* [1990] ECR I-2321 at 2355–2366. In the literature, cf. Lenaerts and Van Nuffel (2011), pp. 629–631; Schaus (1994), p. 79.

[25] Cf. the rulings of the Austrian Constitutional Court published in the official collection *Erkentnisse und Beschlüsse des Verfassungsgerichtshofes* (in acronym *VfSlg.*) 14.863/1997 and 17.022/2003.

Federation in a field in which there is no constitutional basis for federal intervention. The Austrian Court held that this type of intervention would require a constitutional amendment.[26] This is quite a significant statement, considering that the Court had already accepted the principle of primacy of EU law, i.e., that single constitutional provisions should be set aside in the event of a conflict with EU law.[27] This suggests that the protection of the constitutional role and status of the sub-national authorities in the Austrian context can provide an exception even to one of the constitutional cornerstones of the EU system.

The constitutional right and duty of the sub-national authorities to implement, and comply with, EU law, is not an Austrian peculiarity. This principle is *explicitly* (Austria,[28] UK,[29] Italy[30]) or *implicitly* (Germany,[31] Belgium,[32] Spain[33]) embedded also in the constitutional laws of other Member States.

In conclusion, from the perspective of EU law, the State is the only entity responsible for the implementation of EU law/policy, but there are constitutional constraints at national level preventing a central authority from encroaching arbitrarily on the sphere of competence of the sub-national authorities in relation to the implementation of EU law and policy.

---

[26] Cf. the Ruling of the Austrian Constitutional Court in *VfSlg.* 17.022/2003.

[27] Cf. the Ruling of the Austrian Constitutional Court in *VfSlg.* 15.427/1999. In the literature, cf. Eberhard (2011), p. 229.

[28] Art. 23d(5) Federal Constitutional Law (*Bundes-Verfassungsgesetz*, in acronym B-VG).

[29] Section 53 and Paragraph 7(2) of Schedule 5 of the Scotland Act 1998; Paragraph 3(c) of Schedule 2 of the Northern Ireland Act 1998; Section 80 of the Government of Wales Act 2006. Cf. also Paragraph 21 Memorandum of Understanding between UK government and devolved administrations, September 2012 (hereafter 'Memorandum of Understanding' or 'MoU') and Section B4.17 of the Concordat on Co-ordination of European Union Policy Issues (hereafter 'Concordat'). In the UK, the implementation of EU law by the devolved authorities resembles more a 'duty' than a fully fledged 'right'. The Concordat states in clear-cut terms that the UK Parliament and UK Ministers retain the power to legislate to implement EU obligations throughout the UK (cf. Section B4.9; cf. also Paragraph 14 MoU on the right of UK Parliament to legislate on any issue, including those devolved). In relation to local authorities, cf. Part 2 (EU Financial Sanctions) and Part 3 (EU Financial Sanctions: Wales) of the Localism Act 2011.

[30] Art. 117(5) Italian Constitution.

[31] The right of the *Länder* to implement the EU law in matters of their competence can be drawn from Article 30 GG ('GG' is the acronym for *Grundgesetz*, lit. 'Basic Law', which is the German federal constitution), according to which the exercise of State powers and the performance of State functions is a matter for the *Länder*, unless otherwise provided or permitted by the *Grundgesetz*. Cf. Degenhart (2007), p. 1424 (Rn. 6).

[32] This is a result of the principle 'in foro interno et in foro externo', according to which the Belgian Regions and Communities shall enjoy in the EU arena the same powers they enjoy in the domestic jurisdiction. Cf. De Becker (2011), p. 256.

[33] In Spain, this principle can be drawn from Article 1 of Act No. 47 of 27 December 1985, which was passed at the time of the Spanish accession to the Communities. The principle has been confirmed by the Constitutional Court in Ruling No. 236 of 12 December 1991 and No. 79 of 28 May 1992.

2. State Liability and Financial Liability of the Sub-national Authorities in Case of Failure to Comply with Obligations Stemming from the EU

What happens if a sub-national authority does not comply with obligations stemming from the Treaties? In *Konle* and *Haim*, the ECJ recognised that State liability may be triggered by an action or a failure to act of a sub-state entity (a part of the State). In such circumstances, the federation or the central government should not necessarily make the reparation of the damage or the loss. This can be made by the responsible sub-state entity in accordance with domestic law.[34] In this manner, the ECJ legitimised the national legislation imposing exclusively on sub-national authorities the responsibility for a 'loss' or 'damage' attributable to a component of the State.

In some Member States, there is a subsidiary financial liability of the sub-national authorities towards the State, which finds application in the event of a breach of EU obligations originating from the behaviour of a sub-state authority. Such arrangements aim to work as a deterrent against failures to implement, inaccurate implementation or any other breach of obligations deriving from EU membership. Germany is a good example of this approach. Any cost deriving from Germany's violation of 'supranational' or 'international' obligations must be borne by the responsible *Land* or *Länder* in proportion to the respective quota of responsibility.[35]

Similar criteria find application also in other Member States. Austrian law lays down the obligation for the *Länder* and the local authorities to pay the costs that derive from judgments of the Court of Justice in relation to breaches of EU law.[36] Any disputes on the attribution of the financial liability to the sub-state authorities are decided by the Constitutional Court (cf. Art. 137 Federal Constitutional Law). In a similar manner, in Spain the *Tribunal Constitucional* has held that when an Autonomous Community does not implement EU law correctly in an area within its responsibility, that Community shall comply with the findings of the Court of Justice and pay any fine.[37] In the UK too, when a breach of EU obligations originates from the behaviour of one of the devolved authorities in Scotland, Northern Ireland or Wales, or of a local authority, the responsible entity may be required to pay the pecuniary sanction imposed on the UK.[38] A comparable 'right of

---

[34] Cf. Case C-302/97 *Konle v Austria* [1999] ECR I-3099 at 61–64; Case C-424/97 *Haim v Kassenzahnärtztliche Vereinigung Nordrhein* [2000] ECR I-5123 at 31–32. Cf. Craig and De Bùrca (2011), p. 245.

[35] Cf. Art. 104a(6), first subparagraph, GG.

[36] Cf. 2008 Financial Equalization Act (*Finanzausgleichsgesetz* 2008, in acronym FAG 2008), published in Federal Law Gazette (*Bundesgesetzblatt*, BGBl. in acronym) I 2007/103.

[37] Cf. Ruling of the Spanish Constitutional Court No. 79 of 28 May 1992 and later judgments.

[38] In relation to devolved administrations, cf. Section B4.26 of the Concordat on Co-ordination of EU Policy Issues. In relation to local authorities, cf. Part 2 and Part 3 of the Localism Act 2011.

redress' through which the central government can recover any expenditure deriving from the non-fulfilment of EU obligations also exists in Italy,[39] Belgium[40] and the Netherlands.[41]

In summary, from a traditional orthodox EU perspective, only the State is responsible for a breach of EU obligations, but from an internal/constitutional perspective the sub-national authority that causes a financial liability of the State or the State liability may have to pay the fine or the 'loss' or 'damage'. The subsidiary financial liability of the sub-national authorities is anchored to the national constitution (Germany, Spain) or is embedded in rules of constitutional significance, i.e., rules affecting the constitutional autonomy of the sub-national authorities (this is the case of all other analysed case studies). This confirms that the EU multilevel system is far more complicated and articulated than just a linear national–supranational relationship between Member States and the EU.[42]

3. Protecting Local and Regional Self-government from Surreptitious 'Re-centralisation': Constitutional Limitations and Constraints Surrounding the EU-Related Substitution Powers of the State

Another tool often provided by domestic law for ensuring compliance with EU obligations is the substitution power granted to the central government of the State. The practical meaning of such substitution is that the right to enact implementation measures passes *exceptionally* and *temporarily* to central authorities (whether executive or legislature). Typically, the non-compliant territorial authority (regional or local entity) retains the right to implement the obligation at a later stage; i.e., at a later stage, it can replace the measure issued by the central government with an own measure. In Italy, this phenomenon is called *cedevolezza*, i.e., pliability, of the substitute measure. The substitution should be seen as an *extrema ratio*, required to overcome the refusal or inability by a sub-state authority

---

[39] Cf. Art. 43(2) Law No. 234 of 24 December 2012. Art. 43(10) of the same Law establishes that the State has a similar 'right of redress' against the sub-state authorities responsible of a violation of the European Convention on Human Rights (ECHR). Both provisions were originally introduced in 2007.

[40] Cf. Art. 16(3) of the Special Act of 8 August 1980.

[41] Cf. Statute of 24 May 2012 on the correct application of European law by public authorities (*Wet Naleving Europese regelgeving publieke entiteiten*) in: *Staatsblad* (lit. State Gazette), 2012, 245. Cf. Backes and van der Woude (2013), p. 252.

[42] Contra see Cygan (2013), p. 188: 'The paradox arising from the Treaty of Lisbon is that it while it has sought to improve the legitimacy of EU law through competence monitoring by the CoR, the Treaty has failed to sufficiently recognise the political and legislative autonomy of regions, and establish appropriate corresponding mechanisms for their accountability in circumstances when they misapply EU law'.

to comply with EU law. The substitution power is a good example of how, despite the institutional and procedural autonomy principle (cf. supra Sect. D.1), EU integration may produce an impact on the internal distribution of powers in the Member States.[43]

It is possible to draw a distinction between an 'a priori' and a 'post facto' substitution. A priori substitution takes place before the non-fulfilment of an EU obligation, in order to prevent it from occurring (for example, before the expiry of the term for transposing a directive). Post facto substitution takes place after the non-fulfilment of an EU obligation (for example, after the expiry of the term for transposing a directive or after a judgment of the Court of Justice certifying an infringement of EU law).

A priori substitution is problematic in the light of the 'right' of sub-state authorities to implement EU law in their own sphere of competence. The Spanish Constitutional Court dealt with this issue in a case concerning the European Agricultural Guidance and Guarantee Fund. The Court held that the central government has the right to issue substitute provisions implementing EU law in areas of regional competence, but this is allowed only after a non-fulfilment of an EU obligation has taken place. Were the substitution power exercisable regardless of a previous non-compliant behaviour, the entire constitutional distribution of powers between the central government and the Autonomous Communities would be irremediably undermined.[44]

This explains why, in the Member States where it is exceptionally allowed, a priori substitution is surrounded by safeguards in the interest of the sub-state authorities. In the UK, for example, whilst Parliament, in accordance with the principle of parliamentary sovereignty, theoretically retains the right to legislate on *any* issue, devolved or not, the devolved administrations and the UK government may agree that an EU obligation would be best implemented by uniform national measures adopted by the Westminster Parliament.[45] Given that the substitution (not only a priori but also ex post facto) requires that Westminster and the devolved administrations seek an agreement, this mechanism takes into account the prerogatives of the devolved administrations.[46] The constitutional standing of the devolved administrations in the EU multilevel context entails a partial constraint

---

[43] The substitution power can be seen as a manifestation of the principle established at Article 4 (3) TEU: 'The Member States shall take any appropriate measure, general or particular, to ensure fulfilment of the obligations arising out of the Treaties or resulting from the acts of the institutions of the Union'. On the acceptability in principle of transposition of EU law through the subsidiary application of national rules, cf. the Opinion of AG Kokott, 30 May 2013, Case C-151/12, *Commission v Spain* (cf. para. 34). However, in the view of AG Kokott, 'such subsidiary application must be beyond question'.

[44] Ruling of the Spanish Constitutional Court No. 80 of 8 March 1993. Cf. Chicharro Lázaro (2011), pp. 203–204.

[45] This can be inferred from Paragraph 14 MoU.

[46] Under Paragraph 21 MoU, the devolved administrations may even ask the UK government to extend UK legislation to cover their EU obligations.

to the principle of parliamentary sovereignty, which is one of the cornerstones of the UK constitution.

In Italy, until recently, the national government was entitled to implement EU obligations on a yearly basis through the annual 'Community law' (*legge comunitaria*[47]) and the related delegated legislation. This could happen in relation to any subject matter, including those within the legislative responsibility of the Regions. In practice, this system triggered a large-scale, annual, a priori substitution of the regional authorities by the State. However, the substitute laws emanated by the State were characterised for the previously mentioned 'pliability', *cedevolezza*. This implied that every time the State substituted its laws for those of the Regions, then, at a later stage, the Regions were entitled to replace those laws with their own. In this way, they were able to regain control over their sphere of competence.[48] In 2012, this mechanism was replaced by an alternative approach. Under the new regime, the substitution powers of the State shall apply only in case of failure by a Region to comply with EU law (post facto substitution).[49] In this way, the autonomy of the Regions and their *primary* role in implementing EU law and policy find stronger recognition than in the past, with the State intervening only in case of lack of implementation or non-compliance.

In some Member States, substitution can take place only after a judicial decision has been issued by Union Courts. This is the case in Austria and Belgium, where substitution is possible only if/when a Union Court has found against the State on grounds that a *Land* (Austria), or a Region or Community (Belgium), has failed to comply with EU obligations.[50] This is a form of substantial protection of the prerogatives of the sub-state entities since, in the absence of a Union Court's

---

[47] The *legge comunitaria* was a special statute passed by Parliament every year in order to ensure that Italian law was in conformity with all EU directives and regulations issued during the previous year.

[48] On the pre-2012 regime, cf. Villamena (2011), pp. 173–179.

[49] This seems to be the correct interpretation of Art. 41 in conjunction with Art. 37 Law No. 234 of 24 December 2012. The constitutional foundation of the State substitution powers is to be found in Arts. 117(5) and 120(2) of the Italian Constitution. So far, the only example of exercise of substitution powers (apart from the 'ordinary' a priori substitution taking place on the basis of the former *leggi comunitarie* through delegated legislation of the government) is the suspension in 2006 by a Government Decree Law of the application of a statute of the Liguria Region. This statute was in breach of Directive 79/409/EEC of 2 April 1979 on the conservation of wild birds. On this occasion, State intervention followed an Order of the President of the ECJ issued in the context of an infringement case against Italy (cf. Order of the President of the ECJ in the Case C-503/06). In relation to local (i.e., sub-regional) authorities (Municipalities and Provinces), the central government can act for them (i.e., substitute them) when it ascertains the inertia of the local authorities in performing their functions, provided that such inertia constitutes a 'non compliance with the obligations stemming from membership in the EU' or a 'risk of a serious damage to the national interest' (cf. Art. 137 Legislative Decree No. 267 of 18 August 2000, better known as *Testo Unico degli Enti Locali*, lit. Unified Text on Local Authorities, TUEL in acronym).

[50] On Austria, cf. Art. 23d(5) B-VG. This could only be relevant in the case of a judgment of the ECJ pursuant to Art. 260 TFEU (ex Art. 228 TEC). Cf. Öhlinger (1999), Rz. 32. On Belgium, cf. Art. 169 Belgian Constitution and Art. 16 § 3 of Special Act of 8 August 1980 as amended by

judgment, it would remain uncertain whether a sub-state entity has really infringed EU law. However, this protection is not in force in all countries. In some Member States, post facto substitution is possible even in the absence of, or before, a judicial decision. Such is the case in the UK and in Italy, where the central authorities are entitled to exercise substitution powers before a judgment of the Court of Justice.[51]

The exercise of substitution powers by central governments is an exception to the normal constitutional distribution of powers. Therefore, in order to respect the decentralised, federal or regional structure of the State, the substitution procedures must be inspired by principles such as loyal cooperation, respect for regional and local autonomy, proportionality. In Belgium, for instance, the State can only prompt the procedure following a formal finding by the Court of Justice of an infringement of EU law. Additionally, three further conditions must be fulfilled. First, formal notice shall be given to the Community or Region concerned, in order to grant sufficient time to conform to EU obligations before the substitution takes place. Second, the Community or Region concerned must be involved in the whole procedure during the litigation to find a solution for the pending case. Third, the substitution shall involve only those measures that are strictly necessary to comply with the Court of Justice's ruling (proportionality).[52]

In a similar way, in Italy, the substitution procedure takes account of the rights of the Regions. Like in Belgium, the national government must assign a proper timescale to allow the Regions to act, and *only* in the absence of their activity will it enact the necessary measures. The Head of the Executive of the Region concerned has the right to participate in the session of the Council of Ministers deciding on the adoption of the substitute measure. Finally, once again like in Belgium, the principle of proportionality must be respected; i.e., the means must be proportionate to the aims.[53]

In Germany, the Federation has no power to step in and act for a *Land*. Infringements of EU law by the *Länder* are tackled through Federation-*Länder* dialogue or, ex post, through the financial liability of the *Länder* (cf. supra Sect. D.2). An intervention of the federal power in Germany would be theoretically possible under Article 37 GG in order to coerce the *Länder* to comply with their duties (*Bundeszwang*, federal coercion). It must be pointed out, however, that Article 37 GG has never been applied. This is likely to be due to the genuine cooperative attitude of the *Länder* and also to the fact that the use of this provision could prove time consuming and cause political difficulties.[54]

Special Act of 5 May 1993. A judgment passed under Article 263 TFEU (ex Art. 234 TEC) would not trigger the substitution power. Cf. De Becker (2011), pp. 271–272.

[51] On the UK, cf. Section 57 Scotland Act 1998, Section 26(2) Northern Ireland Act 1998, Section 82 Government of Wales Act 2006. On Italy, cf. Art. 8 Law No. 131 of 5 June 2003, Art. 41 Law No. 234 of 24 December 2012, Art. 137 TUEL.

[52] Art. 16 § 3 of the Special Act of 8 August 1980 as modified by the Special Act of 5 May 1993. To date, this special procedure has not found application.

[53] Cf. Art. 8 Law No. 131 of 5 June 2003.

[54] Cf. Huber (2007), p. 217.

EU-related substitution powers are another by-product of the 'EU multilevel system'. These powers are rooted in the national constitutions and aim to face the challenge of timely and proper fulfilment of the obligations arising from EU membership. In the analysed Member States, substitution is an exception to the normal division of powers and constitutes a measure used only in extremis. It is subject to considerable legal/constitutional constraints, which demonstrates the stability and strength of the legal position of the sub-national authorities in the EU multilevel context. The above analysis strengthens the conclusion that the sub-national level of government is an integral part of the EU as the status of the sub-national authorities derives from the combination, the 'fusion', of the EU with the legal systems of the Member States.

4. The Defence of the Sub-state Authorities in Infraction Proceedings

In case of an alleged breach of an EU obligation by a sub-state authority, the Commission instigates infraction proceedings against the respective Member State. Yet, as shown above, according to domestic law the sub-state authority concerned may have to bear the consequences of its non-compliance with EU law by way of financial liability or substitution (cf. supra Sects. D.2 and D.3). This position raises the question of the rights of defence of the sub-state authorities in infraction proceedings. Being the proceedings addressed against a State, and not against a regional/local authority, EU law itself does not contemplate any specific defence for the latter. Accordingly, it is necessary to look at if/how the single Member States protect the rights of their territorial authorities. Specific provisions in relation to this aspect exist in Belgium, Spain, the UK and Germany.

In Belgium, Spain and the UK, the regional authority concerned (Community or Region in Belgium, Autonomous Community in Spain, devolved administration in the UK) is *individually* involved in the entire infraction proceedings. This includes both the pre-judicial and the judicial phase of the proceedings. Accordingly, where a case is referred to the Court of Justice against Belgium, Spain or the UK, the regional authority concerned will contribute to determine the position of the Member State before the Court.[55]

---

[55] In relation to Belgium, cf. Art. 16 § 3 Special Act of 8 August 1980. On Spain, cf. Art. 11 of CARCE Agreement of 11 December 1997 on the participation of the Autonomous Communities in proceedings before the ECJ (*Acuerdo sobre la participación de las Comunidades Autónomas en los procedimientos ante el TJCE*). On the UK cf. Sections B4.23–B4.25 MoU.

An interesting pattern of regional involvement in the infraction proceedings is in place in the UK. Both in the pre-judicial and judicial stages of the proceedings, the UK system requires a high degree of interaction and cooperation between UK government and devolved administrations. More specifically, where infraction proceedings relate to matters falling *entirely* within the responsibility of a devolved administration, the draft reply is prepared by that administration and agreed with the interested Whitehall departments before being submitted to the Commission.[56] Where a case partly concerns the implementation of a devolved matter in England and in one among Scotland, Wales or Northern Ireland, *or* concerns implementation in the devolved regions in relation to a non-devolved matter, the draft reply is prepared by the lead Whitehall department in bilateral consultation with the relevant devolved authority.[57] As to the judicial stage of the infraction proceedings, where a case *partly or entirely* involving the implementation of EU obligations by a devolved administration is referred to the Court of Justice, the devolved administration contributes to the preparation of the UK's submissions to the Court. The devolved administration shall take the lead for those cases solely concerned with implementation in relation to matters falling within its responsibility and shall act in agreement with the relevant Whitehall departments.[58]

Contrary to Spain, Belgium and the UK, German law lays down a *collective* right of the *Länder* to be involved in infraction proceedings affecting them. Accordingly, in infraction proceedings brought against Germany for an alleged breach caused by one or more of the *Länder*, the Federal Government has to agree its defence strategy with the *Bundesrat*, the chamber representing the *Länder* on the federal level.[59]

The traditional, 'orthodox', EU perspective is to consider the Member States as the only entities that are responsible for an infringement of EU obligations. Accordingly, infraction proceedings can be instigated *only* against a Member State, even in the event that a sub-national authority causes an infringement. However, some Member States feature mechanisms to involve the sub-national authorities in the pre- and judicial phases of the infraction proceedings. This involvement ensures that the point of view of the sub-national authorities is taken into account before a financial sanction is issued against the Member State. This is consistent with the constitutional role of the sub-national entities and especially with circumstance that the same entities are responsible *vis-à-vis* the Member State for infringements of EU law.

---

[56] Cf. Section B4.24 MoU (initial part).

[57] Cf. Section B4.24 MoU (final part).

[58] Cf. Section B4.25 MoU.

[59] Cf. § 7(3) Law on the cooperation of Federation and *Länder* in EU related matters (*Gesetz über die Zusammenarbeit von Bund und Ländern in Angelegenheiten der Europäischen Union*, EUZBLG in acronym).

E. The Challenge of Union Acts by the Sub-national Authorities

1. Direct Challenge of Union Acts: The 'State Centric' Jurisprudence of the ECJ

In addition to participating in infraction proceedings (cf. supra Sect. D.4), the sub-state authorities may need to challenge the validity of Union acts, where these, in a way or another, negatively affect them (for example, by encroaching on their sphere of competence or by producing a detrimental impact on local economy). In the view of the Court of Justice, Article 263(2) TFEU does not grant the status of 'privileged applicants' to the sub-state authorities; i.e., in terms of their locus standi, these public authorities fall in the same class as the individuals.[60] They may challenge acts addressed to them without any specific restriction. They may also challenge acts not addressed to them (for example, a decision addressed to a Member State, a regulation), provided that such acts concern them 'directly and individually'. Finally, they may challenge 'regulatory acts' that do not entail implementing measures, provided that such acts concern them 'directly' (albeit not necessarily 'individually').[61] Showing the existence of 'direct' and 'individual concern' could be extremely difficult for sub-national authorities.[62] A few lessons can be learned from the existing case law.

The mere fact that an EU act deals with an issue falling within the responsibility of a sub-state authority is not sufficient in order to entitle that authority to challenge the act. In *Friuli-Venezia Giulia v Commission*, concerning an annex to an EU regulation limiting temporally the right to use the label 'Tocai friulano', a vine variety typical of that region, the Court of First Instance (CFI) held that 'the division of legislative and regulatory powers within a Member State is solely a matter for the constitutional law of that State and has no effect from the point of

---

[60] Cf. ECJ Judgment 11 July 1984 in the Case *Municipality of Differdange v Commission* [1984] ECR 2889, para. 8; ECJ Order of 21 March 1997 in the Case C-95/97, *Région Wallonne v Commission*, ECR [1997] I-1787, paras. 6–7. Cf. also Case C-180/97 *Regione Toscana v Commission* [1997] ECR 1-5245, paras. 7–8; Case T-214/95 *Vlaams Gewest v Commission* [1998] ECR II-717, para. 28. The Order of the General Court (GC) 6 March 2012, Case T-453/10, *Northern Ireland Department of Agriculture and Rural Development v Commission*, ECR [2012], paras. 36–38, dismissed the argument advanced by the applicant that the lack of recognition of locus standi to Northern Ireland goes against the obligation for the EU (stemming from Art. 4(2) TEU) to respect the national identity of the UK, including its regional self-government.

[61] Cf. Art. 263(4) TFEU. The 'direct and individual concern' requirement also applies to actions for wrongful failure to act under Art. 265(3) TFEU brought by a natural or legal person, when the expected act is not addressed to the applicant. Cf. ECJ Judgment 26 November 1996, Case C-68/95, *Port v Bundesanstalt für Landwirtschaft und Ernährung* [1996] ECR I-6065; CFI Judgment 15 September 1998, Case T-95/96, *Telecinco v Commission* [1998] ECR II-3407.

[62] In the literature, cf. Van Nuffel (2001), pp. 871 ff.; Dani (2004), pp. 181 ff.; Lenaerts (2008); Thies (2011), pp. 25 ff.

view of assessing the possible effects of a Community legal measure on the interests of a territorial body'. Accordingly, the Court held that the Region Friuli-Venezia Giulia was not 'individually concerned' by the contested legal provision.[63]

The simple fact that an EU act affects a local interest (for example, the local economy) is not sufficient to ground 'individual concern'. In *Cantabria v Council*, the CFI held that 'any general interest the applicant [Autonomous Community] may have, as a third person, in obtaining a result which will favour the economic prosperity of a given business and, as a result, the level of employment in the geographical region where it carries on its activities, is insufficient, on its own, to enable the applicant to be regarded as "concerned" [...], nor, a fortiori, as being individually concerned'.[64] This argument has been repeated in several cases since.[65]

The status as an 'outermost region' under Article 349 TFEU (ex Art. 299 TEC) does not automatically lead to the recognition of 'individual concern'. In *Azores v Council*, the President of the CFI held that the mere circumstance that an applicant region benefits from specific Treaty protection is not sufficient to show 'individual concern'. 'Otherwise the outermost regions mentioned in Article 299(2) EC [now Art. 349 TFEU, including the Azores] would acquire rights to bring legal proceedings akin to the rights of Member States. Such a result would be contrary to Article 230 EC [now Art. 263 TFEU] which does not entitle, by analogy, regional entities to bring actions under the same conditions as Member States'.[66]

The fact that a sub-state authority is responsible for the implementation of a project funded under the Structural Funds does not automatically give it locus standi to challenge an act cancelling or modifying the financial assistance. In *Sicily v Commission*, concerning a decision withdrawing the funds for a project funded by the ERDF[67] (construction of a river dam in Sicily), the Court of Justice held that the

---

[63] Cf. CFI Order 12 March 2007, Case T-417/04, *Regione autonoma Friuli-Venezia Giulia v Commission* [2007] ECR II-641, para. 62.

[64] Cf. CFI Order 16 June 1998, Case T-238/97, *Comunidad Autónoma de Cantabria v Council* [1998] ECR II-2271, para. 49. The case concerned a regulation on State aid to shipyards. The regulation subjected the State aid to the limitation on ship conversion activities in a publicly owned shipyard in Cantabria.

[65] Cf. CFI Order 23 October 1998, Case T-609/97, *Regione Puglia v Commission* [1998] ECR II-4051, para. 22 (the contested regulation concerned production aid payable to producers of olive oil); ECJ Judgment 10 April 2003, Case C-142/00 P, *Commission v Nederlandse Antillen* [2003] ECR I-3483, para. 69; CFI Order 7 July 2004, Case T-37/04 R, *Região autónoma dos Açores v Council* [2004] ECR II-2153, para. 118; Case T-417/04, *Regione autonoma Friuli-Venezia Giulia v Commission* [2007] ECR II-641, para. 61. The ECJ denied locus standi to the Municipality of Differdange (Luxembourg) for lack of 'direct concern' in Judgment 11 July 1984 in the Case *Municipality of Differdange v Commission* [1984] ECR 2889, paras. 10–12.

[66] Cf. CFI Order 7 July 2004, Case T-37/04 R, *Região autónoma dos Açores v Council* [2004] ECR II-2153, para. 119. An appeal against this decision has been dismissed by the ECJ by Order 26 November 2009, Case C-444/08 P, *Região autónoma dos Açores v Council* [2009] ECR I-200*. See also ECJ Judgment 22 November 2001, Case C-452/98, *Nederlandse Antillen v Council* [2001] ECR I-8973, para. 50.

[67] European Regional Development Fund.

Sicily Region was not 'directly concerned'. The Court stated clearly that 'the position of "authority responsible for the application" [...] does not have the effect of putting the appellant [Region] in a direct relationship with the Community assistance, which [...] was applied for by the Italian Government and granted to the Italian Republic'.[68]

Union Courts take the same strict approach in relation to cases regarding financial assistance granted by the Cohesion Fund. On 10 September 2008, for instance, an Order of the CFI declared inadmissible, due to lack of 'direct concern', an application brought by the Município de Gondomar (Portugal) for the annulment of a Commission decision cancelling the financial assistance for a project for the redevelopment of Grande Porto Sul, Subsistema de Gondomar.[69] The CFI also declared inadmissible, due to lack of 'direct concern', an application brought by the Community of Grammatiko (Greece) against a Commission decision to finance a project for the construction of a landfill site in that location.[70] The applicant had claimed to be entitled to challenge the decision 'because it is a public body responsible for the protection of public health and the environment in the area where the project that is being financed is located'.[71]

The approach of Union Courts is more open in cases concerning State aid. Sub-state entities are entitled to challenge Union acts that prevent them from

---

[68] Cf. ECJ Judgment 22 March 2007, Case C-15/06, *Regione Siciliana v Commission* [2007] ECR I-2591, para. 36. In this way the ECJ overturned the CFI's ruling in Case T-60/03, *Regione Siciliana v Commission* [2005] ECR II-4139, where the CFI had admitted the locus standi of Sicily. See also CFI Order 11 December 2007, Case T-156/06, *Regione Siciliana v Commission* [2007] ECR II-168*, Summary publication, where the CFI denied the locus standi of the Sicily Region in a case concerning a reduction in financial assistance from the European Social Fund for an operational programme in Sicily; ECJ Judgment 2 May 2006, Case C-417/04 P, *Regione Siciliana v Commission* [2006] ECR I-3881, paras. 26–32, where the ECJ denied the locus standi of Sicily for lack of 'direct concern' in a case concerning a Commission decision withdrawing the financial assistance from the ERDF for the Messina–Palermo Motorway. In another case, the CFI held admissible a direct action of annulment brought by a public law consortium (comprising the Italian State, the Campania Region, the Province of Naples and a number of municipalities located in the area of the Vesuvius), whose object is to protect and improve the complex sites of the *Ville Vesuviane* (a number of historic villas located in the area around the Vesuvius). Cf. CFI Judgment 18 July 2007, Case T-189/02, *Ente per le Ville Vesuviane v Commission* [2007] ECR II-89*, Summary publication. However, the ECJ set aside the CFI's judgment for lack of 'direct concern' of *Ente*. Cf. ECJ Judgment 10 September 2009, Case C-445/07 P, *Commission v Ente per le Ville Vesuviane* [2009] ECR I-7993, para. 67.

[69] Cf. CFI Order 10 September 2008, Case T-324/06, *Município de Gondomar v Commission* [2008] ECR II-173, paras. 37–52. The applicant brought an appeal before the ECJ submitting that the CFI had erred in law when denying the applicant's locus standi. The ECJ dismissed the appeal with the Order 24 September 2009, Case C-501/08 P, *Município de Gondomar v Commission* [2009] ECR I-152.

[70] Cf. CFI Order 8 October 2008, Case T-13/08, *Koinotita Grammatikou v Commission*. See OJ 7 February 2009, C 32/35. Interestingly, unlike in the other analysed cases, the applicant challenged the financial assistance from Cohesion Fund, i.e., the applicant was trying to prevent the construction of the landfill. No appeal has been brought against this decision.

[71] See the Application in OJ 29 March 2008, C 79/29.

adopting aid measures or that require them to withdraw such measures.[72] In *Vlaams Gewest (Flemish Region) v Commission*, for example, the CFI acknowledged that 'The contested decision [concerning aid granted by the Flemish Region to a Belgian airline] has a direct and individual effect on the legal position of the Flemish Region [since] [such decision] directly prevents [that Region] from exercising its own powers, which here consist of granting the aid in question, as it sees fit'.[73] In *Freistaat Sachsen (Land Saxony) and Volkswagen v Commission* and in *Friuli-Venezia Giulia v Commission*, the CFI recognised the locus standi of the applicant sub-state entity, given that the contested act required the sub-state authority to recover from the recipients an aid previously granted.[74] In 2000, the Sicily Region challenged a Commission decision that stated, *inter alia*, that the State aid established by a regional law in favour of undertakings operating in the agriculture or fisheries sector was incompatible with EU law and, accordingly, the aid in question had to be withdrawn. The Commission did not seek to argue that the measure was not of 'direct and individual concern' to the applicant, and the CFI held the action admissible, after verifying that it had been brought within the correct time frame.[75] In a number of cases since, the question of locus standi in actions brought by sub-national authorities in relation to State aid has no longer been required to be addressed in Union Courts.[76]

---

[72] Cf. CFI Judgment 1 July 2008, Case T-37/04, *Região autónoma dos Açores v Council* [2008] ECR II-103*, at para. 82, referring to: T-214/95, *Vlaams Gewest v Commission* [1998] ECR II-717, para. 29; Joined Cases T-346/99 to T-348/99, *Diputación Foral de Álava and Others v Commission* [2002] ECR II-4259, para. 37; Joined Cases T-366/03 and T-235/04, *Land Oberösterreich and Austria v Commission* [2005] ECR II-4005, para. 28. The CFI pointed out in *Região autónoma dos Açores*, at para. 82, that the cases listed above concerned decisions on 'aid paid by the applicant local bodies, so that the lawfulness of that aid depended on the outcome of the proceedings'.

[73] Cf. CFI Judgment 30 April 1998, Case T-214/95, *Vlaams Gewest (Flemish Region) v Commission* [1998] ECR II-717, para. 29. This ruling was in line with earlier cases concerning a decision affecting, *inter alia*, a Region's power to grant State aid, in which the admissibility of the action had not been contested by the Commission. Cf. Joined Cases 62/87 and 72/87, *Exécutif régional wallon v Commission* [1988] ECR 1573, paras. 6 and 8.

[74] Cf. Joined Cases T-132/96 and T-143/96, *Land Saxony and Volkswagen v Commission* [1999] ECR II-3663, paras. 84–86; Case T-288/97, *Friuli Venezia Giulia v Commission* [1999] ECR II-1871, paras. 31–32.

[75] Cf. Case T-190/00, *Regione Siciliana v Commission* [2003] ECR II-5015, paras. 29–33 (dismissed as unfounded).

[76] See, e.g., Joined Cases T-228/99 and T-233/99, *Westdeutsche Landesbank and Land Nordrhein-Westfalen v Commission* [2003] ECR II-435; Case T-318/00, *Freistaat Thüringen v Commission* [2005] ECR II-4179; Case T-357/02, *Freistaat Sachsen v Commission* [2007] ECR II-1261; Case T-357/02 RENV, *Freistaat Sachsen v Commission* [2011] ECR II-5415; Case T-369/00, *Dé partement du Loiret v Commission* [2003] ECR II-1789, and [2007] ECR II-851; Joined Cases T-211/04 and T-215/04, *Government of Gibraltar and UK v Commission* [2008] ECR II-3745; Case T-394/08, *Regione autonoma della Sardegna v Commission* [2011] ECR II-6255. In GC Judgment 24 March 2011, Case T-443/08, *Freistaat Sachsen and Land Sachsen-Anhalt v Commission* [2011] ECR II-1311, concerning a State aid to DHL, the GC held inadmissible the application of the applicant German *Länder* on grounds of lack of a relevant legal interest. The

Union Courts appear reluctant to admit the locus standi in cases concerning a cancellation or reduction of EU funding under the Common Agricultural Policy (CAP). In *Northern Ireland Department of Agriculture v Commission*, concerning a Commission decision excluding from EU financing certain expenditures incurred by certain Member States (including the UK) in the context of the CAP, the General Court (GC) denied the locus standi of the applicant sub-state authority (Northern Ireland Department of Agriculture) for lack of 'direct concern'.[77] According to the Court, the Commission decision had a direct impact only on the Member State's budget. The impact on the applicant's budget derived from a decision of Westminster (which refused to cover the expenditure) and was only an *indirect* consequence of the Commission decision. The Court also explained the difference between State aid cases and the present case: 'Unlike the practice generally adopted by the Commission with regard to State aid declared incompatible with the common market whereby the Commission decisions contain provisions calling upon the Member States to recover the sums wrongly paid from the beneficiaries, the contested decision did not place the Member State concerned under any obligation to recover the sums in question from the ultimate beneficiary [. . .]. The outcome cannot be any different where a decision does not place the Member State concerned under an obligation to set those sums against the applicant's budget'.[78]

The challenge against 'regulatory acts' addressed to other people and that 'do not entail implementing measures' requires only 'direct concern'. Article 263(4) TFEU stipulates: 'Any natural or legal person may [. . .] institute proceedings [. . .] against a regulatory act which is of direct concern to them and does not entail implementing measures'. The meaning of 'regulatory acts' is still controversial; however, a recent Order of the General Court pointed out that 'regulatory acts' are 'non-legislative acts of general application'.[79]

It emerges from the above analysis that (with the exception of 'regulatory acts') it is extremely difficult for the sub-state authorities to challenge the validity of Union acts that are not addressed to them. However, Union Courts maintain that

---

GC did not deal with the question of direct and individual concern. In the Case T-461/12, *Hansestadt Lübeck v Commission* (9 September 2014, not yet published), concerning State aid to the airport of Lübeck, the CG recognised the locus standi of the City of Lübeck (successor of the society Flughafen Lübeck in controlling the airport), which had been contested by the Commission (cf. para. 20 ff. of the judgment).

[77] Cf. GC Order 6 March 2012, Case T-453/10, *Northern Ireland Department of Agriculture and Rural Development v* Commission, ECR [2012], paras. 47–48 and 52.

[78] Cf. GC Order 6 March 2012, Case T-453/10, *Northern Ireland Department of Agriculture and Rural Development v* Commission, ECR [2012], para. 56. The GC decision has been fully confirmed by the CJ on appeal. Cf. Order 6 March 2014, Case C-248/12 P, *Northern Ireland Department of Agriculture and Rural Development v Commission*, not yet published in ECR.

[79] Cf. Order 6 September 2011, Case T-18/10 *Inuit Tapiriit Kanatami v Parliament and Council*, [2011] ECR II-5099. In her Opinion in preparation of the appeal case before the ECJ, AG Juliane Kokott validated this interpretation with plenty of supporting arguments. Cf. Opinion delivered on 17 January 2013 in Case C-583/11 P, para. 25 ff., cf. also Craig and De Bùrca (2011), pp. 508–509; *contra* cf. Panara (2008), p. 608.

there is no gap in the legal protection afforded by the EU. The CFI in *Azores v Council* pointed out that regional authorities are able 'either indirectly to plead the unlawfulness of such acts before the Community judicature under Art. 241 EC [now Art. 277 TFEU] or to do so before the national courts and ask them [...] to make a reference to the Court of Justice for a preliminary ruling [under Art. 234 TEC, now Art. 267 TFEU] as to lawfulness'.[80] In reality, Article 277 and Article 267 TFEU do not seem to overcome the lack of locus standi. According to Article 277 TFEU, it is possible to invoke the 'inapplicability' of an 'act of general application' in the context of other proceedings before the Court. More specifically, where an applicant challenges the validity of an act implementing an 'act of general application' (for example, a regulation), which forms the legal basis of the other act, the applicant may ask the Court to declare 'inapplicable' the 'act of general application'.[81] However, if an applicant does not have locus standi to challenge the act in the main proceedings, then there would be no opportunity for him to obtain the declaration of 'inapplicability' of the 'act of general application'. As to preliminary rulings (Article 267 TFEU), they do not adequately fill the gap in legal protection. First, the protection would depend on the existence of a legal remedy under domestic law, for example, the right to challenge the validity of a national measure implementing an EU act. Second, since domestic courts would act as a 'filter' prior to the referral of a question to the ECJ, such 'filter' could prevent a plea for invalidity of an EU measure from being referred to the ECJ.[82]

---

[80] See CFI Judgment 1 July 2008, Case T-37/04, *Região autónoma dos Açores v Council* [2008] ECR II-103*, at para. 92, referring to: ECJ Judgment 25 July 2002, Case C-50/00 P, *Unión de Pequeños Agricultores v Council* [2002] ECR I-6677, para. 40; ECJ Order 16 February 2005, Case T-142/03, *Fost Plus v Commission* [2005] ECR II-589, para. 75.

[81] The role of Art. 277 TFEU is very well explained in Judgment 6 March 1979, Case 92/78, *Simmenthal v Commission* [1979] ECR 777, para. 39: 'Article 184 of the EEC Treaty [now Art. 277 TFEU] gives expression to a general principle conferring upon any party to proceedings the right to challenge, for the purpose of obtaining the annulment of a decision of direct and individual concern to that party, the validity of previous acts of the institutions which form the legal basis of the decision which is being attacked, *if that party was not entitled under Article 173 of the Treaty [now Art. 263 TFEU] to bring a direct action challenging those acts by which it was thus affected without having been in a position to ask that they be declared void*' (emphasis added).

[82] Furthermore, the preliminary ruling cannot reopen the time limit for challenging the validity of an EU act. Accordingly, if an applicant failed to attack an act within the mandatory time limit through a direct action, then he is not entitled to call in question the validity of that act before a national court. Cf. ECJ Judgment 9 March 1994, Case C-188/92, *TWD Textilwerke v Germany* [1994] ECR I-833, para. 17. In a later case, the ECJ stated that in such event (expiry of the deadline for direct action), the preliminary ruling could still be instigated *ex officio* by the domestic court. However, this possibility does not overcome the lack of legal protection for a non-privileged applicant, given that a person would have to rely on the totally uncertain initiative of a domestic court. Cf. ECJ Judgment 10 January 2006, Case C-222/04, *Ministero dell'Economia v Cassa di Risparmio di Firenze* [2006] ECR I-289, para. 72.

2. The Way Out of the Conundrum: The Judicial Defence of the Rights of the Sub-state Authorities at EU Level Through the National Government

In *Friuli-Venezia Giulia v Commission*, the CFI stated that 'In the Community [now Union] legal order, it is for the authorities of the State to represent any interests based on the defence of national legislation, regardless of the constitutional form or the territorial organisation of that State'.[83] However, given that the central government may have no obvious incentive (for example, financial interest) to bring an action, to rely on the mere good will of the central government could be problematic.[84] Accordingly, it has to be looked at whether/to what extent the domestic law creates tools enabling the sub-state authorities to trigger an action for direct annulment before the Court of Justice. In relation to this aspect, three different patterns can be identified.

The first pattern features the right of a single regional authority to oblige the central government of the Member State to bring a direct claim for judicial review under Article 263(2) TFEU. Two federal States, Belgium and Austria, adopt this approach. In both countries, the State government has a duty to bring a claim if an EU act concerns a matter falling within the responsibility of a regional authority (Region or Community in Belgium, *Land* in Austria).[85] In Austria, the State government is not obliged to challenge an act on behalf of a *Land*, where another *Land* disagrees or there are compelling 'reasons of foreign and integration policy'. This 'safety clause' could weaken the position of the *Länder* since no procedure exists to overcome possible disagreements with the Federation. Until now, no direct challenge has been brought by Austria on request from the *Länder*.

A second pattern features the right of the *majority* of the regional authorities to oblige the central government to challenge an EU act. This system is in place in Italy and Germany. In Italy, the State-Regions Conference,[86] by absolute majority,

---

[83] CFI Order 12 March 2007, Case T-417/04, *Regione autonoma Friuli-Venezia Giulia v Commission* [2007] ECR II-641, para. 62.

[84] This is the submission of the applicant in GC Order 6 March 2012, Case T-453/10, *Northern Ireland Department of Agriculture and Rural Development v* Commission, not yet reported in ECR, para. 32.

[85] On Belgium, cf. Cooperation Agreement of 11 July 1994. The duty for the State government to bring an action before the ECJ applies only to EU acts involving exclusive responsibilities of a Community or Region. Where an EU act affects a shared responsibility, the government will bring an action only where it considers it expedient. Cf. Lenaerts (2008), pp. 8–9. On Austria, cf. Art. 10 (1) of the 1992 Agreement concerning the right of the Austrian *Länder* and Municipalities to participate in matters of European integration, published in *Bundesgesetzblatt* (Federal Law Gazette, *BGBl.* in acronym) 1992/775. Cf. Eberhard (2011), pp. 227–228.

[86] The State-Regions Conference is a committee where the national and the regional governments are both represented. The Italian Constitutional Court stated that this body 'is the privileged forum for discussion and negotiation of policy between the State and the Regions' (cf. Ruling No. 116 of 23 March 1994).

may oblige the State government to challenge an EU act concerning a matter of regional competence.[87] In Germany, the *Bundesrat* (the legislative chamber representing the *Länder* at federal level) may request the Federal Government to make use of the actions provided by the Treaty against acts or failures to act of the Union that affect issues falling within the competence of the *Länder*. However, the Federal Government may refuse to bring the action on grounds of its 'responsibility for the whole state', including concerns of 'foreign, defence, and [European] integration policy'.[88]

The third pattern does not provide an obligation for the State government to bring an action before the Court of Justice. This is the position, for example, in Spain, France, and the UK. In these countries, one or more sub-state authorities may certainly request the State government to put an application for judicial review. However, it will be for the State government to decide whether to file or not the action.[89] The ability of a sub-state entity or of a group of sub-national authorities to persuade the State government might well depend on extra-legal factors (for example, the political weight of a certain Autonomous Community or Region).

A holistic analysis shows that the European multilevel system, inclusive of the EU and the Member States, entails some rights for the sub-national authorities to instigate judicial proceedings under Article 263 TFEU. Yet the mechanisms set up at national level do not compensate entirely the lack of 'privileged applicant' status of these authorities. Even in Austria, where a single *Land* has the right to request the Federation to bring an action, or in Germany, where the majority within the *Bundesrat* has the same right, there are 'safety clauses' that allow the central government to refuse to put an application to Court. Belgium is the only country where there is a fully fledged duty for the central government to challenge an act on request from an individual Region or Community. However, this system is in place only in relation to EU acts affecting matters that fall within the exclusive responsibility of the Belgian Regions or Communities; if a topic belongs to a different category, the central government may decide not to espouse the regional request.

The position of the sub-state authorities may have been strengthened by the Protocol on Subsidiarity and Proportionality, annexed to the Treaty of Lisbon, according to which any national parliament, or 'any chamber thereof', is entitled to require the respective Member State to 'notify', on its behalf, a direct action for

---

[87] Art. 5(2) Law No. 131 of 5 June 2003. To date, no direct action for annulment has been proposed by the Italian government under Art. 5(2) Law No. 131 (last checked September 2014). According to Art. 5(2) Law No. 131, the government has no obligation to bring a case on a request from a single Region.

[88] Cf. § 7(1) EUZBLG.

[89] On Spain, cf. *Acuerdo sobre la participación de las Comunidades Autónomas en los procedimientos ante el TJCE* of 11 December 1997 (published in *Boletín Oficial del Estado*, *BOE* in acronym, of 2 April 1998). In the UK, neither the MoU nor the Concordats between the UK and its devolved authorities include an obligation for the Westminster government to commence an action before the ECJ. In France, there is no specific legal provision on this issue.

annulment of EU legislative acts on grounds of an infringement of subsidiarity.[90] The expression 'any chamber thereof' embraces also those national legislative houses that represent local and/or regional sub-state authorities. The Protocol also grants the Committee of the Regions the right to challenge an EU legislative act, for whose adoption the consultation of the Committee is mandatory, on grounds of an infringement of subsidiarity.[91]

F. Concluding Remarks

The previous analysis demonstrates that the EU is a multilevel system in which the sub-national authorities are an integral part of the European edifice and enjoy 'rights' and 'duties' in accordance with the asymmetric 'constitutional mosaic' resulting from the combination of EU and domestic constitutional laws. A number of elements corroborate this conclusion:

1) In the EU multilevel system, Treaty making/amendment is not an exclusive prerogative of the Member States. In some Member States, the sub-national authorities are involved in these processes, and in the case of Belgium each regional parliament can veto the entry into force of a new Treaty.
2) The lawmaking process in the Council is not entirely 'State dominated'. The sub-national entities enjoy participation rights that result from the combination of EU and national processes.
3) The sub-national authorities have a duty to comply with EU obligations and at the same time a right to implement EU law/policy in the areas falling within their responsibility. In a number of Member States, failure by a sub-national authority to comply with EU obligations causes financial liability to be imposed upon the responsible sub-national authority and could also justify the exercise of EU-related State substitution powers. At the same time, infringement proceedings initiated by the Commission are not necessarily a matter regarding exclusively the Member State; the sub-national authorities in some Member States are involved in those proceedings.
4) The ECJ's jurisprudence on locus standi is rather 'State centric', insofar as the sub-national authorities are granted limited rights to challenge Union acts *directly* before Union Courts. However, a holistic analysis embracing both the EU level and the Member State level reveals that in some Member States the sub-national authorities can oblige the Member State to initiate judicial proceedings on their behalf. The Treaty of Lisbon introduced the Committee of the Regions' right to bring a direct challenge before the ECJ on grounds of subsidiarity, as well as the right of each chamber of national parliament (including

---

[90] Cf. Art. 8(1) Protocol on Subsidiarity and Proportionality.
[91] Cf. Art. 8(2) Protocol on Subsidiarity and Proportionality.

'second chambers' representing the sub-national authorities) to oblige the State to bring a direct challenge before the ECJ on grounds of subsidiarity.

The status of the sub-national authorities in the EU multilevel system (i.e., the EU-related 'rights' and 'duties' of the sub-national authorities) enjoys a considerable degree of strength and stability. The legal position of these authorities is an outcome of the EU as a 'compound of constitutions' since their position is rooted in the EU primary law (the 'constitutional charter' of the Union) and in the State constitution. Accordingly, multilevel governance is not a concept that can remain confined to 'politics' or 'soft law'; it is a legal concept rooted in the constitutional law of the Union and of the Member States. This aspect will be further developed in the next chapter.

References

C. Backes, W. van der Woude, Local authorities in the polder-Dutch municipalities and provinces, in *The Local Government in Europe: The 'Fourth Level' in the EU Multi-Layered System of Governance*, ed. by C. Panara, M. Varney (Routledge, London, 2013). pp. 231 ff

P. Birkinshaw, *European Public Law* (Butterworths, London, 2003)

A. Chicharro Lázaro, The Spanish Autonomous Communities in the EU: 'The Evolution from the Competitive Regionalism to a Cooperative System', in *The Role of the Regions in EU Governance*, ed. by C. Panara, A. De Becker (Springer, Heidelberg, 2011). pp. 185 ff

P. Craig, G. De Bùrca, *EU Law. Text, Cases and Materials*, 5th edn. (OUP, Oxford, 2011)

A. Cygan, Regional governance, subsidiarity and accountability within the EU's multi-level polity. Eur. Public Law **19**(1), 161 f. (2013)

M. Dani, Regions standing before the EU courts – towards a constitutional theory on "Direct and Individual" participation of the regions in the EU decision-making processes, in *An Ever More Complex Union*, ed. by R. Toniatti et al. (Nomos, Baden-Baden, 2004), pp. 181 ff

A. De Becker, Belgium: the state and the sub-state entities are equal, but is the state sometimes still more equal than the others? in *The Role of the Regions in EU Governance*, ed. by C. Panara, A. De Becker (Springer, Heidelberg, 2011). pp. 251 ff

C. Degenhart, [Commentary to] *Art. 70 GG*, in *Grundgesetz. Kommentar*, ed. by M. Sachs (C.H. Beck, München, 2007), pp. 1422 ff

H. Eberhard, Austria: the role of the Länder in a 'Centralised Federal State', in *The Role of the Regions in EU Governance*, ed. by C. Panara, A. De Becker (Springer, Heidelberg, 2011). pp. 215 ff

G. Guillermin, Le principe de l'équilibre institutionnel dans la jurisprudence de la Cour de Justice des Communautés européennes. J. de Droit Int. **119**(2), 319 f. (1992)

A. Gunlicks, *The Länder and German Federalism* (Manchester University Press, Manchester, 2003)

L. Hooghe, G. Marks, *Multi-Level Governance and European Integration* (Rowman & Littlefield, Lanham, 2001)

P.M. Huber, Die Europatauglichkeit des Art. 23 GG, in *Die Zukunft des Föderalismus in Deutschland und Europa*, ed. by D. Merten (Duncker & Humblot, Berlin, 2007). pp. 209 ff

K. Lenaerts, *Access of the Regions with Legislative Power to the ECJ*. Conference on Subsidiarity organized by the Committee of the Regions (25 August 2008), http://cor.europa.eu/en/news/highlights/documents/2e30bc34-7ce2-427d-8d35-53f2c7b50a8a.pdf. Accessed Sept 2014

K. Lenaerts, P. Van Nuffel, *European Union Law*, 3rd edn. (Sweet & Maxwell, London, 2011)

G. Marks et al., European integration from the 1980s: State Centric v. Multi-level Governance. J. Common Mark. Stud. **34**(3), 341 f. (1996)

M. Nettesheim, Wo "endet" das Grundgesetz? – Verfassungsgebung als grenzüberschreitender Prozess. Der Staat **51**(3), 313 f. (2012)

T. Öhlinger, [Commentary to] *Art. 23d B-VG*, Rz. 32, in *Österreichisches Bundesverfassungsrecht, Kommentar*, ed. by K. Korinek, M. Holoubek (Springer, Wien New York, 1999)

C. Panara, The German Länder in the process of European Integration between Föderalismusreform and Reform Treaty. Eur. Public Law **14**(4), 585 f. (2008)

C. Panara, A. De Becker, The role of the regions in the European Union: the "Regional Blindness" of both the EU and the Member States, in *The Role of the Regions in EU Governance*, ed. by C. Panara, A. De Becker (Springer, Heidelberg, 2011). pp. 297 ff

I. Pernice, The treaty of Lisbon: multilevel constitutionalism in action. Columbia J. Eur. Law **15**(3), 349 f. (2009)

I. Pernice, Verfassungsverbund, in *Strukturfragen der Europäischen Union*, ed. by C. Franzius (Nomos, Baden-Baden, 2010). pp. 102 ff

S. Ricci, The Committee of the Regions and the challenge of European Governance, in *The Role of the Regions in EU Governance*, ed. by C. Panara, A. De Becker (Springer, Heidelberg, 2011). pp. 109 ff

F. Rubio Llorente, J. Alvarez Junco (eds.), *El informe del Consejo de Estado sobre la reforma constitucional: Texto del informe y debates academicos* (Centro de Estudios Constitucionales, Madrid, 2006)

A. Schaus, L'exécution des traités. Revue belge de droit international **27**(1), 66 f. (1994)

A. Thies, The Locus Standi of the regions before EU Courts, in *The Role of the Regions in EU Governance*, ed. by C. Panara, A. De Becker (Springer, Heidelberg, 2011). pp. 25 ff

T. Tridimas, *The General Principles of EU Law*, 2nd edn. (OUP, Oxford, 2006)

P. Van Nuffel, What's in a Member State? Central and decentralized authorities before the Community Courts. Common Mark. Law Rev. **38**(4), 871 f. (2001)

S. Villamena, State and regions vis-a-vis European integration: the 'Long (and Slow) March' of the Italian Regional State, in *The Role of the Regions in EU Governance*, ed. by C. Panara, A. De Becker (Springer, Heidelberg, 2011). pp. 157 ff

J.H.H. Weiler, The community system: the dual character of supranationalism. Yearb. Eur. Law **1**, 267 f. (OUP, Oxford, 1981)

W. Wessels, An ever closer fusion? A dynamic macropolitical view on integration processes. J. Common Mark. Stud. **35**(2), 268 f. (1997)

Chapter 3
Multilevel Governance in the EU

A. Introduction

In the previous chapter, it was shown that the EU is a 'multilevel system', of which the sub-national authorities are an integral part. The existence of such a 'multilevel' and 'multidimensional' EU requires the development of principles and tools coordinating the action of the different levels of government. This explains why concepts such as multilevel governance and subsidiarity are increasing in importance in the EU. Whilst most studies of multilevel governance deal with this concept from a political science or economic perspective, legal scholars use the same notion as a descriptive formula illustrating the existence and role of the sub-national authorities in the EU. However, multilevel governance has never been studied as a legal concept, nor have its constitutional foundation, rationale and legal consequences been explored. For the first time, this chapter analyses multilevel governance in the EU, specifically from a legal perspective. It will be argued that multilevel governance is a legal/constitutional principle stemming from the European 'constitutional composite'. This principle is 'procedural' in that it commands a 'method of governance' consisting in the involvement of sub-national authorities in the EU decision-making process and in the implementation of EU law/policy (Sect. B). In this way, multilevel governance contributes *legitimacy* to the participation of the Member States in the EU and to EU decision-making activity (Sect. C).

© Springer International Publishing Switzerland 2015
C. Panara, *The Sub-national Dimension of the EU*,
DOI 10.1007/978-3-319-14589-1_3

B. Content and Constitutional Foundation of Multilevel Governance

1. The Emergence of Multilevel Governance in the EU

The emergence of the 'third level' within the EU, in particular since the second half of the 1980s (due to the combined impact of decentralisation processes at national level and the progressive opening up of the Union to input from the sub-national authorities), led scholars in the late 1980s and in the early 1990s to rethink the structure of the European decision-making in view of the role played by the sub-national level. A crucial development occurred in 1988, when a major reform of structural funding took place.[1] Under the new regime, the funds had to be administered through partnerships established within the Member States, consisting of representatives of national and regional and/or local authorities and the Commission. It was indeed from the study of the renewed European structural policy and particularly of the partnership principle that in the early 1990s Gary Marks developed and launched the notion of 'multilevel governance'.[2]

The multilevel governance analysis framework was later extended to the whole spectrum of EU action, and in this way multilevel governance became a general theory on the functioning of the EU (albeit, more precisely, the multilevel governance paradigm is usually applied only to the former 'First Pillar',[3] due to the mainly intergovernmental nature of the 'Second Pillar' and 'Third Pillar'[4]).[5] Over

---

[1] See Council Regulation (EEC) No. 2052/88 of 24 June 1988 on the tasks of the Structural Funds and their effectiveness and on coordination of their activities between themselves and with the operations of the European Investment Bank and the other existing financial instruments, in OJ L 185, 15 July 1988, pp. 9–20.

[2] The concept of 'multilevel governance' was developed by Gary Marks in two studies on the structural policy: cf. Marks (1992), pp. 191 ff.; Marks (1993), pp. 391 ff. On multilevel governance in the EU regional policy, see also Bache (2004), pp. 165 ff.; Bovis (2011), pp. 81 ff. In the *Sixth Periodic Report on the Social and Economic Situation and Development of the Regions of the EU*, published in 1999, the Commission itself used for the first time the expression multilevel governance in an official document, where it argued that 'the delivery system developed for the structural funds is characterized by multi-level governance, i.e., the Commission, national governments, and regional and local governments are formally autonomous, but there is a high level of shared responsibility at each stage of the decision making process. The relationship between these is, accordingly, one of partnership and negotiation, rather than being a hierarchical one' (ibid. p. 143).

[3] This is the 'Community Pillar', including the former European Community (EC) and the Euratom. Until 2002, the First Pillar included also the European Coal and Steel Community (ECSC).

[4] The Common Foreign and Security Policy (Second Pillar) and the Police and Judicial Cooperation in Criminal Matters (Third Pillar).

[5] Cf. Marks et al. (1996), pp. 341 ff. The multilevel governance paradigm has been applied by Michael Smith to the EU Common Foreign and Security Policy. However, in his article, Smith does not take into account the local/regional level, which is not at the forefront in foreign policy

the last 20 years, also thanks to research into multilevel governance, it became increasingly clear that sub-national authorities perform a role in EU decision-making (for example, through consultation with the Commission or through national participation channels) and are involved in the implementation of EU law and policy (in some Member States, they are responsible for the transposition of directives and for the implementation of the structural or cohesion policy[6]). According to multilevel governance theory, in the atypical European 'multilevel polity', decision-making in a number of policy areas in the former First Pillar is not dominated by national governments, as put by liberal intergovernmentalism,[7] nor is it entirely in the hands of supranational institutions. In those policy areas and to a varying degree across the different Member States, European decision-making rather reflects a 'triangulation of political relationships' among national, supranational and sub-national players,[8] i.e., a system of multilevel 'co-governance' in accordance with the constitutional structure of the Member States (federal, regionalised or otherwise decentralised).

Over the years, the multilevel governance paradigm has been fundamentally accepted by the majority of legal and political scholars and became a key pattern for understanding the functioning of the EU and its territorial dynamics.[9] The summa divisio in the field of multilevel governance is between two ideal types. The first

---

matters. Cf. Smith (2004), pp. 740 ff. On the different conjugations of multilevel governance, cf. Stephenson (2013), pp. 817 ff. See also Piattoni (2010), pp. 17 ff.; Piattoni (2009), pp. 163 ff.

[6] The Committee of the Regions' *White Paper on Multilevel Governance* reports that in the EU-27, the sub-national authorities are responsible for the implementation of nearly 70 % of Union legislation. Cf. Committee of the Regions (2009), p. 3. Bauer and Börzel believe that this claim might well be called into question, but at the same time they admit that 'there is little doubt that many EU policies have serious repercussions for regional and local levels'. Cf. Bauer and Börzel (2010), p. 254.

[7] See, for example, the approach of Andrew Moravcsik. Cf. Moravcsik and Schimmelfenning (2009), pp. 67 ff.

[8] Cf. Marks (1997), p. 32. The term 'player' used in the text is intentionally generic. Whilst examining the interactions between state and sub-state authorities in reality, we analyse the behaviour of the political leaders who rule the state and the sub-state institutions. This aspect is highlighted by Gary Marks, ibid., pp. 34–35. See also Hooghe and Marks (2001), passim but especially Chap. 2.

Littoz-Monnet (2010) argues that EU integration dynamics can only be fully understood within a process of interaction and reciprocal feedback between actors at different levels of governance.

The focus of this study is limited to the EU. However, scholars apply the multilevel governance paradigm also to other forms of global (e.g., UN, global trade, global economic governance) or regional governance (e.g., NAFTA, ASEAN, Mercosur), often establishing comparisons and parallels between these systems and the EU. See, for example, Sbragia (2010), pp. 267 ff.

[9] The research interest in multilevel governance is demonstrated by the fact that 'the development of forms of multi-level governance which are accountable, legitimate, and sufficiently robust and flexible to address societal change including integration and enlargement' is one of the research priorities for the EU for the period 2002–2006. Cf. Council Decision of 30 September 2002 adopting a specific programme for research, technological development and demonstration: 'Integrating and strengthening the European Research Area' (2002–2006), in OJ L294/1, 29 October 2002, Annex I, pp. 5 ff.

(Type I multilevel governance), whose prototype is federalism, includes general-purpose territorial jurisdictions (states, regional and local authorities). These 'bundle together multiple functions, including a range of policy responsibilities, and in many instances, a court system and representative institutions'. In this context, 'every citizen is located in a Russian Doll set of nested jurisdictions, where there is one and only one relevant jurisdiction at any particular scale'. The second type of multilevel governance (Type II) embraces 'task-specific jurisdictions', such as specialised agencies and task-specific organisations that provide a certain local service, select a product standard, monitor water quality in a particular river and so forth. This study is concerned with Type I multilevel governance only, as it focuses on the role and mutual interaction of territorial authorities that are expression of regional and local communities (general-purpose territorial jurisdictions).[10]

2. The White Papers' Approach to Multilevel Governance

Concerns relating to Type I multilevel governance are at the forefront in the Commission's *White Paper on European Governance* of 2001 and in the Committee of the Regions' *White Paper on Multilevel Governance* of 2009.[11] In the *White Paper on European Governance*, the Commission places substantial emphasis on the interaction and dialogue between the EU and the sub-national authorities and lays down recommendations (for example, 'There needs to be a stronger interaction with regional and local governments', 'Establish a more systematic dialogue with representatives of regional and local governments through national and European associations at an early stage in shaping policy', 'Bring greater flexibility into how Community legislation can be implemented in a way which takes account of regional and local conditions'[12]). 'Multilevel governance' is expressly mentioned at p. 34 of the document in relation to how competence is shared, not separated, between the EU and the Member States:

> The Union needs clear principles identifying how competence is shared between the Union and its Member States. In the first place this is to respond to the public's frequent question 'who does what in Europe?' A common vision is needed to answer this question. The White Paper has highlighted [...] a Union based on multilevel governance in which each actor contributes in line with his or her capabilities or knowledge to the success of the overall exercise. In a multi-level system the real challenge is establishing clear rules for how

---

[10] On the Type I–Type II distinction, see Marks and Hooghe (2004), pp. 15 ff. The quotes in the text can be retrieved, ibid. pp. 16–17. Cf. also Hooghe and Marks (2003), pp. 233 ff.; Hooghe and Marks (2010), pp. 17 ff.

[11] EU Commission (2001) and Committee of the Regions (2009). See also the Opinion of the Committee of the Regions (2012).

[12] EU Commission (2001), p. 4. See also pp. 12 et seq. The role of the sub-state level of government is emphasised also in the Commission's Commission of the European Union et al. (2008).

competence is shared – not separated; only that non-exclusive vision can secure the best interests of all the Member States and all the Union's citizens.[13]

This idea of interwoven and overlapping competences between the different tiers of government is strongly rooted in cooperative federalism theory[14] and constitutes the foundation of multilevel governance. The key challenge for multilevel governance is bringing together and coordinating the action of different territorial levels. The specific instruments identified by the Commission to this purpose are the 'structured dialogue' and the 'tripartite agreements and contracts'.[15] The 'structured dialogue' consists of regular meetings between the Commission and the European and national associations of sub-national authorities. These meetings may concern issues of broad interest, such as the annual work programme of the Commission (general dialogue), or a specific policy area (thematic dialogue).[16]

The 'tripartite agreements and contracts' are stipulations between the Commission, a Member State and one or more sub-national authorities concerning the implementation of binding law (contracts) or soft law (agreements).[17] Up to now, this instrument has found only limited application, despite the submission of some

---

[13] EU Commission (2001), p. 34. Specific recommendations contained in the Commission's *White Paper* include (cf. p. 14) the following:

For the Commission:

– Establish a more systematic dialogue with European and national associations of regional and local government at an early stage of policy shaping.
– Launch pilot 'target-based contracts' within one or more areas as a more flexible means of ensuring implementation of EU policies.

For the Committee of the Regions:

– Play a more proactive role in examining policy.
– Promote exchange of best practice on how sub-national authorities are involved in the preparatory phase of European decision-making at national level.
– Review the local and regional impact of certain directives.

For the Member States:

– Examine how to improve the involvement of sub-national actors in EU policymaking.
– Promote the use of contractual arrangements with their regions and localities.

[14] On the application of cooperative federalism theory to the EU, cf. Benson and Jordan (2011), pp. 1 ff., who construe EU policymaking as a 'multilevel cooperative game'. On the distinction between dual and cooperative federalism, the literature is huge. Cf. Bognetti (1994), pp. 273 ff.; Reposo (2005), pp. 119 ff.

[15] The *White Paper* mentions only the 'tripartite contracts', not the 'agreements'.

[16] On the 'structured dialogue', cf. Communication from the Commission COM (2003)811 final of 19 December (2003) and Committee of the Regions' (2004). In the literature, see Vara Arribas (2005), pp. 19 ff.; Domenichelli (2007), pp. 71 ff. The associations of local and regional authorities to be involved in the 'structured dialogue' are chosen by the Commission with the help of the Committee of the Regions. The Committee of the Regions is the host of the meetings of the 'structured dialogue'.

[17] On the 'tripartite contracts and agreements', cf. Commission's Communication 'A framework for target-based tripartite contracts and agreements between the Community, the States and regional and local authorities' COM (2002) 709 final. In the literature see Vara Arribas (2005), pp. 19 ff.; Domenichelli (2007), pp. 76 ff.

projects concerning environmental protection in Birmingham (UK), Lille (France) and Pescara (Italy). The first and to date only tripartite agreement was signed on 15 October 2004 by the Commission, the Italian Government and the Region Lombardy in relation to sustainable mobility.[18] Although tripartite stipulations have not found extensive application, probably due to the lack of planned European funding,[19] their existence is emblematic, as it shows that the EU ascribes to the sub-national authorities the status of contractual partners on an equal footing with other tiers of government and the ability to negotiate contracts and agreements with the Commission. Only the Member State is responsible *vis-à-vis* the EU in case of non-compliance with the contract or agreement. However, as shown previously (cf. supra Chap. 2), in some Member States with federal or regional structure, there are mechanisms ensuring that a sub-national authority that causes a non-compliance with EU obligations is held financially accountable and is involved by the Member State in the pre-judicial and judicial phases of the infraction proceedings. This corroborates the submission that in the EU multilevel system the status of the sub-national authorities derives from the combination, 'amalgamation', of rules emanating from the European and the national levels.

Eight years after the Commission's *White Paper*, the Committee of the Regions published the *White Paper on Multilevel Governance*, which defines multilevel governance as follows:

> coordinated action by the European Union, the Member States and local and regional authorities, based on partnership and aimed at drawing up and implementing EU policies.[20]

The document further specifies:

> Multilevel governance is not simply a question of translating European or national objectives into local or regional action, but must also be understood as a process for integrating the objectives of local and regional authorities within the strategies of the European Union. Moreover, multilevel governance should reinforce and shape the responsibilities of local and regional authorities at national level and encourage their participation in the coordination of European policy, in this way helping to design and implement Community policies.[21]

In the light of this definition, multilevel governance appears to be a dynamic concept ('coordinated action', 'translating into local or regional action', 'process for integrating the objectives', etc.) consisting of two major elements:

---

[18] On this agreement, cf. Mazzoleni (2006), pp. 263 ff.

[19] See Vara Arribas (2005), pp. 23 ff.

[20] Committee of the Regions (2009), at front-page. See also the Preamble to the Charter for Multilevel Governance in Europe: 'We stand for a multilevel-governance Europe "based on coordinated action by the European Union, the Member States and regional and local authorities according to the principles of subsidiarity, proportionality and partnership, taking the form of operational and institutional cooperation in the drawing up and implementation of the European Union's policies"'. In the literature, cf. Warleigh (1999), pp. 6–7.

[21] Committee of the Regions (2009), p. 7.

- implementation of EU and national laws and policies at regional and local levels ('translating European or national objectives into local or regional action').
- involvement of local and regional authorities in EU lawmaking and policymaking both at EU level and at national level ('integrating the objectives of local and regional authorities within the strategies of the European Union (. . .) and encourage their participation in the coordination of European policy').

The 'dynamic' notion of multilevel governance emerging from the Committee of the Regions' *White Paper* is fundamentally 'procedural', as it lays down certain guidelines in relation to *how* decisions are to be made.[22] Multilevel governance emerges as a 'method' or an 'approach',[23] the appropriate method or approach according to the Committee, for bringing together and coordinating the action of the different layers of government in the EU multilevel system.

3. Towards a Legal Notion of Multilevel Governance: A) EU Primary Law

So far, the notion of multilevel governance has remained mainly the province of students of politics and of official statements or policy documents of Union bodies and institutions. However, whilst political studies deserve great credit for defining the concept and for explaining its importance for the functioning of the EU, the notion has remained mainly descriptive.[24] From a legal perspective, we need to

---

[22] In the Committee of the Regions' document entitled *Scoreboard for monitoring Multilevel Governance (MLG) at the European level 2011* (research coordinated by Gracia Vara Arribas and Martin Unfried, published on December 2011), a distinction is made between procedures and content of multilevel governance practices (cf. p. 5). However, what the authors of the research indicate as 'content' is in reality largely procedural: territorial/integrated/place-based policy, smart regulation mechanisms, innovative instruments for implementation and partnership. The reflection paper emanating from the Co-creation Workshop of 16 April 2012 concerning the European Charter on Multilevel Governance identifies the guiding principles constituting the European multilevel governance approach. A number of principles are clearly procedural: 'strengthen proximity and local governance by promoting participative procedures'; 'respect and further strengthen "vertical". . . and "horizontal partnerships"'; 'commit towards the sharing of knowledge, enhanced inter-institutional and administrative dialogue and cooperation with other public authorities and with neighbouring authorities in particular'; 'endeavour to connect and network your territory at all levels of governance, including at EU level' (p. 3).

[23] The Protocol of 16 February 2012 on cooperation between the European Commission and the Committee of the Regions says that 'the multilevel governance approach is an important tool for designing and implementing EU policies' (Point C of the Preamble).

[24] Cf., for example, Hooghe and Marks (2001), p. xi: 'Multi-level governance . . . describes the dispersion of authoritative decision making across multiple territorial levels'. George does not depart fundamentally from the same descriptive pattern when he suggests that multilevel governance is not a description of the EU but a theory on the EU: 'As a distinct perspective on the European Union, multi-level governance offers not a description, but a theory of what sort of organization the European Union is. It is hypothesized to be an organization in which the central

move from a descriptive to a prescriptive notion of multilevel governance. Law is not only concerned with 'what is' but principally with 'what ought to be'. *If*, as this study shall demonstrate, multilevel governance is a legal concept, it will determine *how* the EU has to handle the territorial pluralism within it. The Committee of the Regions' *White Paper*, due to its objective to shape future European integration, is an essential starting point for formulating a hypothesis in relation to the legal content of multilevel governance.[25]

In light of the definition of multilevel governance in the *White Paper* ('coordinated action by the European Union, the Member States and local and regional authorities, based on partnership and aimed at drawing up and implementing EU policies'[26]), the working hypothesis is that, as a minimum, multilevel governance should include the following:

α) the sharing of authoritative decision-making between different levels of government within the EU,[27] which in turn presupposes a substantial degree of autonomy of each level of government in dealing with the welfare needs of the respective population; this element suggests the existence of a close link between multilevel governance and subsidiarity[28];

β) the coordination of the action of the different levels of government in accordance with the principle of partnership;

---

executives of states do not do all the governing but share and contest responsibility and authority with other actors, both supranational and subnational'. Cf. George (2004), p. 125. Even if the illustrated hypothesis proved valid, still we would only know more in relation to the nature and functioning of the Union. However, we would know nothing or very little in relation to how the EU ought to be organised to comply with multilevel governance. Especially, we would not know *if* or *why* the EU ought to be organised and the decision-making structured in a certain way.

[25] The shift from a descriptive to a normative (if not prescriptive) notion of multilevel governance is present also in the document of the Committee of the Regions entitled *Scoreboard for monitoring Multilevel Governance (MLG) at the European level 2011* (published on December 2011, research coordinated by Gracia Vara Arribas and Martin Unfried). Cf. p. 2: 'Against this background, the Committee of the Regions (CoR) wants to strengthen MLG in the different strategic priorities of the EU and in the different stages of the decision-making process at European level. MLG thus acquires a new quality: from analytical tool it becomes a principle and a programme for action. This demands very concretely the establishment of structured political processes for monitoring and analysing governance in the EU'.

[26] Committee of the Regions (2009), front page.

[27] See also Hooghe and Marks (2001), p. 70: 'Multi-level governance [. . .] is present to the extent that authority is shared by governments at different territorial levels'.

[28] On the concept of autonomy of the sub-national authorities, see the Judgment of the Court of Justice of 6 September 2006 in the Case C-88/03 *Portugal v Commission* [2006] ECR I-7115 concerning State aid. In this case, the Court (Grand Chamber) found that it is not State aid incompatible with EU law when autonomous entities reduce the tax rate within their territory, provided that the tax rate reduction has been decided autonomously by the infra-State entity and that it applies to all the undertakings operating within its territory. Political and fiscal autonomy from the central government require that the infra-State entity must bear the political and financial consequences of its decision. In particular, the financial consequences of a reduction of the national tax rate for undertakings in the region must not be offset by aid or subsidies from other regions or the central government (cf. paras. 67 ff. of the judgment).

γ) the appropriate involvement of sub-national authorities in the EU lawmaking and policymaking, as well as in the implementation of EU law and policy at both EU and national levels.

The foundation of multilevel governance lies in the first place in the Treaties (constitutional charter of the EU):

(1) TEU Preamble: '[The Member States are] RESOLVED to continue the process of creating an ever closer union among the peoples of Europe, in which decisions are taken as closely as possible to the citizen in accordance with the principle of subsidiarity'. This statement is particularly relevant to the sharing of authoritative decision-making between different levels of government within the EU (α). More in general, it assumes the fundamental role of the sub-national authorities for decisions to be taken 'as closely as possible to the citizen' (closeness).

(2) Article 4(2) TEU: 'The Union shall respect the equality of Member States before the Treaties as well as their national identities, inherent in their fundamental structures, political and constitutional, inclusive of regional and local self-government'. This Treaty article is the foundation of the constitutional role of the sub-national authorities in the EU. Accordingly, it is one of the bases of multilevel governance in the EU.

(3) Article 5(3) TEU: 'Under the principle of subsidiarity, in areas which do not fall within its exclusive competence, the Union shall act only if and in so far as the objectives of the proposed action cannot be sufficiently achieved by the Member States, either at central level or at regional and local level, but can rather, by reason of the scale or effects of the proposed action, be better achieved at Union level'. Subsidiarity is one of the key principles of the EU system, in that it presides over the relationship between EU and Member States. Since Lisbon, the Treaty lays down a notion of subsidiarity that includes the 'regional and local level'. In this way, this principle is relevant to all the elements of multilevel governance.

(4) Article 10(3) TEU: 'Every citizen shall have the right to participate in the democratic life of the Union. Decisions shall be taken as openly and as closely as possible to the citizen'. This article lays down the principle of closeness. This principle is particularly relevant to α) and γ) and creates a bridge between multilevel governance and 'participatory democracy' as a fundamental element of the democratic life of the Union.

(5) Article 13(4) TEU: 'The European Parliament, the Council and the Commission shall be assisted by [. . .] a Committee of the Regions acting in an advisory capacity'. The Committee of the Regions is the institutionalised form of multilevel governance in the EU in that it promotes coordination between levels of government (β) and participation of the sub-national authorities in the EU decision-making process (γ).

(6) Article 16(2) TEU: 'The Council shall consist of a representative of each Member State at ministerial level, who may commit the government of the Member State in question and cast its vote'. This provision opens the door to the

participation of regional ministers in Council meetings. In this way, it promotes the involvement of sub-national authorities in the EU decision-making process (γ).

(7) Article 2 of the Protocol on Subsidiarity and Proportionality—'Before propos-ing legislative acts, the Commission shall consult widely. Such consultations shall, where appropriate, take into account the regional and local dimension of the action envisaged'—and Article 6(1) of the same Protocol—'Any national Parliament or any chamber of a national Parliament may, within eight weeks from the date of transmission of a draft legislative act, in the official languages of the Union, send to the Presidents of the European Parliament, the Council and the Commission a reasoned opinion stating why it considers that the draft in question does not comply with the principle of subsidiarity. It will be for each national Parliament or each chamber of a national Parliament to consult, where appropriate, regional parliaments with legislative powers'. These provisions reflect all the elements of multilevel governance (sharing of authoritative decision-making, coordination, involvement in EU lawmaking and policymaking).

The constitutive elements of the notion of multilevel governance are mirrored in the EU primary law. However, despite the fact that the roots of multilevel gover-nance are in EU primary law, and that the EU lays down a framework for regional and local participation, it cannot oblige the Member States to create participation channels for the sub-national authorities or to use those prompted at Union level. For example, participation in the Council is dependent not only on the EU but especially on *if* and *to what extent* each Member State allows the sub-state entities to be involved in the Council activity (cf. infra Sect. C.2). In accordance with the 'united in diversity' motto, the EU cannot impose uniform patterns to *all* the Member States. The EU can open doors and windows, but it is largely up to the Member States and their regions to seize the opportunity. Therefore, the legal source of multilevel governance cannot be the EU primary law *only*. There are two parallel dimensions of multilevel governance in the EU, one supranational (the EU) and one national (the Member States).[29] Furthermore, the insights offered by the EU primary law are rather minimal. Whilst the EU opens up its processes to

---

[29] A similar phenomenon can be observed in relation to the principle of supremacy of EU law. Cf. Weiler (1981), pp. 267 ff. The Committee of the Regions' *White Paper on Multilevel Governance* itself stresses: 'The conditions for good multilevel governance depend on the Member States themselves. The principles and mechanisms of consultation, coordination, cooperation and evaluation recommended at Community level must firstly be applied within the Member States' (p. 7). The reflection paper emanating from the Co-creation Workshop of 16 April 2012 concerning the European Charter on Multilevel Governance proposes recommendations addressed to the Member States. These include 'stimulate regionalisation and decentralisation'; 'cooperation between national parliament and regional parliaments, notably on subsidiarity scrutiny'; 'partic-ipation of RLA [= regional and local authorities] into all stages of the EU policy cycle'; 'further develop participation of RLA into the national delegation to the Council formal/informal meetings and comitology'; etc. (p. 4).

forms of regional and local participation inspired to multilevel governance (e.g., Council, Committee of the Regions, involvement of regional parliaments in the 'early warning system'), there is little prescriptive indication of how these forms of participation should work in practice. For example, the decision on the composition of each (sub-)national delegation to the Committee of the Regions is left to the Member States, so it is up to each Member State to strike a balance in relation to the representation of the different tiers of government (regional and/or local).[30] *Alone*, the opportunities prompted by the EU primary law do not offer the whole picture of regional and local participation in the EU. Multilevel governance, far from being a monolithic notion finding application everywhere in the same way, is a largely *asymmetrical* concept receiving differentiated application in each Member State. Accordingly, there is no single pathway to enforcing multilevel governance but potentially 28 *partly* different pathways.

4. Towards a Legal Notion of Multilevel Governance: B) EU Secondary Law

The concept of multilevel governance is no longer confined to political discourse or theory. As well as being rooted in EU primary law as a concept embracing potentially all fields of Union action, it is also reflected in EU secondary law specifically concerning energy policy, as well as economic, social and territorial cohesion.

Regulation (EU) No 1233/2010 concerning EU financial assistance to projects in the field of energy[31] contains a strong reference to multilevel governance. Point 3 of the Preamble states that 'Cooperation among the various tiers of government (multi-level governance) is essential in th[e] context [of the development of further renewable energy sources and the promotion of energy efficiency]'. Regulation No 1233 also creates a dedicated financial facility in support of investment projects related to energy efficiency and renewable energy by local, regional and national public authorities (cf. Point 4 of the Preamble and Annex II). The notion of multilevel governance as 'cooperation' incorporates the idea of partnership-inspired 'coordinated action', synergy for the achievement of Union objectives (β) and also the respect for the role of the sub-national authorities in conformity

---

[30] In relation to the composition of the Committee of the Regions, Article 305(1) TFEU only establishes that the number of members of the Committee shall not exceed 350. According to Article 300(3) TFEU, the members of the Committee must be representatives of regional and local authorities, who either hold a regional or local authority electoral mandate or are politically accountable to an elected assembly. Within such minimal framework laid down by the Treaty, each Member State determines how to select its representatives in the Committee.

[31] Regulation (EU) No 1233/2010 of the European Parliament and of the Council of 15 December 2010 amending Regulation (EC) No 663/2009 establishing a programme to aid economic recovery by granting Community financial assistance to projects in the field of energy.

with subsidiarity (α). For example, Regulation No 1233 establishes that the Union financial support shall facilitate the financing of investments in energy saving, energy efficiency and renewable energy projects by local, regional and, 'in duly justified cases', national public authorities (cf. Annex II). An interesting aspect of Regulation No 1233 is that it highlights a 'positive dimension' of multilevel governance in the EU. Through its financial intervention, the EU enhances the role of regional/local authorities in achieving the Union's objectives.

The strongest reference to multilevel governance can be found in Regulation (EU) No 1303/2013 on EU funding promoting economic, social and territorial cohesion.[32] This act indicates multilevel governance as a 'principle' that, along with subsidiarity and proportionality, must be 'respected' by the Member States when creating partnerships with the sub-national authorities and other economic and social actors for the implementation of the EU economic, social and territorial cohesion policy.

Like in the Committee of the Regions' *White Paper*, also in Regulation No 1303 multilevel governance emerges as a 'procedural' concept, i.e., as a 'governance method' that requires the involvement of the sub-national authorities ('In accordance with the multi-level governance approach, the partners (. . .) shall be involved by the Member States in the preparation of Partnership Agreements and progress reports and throughout the preparation and implementation of programmes'[33]) and that requires 'coordinated action' between the different levels of government ('In order to respect [the] principles [of partnership and multi-level governance] coordinated action is required, in particular between different levels of governance'[34]).

Regulation No 1303 also contains indications concerning the raison d'être of multilevel governance, where it says that respect for the principles of partnership and multilevel governance is required 'in order to facilitate achieving social, economic and territorial cohesion and delivery of the Union's priorities of smart, sustainable and inclusive growth'.[35] Accordingly, in the view of the EU legislator, the partnership with the sub-national authorities finds its justification in the need to enhance the effectiveness of the EU social and cohesion policy. Similarly, Regulation No 1303 also highlights that the ultimate purpose of a partnership in the context of the EU regional policy is 'to ensure the ownership of planned interventions by stakeholders and build on the experience and the know-how of relevant actors' (Point 11 of the Preamble). The phrase 'ownership by stakeholders' suggests that the participation of sub-national authorities in the EU regional policy could

---

[32] Regulation (EU) No 1303/2013 of the European Parliament and of the Council of 17 December 2013 laying down common provisions on the European Regional Development Fund, the European Social Fund, the Cohesion Fund, the European Agricultural Fund for Rural Development and the European Maritime and Fisheries Fund and laying down general provisions on the European Regional Development Fund, the European Social Fund, the Cohesion Fund and the European Maritime and Fisheries fund and repealing Council Regulation (EC) No 1083/2006.

[33] Art. 5(2) of Regulation (EU) No 1303/2013.

[34] Point 5.1 (1) of Annex I of Regulation (EU) No 1303/2013.

[35] Point 5.1 (1) of Annex I of Regulation (EU) No 1303/2013.

contribute to strengthen acceptance of these policies, i.e., to their *legitimacy* ('ownership') as well as to their effectiveness ('build on the experience and the know-how of relevant actors').

The inclusion of multilevel governance as a key principle of the EU regional policy sets aside any remaining doubt in relation to the nature of multilevel governance as a legal concept. Multilevel governance emerges as a principle of procedural nature (i.e., it requires a certain 'method' or 'approach'), which must be respected by the Member States in the field of economic, social and territorial cohesion. In the context of this policy field, multilevel governance is a concept, more specifically defined as a 'principle', established by Union law, and as such its interpretation may be referred to the ECJ in preliminary rulings stemming from legal disputes in domestic courts. However, given that constitutional arrangements vary asymmetrically across the Union, the ECJ is likely to stick to a minimal notion of multilevel governance whilst applying it to a specific State context, rather than dictating prescriptive solutions for the Member States. The Union notion of 'multilevel governance' must necessarily be minimal and procedural. It must be minimal because the Union can require the Member States to respect a certain 'method' or 'approach' when implementing Union policies; however, it cannot impose a specific multilevel structure on them. The multilevel governance 'method' shall include an appropriate involvement of the sub-national authorities and of other relevant players in the preparation and execution of projects in the EU economic, social and cohesion policy. In this way, far from laying down a set of prescriptive rules, multilevel governance in this policy area emerges as a principle and, more specifically, as a 'procedural principle' indicating in general *how* decisions are to be made and policies implemented. The expected results and added value of that method are the effectiveness and legitimacy of EU policies.

5. Towards a Legal Notion of Multilevel Governance: C) Article 4(2) TEU and the Constitutional Identity of the Member States

All Member States have a constitutional framework that includes regional and/or local self-government. Given that the Member States are also part of the EU, and that almost all EU policies interfere with the competences of the regional or local level, we are faced with mutually contradicting propositions. On the one hand, the Member States' constitutions value regional/local autonomy, but, on the other, a considerable degree of that autonomy has been handed over through the acceptance of the EU membership. These are opposite poles pulling into different directions, regional and/or local autonomy *vs.* creation of a supranational entity dragging a substantial part of that autonomy away from the sub-national level. Can a constitution command one thing and its opposite at the same time? Is it possible to reconcile such conflicting propositions? Whilst contradictions and inconsistencies may exist in any human artefact, including a constitution, the duty of lawyers is to identify and to resolve them.[36]

A first hypothetical but simplistic way to reconcile local/regional autonomy and the growing role of the EU could be the principle of supremacy of EU law. According to that principle, as construed by the Court of Justice in *Internationale Handelsgesellschaft*,[37] EU law shall prevail over any rule of domestic law, including constitutional law. By analogy, one may argue that the centripetal push towards European integration could legitimately forfeit the autonomy of the sub-national authorities. However, it is well known that the national courts have set limits to the prevalence of EU law in order to protect the Member States' constitutional identity.[38] After the Treaty of Lisbon, the constitutional identity of the Member States is protected also by EU primary law. Article 4(2) TEU includes regional and local self-governments among the 'fundamental constitutional structures', which are part of the 'national identity' of the Member States that the Union is obliged to respect.[39] The constitutional laws of the Member States underpin and add new vigour to this conclusion. Some examples will illustrate the point more effectively.

The Swedish Instrument of Government stipulates that 'Swedish democracy is founded on the free formation of opinion and on universal and equal suffrage. It shall be realised through a representative and parliamentary polity and through local self-government' (Chapter 1, Section 1, para. 2, Instrument of Government). It emerges clearly from this constitutional provision that the existence of local self-

---

[36] Carl Schmitt deals with a conceptually similar problem in relation to the antinomy between the first and the second parts of the German Constitution of Weimar. Cf. Schmitt (2004 [1932]). A paradox or contradiction similar to regional/local autonomy *vs.* European integration can be seen between the democratic principle and European integration in relation to the shift of powers of the national parliaments to the EU.

[37] Case 11/70, *Internationale Handelsgesellschaft mbH v. Einfuhr- und Vorratsstelle für Getreide und Futtermittel* [1970] ECR 1125.

[38] Cf., for example, the jurisprudence of the German Federal Constitutional Court in *Solange I* (Ruling of 29 May 1974, published in *Entscheidungen des Bundesverfassungsgerichts* [hereafter *BVerfGE*] Vol. 37, p. 271 ff.), and *Solange II* (Ruling of 22 October 1986, published in *BVerfGE* Vol. 73, pp. 339 ff.). See also the 'controlimiti doctrine' of the Italian Constitutional Court: cf. Ruling No. 183 of 27 December 1973 and Ruling No. 170 of 8 June 1984. On this aspect, cf. Huber (2008), pp. 442–448.

[39] On the key importance of local/regional self-government for the protection of the national identity of the Member States, cf. Pernice (2009), p. 394. Cf. also the Opinion of AG Trstenjak [delivered 4 June 2008] in the Case C-324/07 *Coditel Brabant SPRL v Commune d'Uccle and Région de Bruxelles-Capitale* [2008] ECR I-8457: 'The right to municipal self-government is not reflected only in the legal provisions of the Member States but [...] also in the European Charter on Local Self-Government drawn up within the framework of the Council of Europe signed by all EU Member States and also ratified by most of them. Article 263 of the EC Treaty makes provision for the Committee of the Regions comprising representatives of regional and local authorities. Inherent in this provision is a certain recognition of self-government alongside the possibility of providing institutionalised machinery for bringing to bear regional and municipal perspectives. Finally the Treaty of Lisbon stresses the role of regional and local self-government for the relevant national identity to which heed is to be paid'. [para. 85]. On the problematic relationship between supremacy and national identity, cf. von Bogdandy and Schill (2011), pp. 1417 ff.

government is a qualifying feature of Swedish democracy and of the Swedish State. Similarly, in the Czech Republic, the right to self-government is regarded as one of the fundamental and inalienable rights of local communities (cf. Art. 100 Const.), whilst in Italy local autonomy and decentralisation are fundamental principles of the Constitution (cf. Art. 5 Const.).[40]

These examples underpin the opinion that self-government and local autonomy are constitutional cornerstones. Parliaments cannot *sic et simpliciter* abolish or restrict them. In some Member States, this would be limited or impossible even through an ordinary constitutional revision. For example, in Austria, the federal principle is a core element of the constitutional setting. This implies that the suppression of the *Länder* or of the Municipalities, or a major restriction to their power, would require a total revision of the Federal Constitution pursuant to Article 44(3) of the Federal Constitutional Law. In addition to the passage of a constitutional amendment by the National Council and the Federal Council by two-thirds majority, a total revision would also require a referendum.[41]

Similarly, in Germany, Article 79(3) of the Basic Law rules out any constitutional amendment affecting the division of the country into *Länder*, their participation on principle in the legislative process and the federal character of the State. These limits to constitutional revision do not apply only *internally* within Germany but also in relation to transfers of powers to the EU (cf. Art. 23(1) Basic Law). Furthermore, the German Federal Constitutional Court held that the *Länder* are endowed with a 'hard core' of responsibilities that cannot be taken away from them.[42]

Due to the fluidity of its unwritten constitution, a very interesting pattern in this context is the UK. According to the orthodox doctrine of parliamentary sovereignty,[43] the UK Parliament can modify any earlier statute, i.e., in principle it would have the power to give any responsibility to the local authorities, but it could also take everything away from them. However, over the last few decades, the doctrine of parliamentary sovereignty, in its traditional form, has been repeatedly challenged. Notably, in the case *Thoburn v Sunderland*, Laws LJ held that the doctrine of implied repeal did not apply to the conflict between an earlier 'constitutional

---

[40] On Sweden, cf. Persson (2013), pp. 305 ff. On the Czech Republic, cf. Pomahač (2013), pp. 52 ff. On Italy, cf. Villamena (2013), pp. 183 ff.

[41] Cf. the following cases published in the official collection of the rulings of the Austrian Constitutional Court (*Erkentnisse und Beschlüsse des Verfassungsgerichtshofes*, in acronym VfSlg.): VfSlg. 6697/1972, 7830/1976, 9373/1982. In the literature, cf. Neuhofer (2008), Rz. 45.

[42] The ruling referred to in the text is published in *BVerfGE* Vol. 34 pp. 9 et seq. (pp. 19 et seq.). Cf. Sommermann (2008), pp. 17–18 (Rn. 26).

[43] The traditional definition of the doctrine of parliamentary sovereignty can be traced back to the work of Oxford academic Albert Venn Dicey. Cf. Dicey (1959): 'These then are the three traits of Parliamentary sovereignty as it exists in England: first, the power of the legislature to alter any law, fundamental or otherwise, as freely and in the same manner as other laws; secondly, the absence of any legal distinction between constitutional and other laws; thirdly, the non-existence of any judicial or other authority having the right to nullify an Act of Parliament, or to treat it as void or unconstitutional' (p. 91).

statute' and a later one.[44] According to Laws LJ, the category of constitutional statutes includes any statute that '(a) conditions the legal relationship between citizen and State in some general, overarching manner, or (b) enlarges or diminishes the scope of what we would now regard as fundamental constitutional rights'. In Laws LJ's view, any statute not fitting this description can be classed as an 'ordinary statute'. Important examples of constitutional statutes are the Magna Charta of 1215, the Bill of Rights 1689 and the Act of Union 1707 and also more recent statutes such as the Human Rights Act 1998, the Scotland Act 1998, the Government of Wales Act 1998 and the European Communities Act 1972.[45] The Localism Act 2011 contains an interesting development in relation to local government in England.[46] Section 2(4) stipulates that the powers of local government are not subject to implied repeal. By contrast, the acts that *Thoburn* considered did not include explicit provisions on implied repeal. Laws LJ actually stated that the constitutional acts were such 'by force of the common law'. The further question of *whether* (expressly, of course) it is legally possible for Parliament to remove local government or devolution goes completely to the heart of the constitution in the UK. If Parliament ever tried to remove local government or devolution or to render them irrelevant, most certainly there would be court cases that would test the courts' adherence to the principle of parliamentary sovereignty to the maximum extent. To date, the only case to have suggested a possible willingness of the courts to find certain legislation passed by Parliament to be unlawful is *R (Jackson) v Attorney General*. The House of Lords found, in an obiter dictum, that the courts could find a statute to be in breach of the principle of legality.[47] However, whilst, *politically*, the abolition of local self-government or of devolution is currently unthinkable, it would appear uncertain, to say the least, whether Parliament would be *legally* authorised to dismantle them. Such uncertainty demonstrates that, even in a flexible constitutional system like the UK, the regional and local self-governments are so deeply rooted in the constitutional tradition that they could even limit the principle of parliamentary sovereignty.

The above examples corroborate the conclusion that local/regional autonomy is an essential element of the constitutional identity of the Member States. The key

---

[44] According to the doctrine of implied repeal, if Parliament passes a statute featuring provisions in conflict with an earlier statute, the affected part of the earlier statute is impliedly repealed.

[45] The case *Thoburn v Sunderland City Council* [2002] EWHC 195 (Admin) specifically concerned the application of the doctrine of implied repeal to the European Communities Act 1972.

[46] Different regimes are in place in Scotland, Northern Ireland and Wales. The present system of local government in Scotland is based upon the Local Government (Scotland) Act 1973 and on the reforms brought about by the Local Government (Scotland) Act 1994. The present system of local government in Northern Ireland is based on the Local Government Act 1972 (Northern Ireland). The Welsh Government is the only devolved government that has already taken steps to legislate on local government in a way that makes changes to the framework for local government within its jurisdiction. Cf. Local Government (Wales) Measure 2011.

[47] *R (Jackson) v Attorney General* [2005] UKHL 56.

importance of local/regional autonomy for the constitutional identity of the Member States can be seen also in the European Charter of Local Self-Government of the Council of Europe, which has been ratified by *all* the EU Member States. Multilevel governance, by commanding the involvement of the sub-national authorities in the EU decision-making process and in the implementation of EU law/policy, enables the sub-national authorities to maintain and possibly expand their constitutional role whilst being involved in supranational integration. This (and not supremacy) is the correct way for reconciling regional and local autonomy with European integration. Multilevel governance has a key constitutional function to play in the EU context. It is *constitutionally* required by both the Member States and the Union primary law for the protection and the development of an essential part of the Member States' constitutional identity.

6. Towards a Legal Notion of Multilevel Governance: D) The Role of the CJEU for the Definition and Enforcement of Multilevel Governance

The justiciability of a principle is not essential in order to conclude that it is a juridical and not a philosophical or political notion. For example, in the next chapter, it will be argued that the justiciability of the principle of subsidiarity is limited and yet that subsidiarity remains a legal principle and one of the constitutional cornerstones of the EU.[48] Like subsidiarity, multilevel governance too lives on the edge between law and politics. The judicial enforcement of multilevel governance in Union courts is not the primary route for the application of that principle on the EU level. The principal sanction in case of non-compliance with the requirements of multilevel governance by the EU or the Member States is the loss of *legitimacy* of Union action or of the Member States' participation in the EU. Still, Union courts have an important role to play in enforcing and shaping multilevel governance. There are fundamentally three ways in which Union courts can play a role: *1)* in relation to the Treaty articles embodying the idea of multilevel governance indicated supra at Sect. B.3, *2)* in relation to the concept of 'national identity' of Article 4(2) TEU and *3)* in relation to acts of secondary law that contain reference to the concept (principle) of multilevel governance.

1) In relation to those norms of EU primary law that embody or reflect multilevel governance, Union courts play the ordinary role they would play in relation to any other primary law rule. For example, at least in theory, an infringement of the principle of closeness to the citizen could lead to the annulment of an EU

---

[48] With specific reference to subsidiarity, Nettesheim has recently proposed the oxymoronic notion of 'politisches Recht' ('political law'), indicating those legal provisions that are only or principally enforceable through forms of political coordination (*politische Koordination*). Cf. Nettesheim (2014), passim. See also infra Chap. 4.

act.[49] Also, the lack of consultation of the Committee of the Regions when this is compulsory could lead to the invalidation of the relevant act. The Committee itself could require the annulment through a direct action in accordance with Article 263(3) TFEU.

2) Article 4(2) TEU appears likely to lend itself to judicial enforcement of the principle of multilevel governance only in extreme circumstances. Probably, like for subsidiarity, only a clear abuse, such as an EU regulation on economic, social and cohesion policy ignoring completely the role of the sub-national authorities in that policy area, would find Union courts willing to annul it for a breach of Article 4(2) TEU. An analysis of the jurisprudence of Union courts on Article 4 (2) TEU in relation to the protection of regional and local autonomy offers important insights on multilevel governance. In a recent case concerning two French sub-state authorities, the General Court (GC) observed that, even where aid is granted by a sub-state authority, the administrative procedure of Article 108(2) TFEU concerning State aid is opened *only* against the Member State, whilst respect for constitutional identity does not confer on 'infra-State bodies' that grant aid the same rights of defence. However, in this procedure, these bodies (like the undertakings receiving the aid and their competitors) are considered 'interested parties' and 'have the right to be involved in the procedure to the extent appropriate in the light of the circumstances of the case'.[50] In this way, albeit not on the basis of Article 4(2) TEU and not exclusively in relation to sub-state public authorities, the CG pointed into the direction required by 'multilevel governance', of an involvement of the sub-state units in the decisional procedures of the EU.

In relation to the participation of the sub-state units in the implementation of EU obligations, an interesting statement can be found in the Opinion that Advocate General Kokott delivered in a case concerning the lack of implementation of a directive by the Spanish Autonomous Communities. In response to Spain's argument that a national regulation transposing the directive ensured full

---

[49] So far, the ECJ has not pronounced on the principle of closeness. Occasionally, this principle has been referred to by the Advocates General. See the Opinion of AG Sharpston delivered on 15 October 2009 in Case C-28/08 P, *Commission v Bavarian Lager Co. Ltd* (para. 212: 'Few things would appear to be more *necessary in a democratic society* than transparency and close involvement of citizens in the decision-making process', emphasis in the original). Closeness to the citizen is defined an 'aspiration' by AG Fennelly in the Opinion of 15 June 2000 concerning the Joined Cases C-376/98, *Germany v Parliament and Council*, and C-74/99, *The Queen v Secretary of State for Health* (cf. para. 133). See also the Opinion of AG Trstenjak delivered on 3 February 2009 in Case C-428/07, *Mark Horvath v Secretary of State for Environment, Food and Rural Affairs* (para. 93).

[50] It has to be noted that the status of 'interested party' does not derive from Article 4(2) TEU. Cf. Judgment of the General Court (Eight Chamber) of 12 May 2011, Joined Cases T-267/08 and T-279/08, *Région Nord-Pas-de-Calais* and *Communauté d'agglomération du Douaisis (France) v Commission*, [2011] ECR II-1999, paras. 70 et seq. The Member States could decide to involve the sub-state authorities in the exercise of the rights of defence of the Member State in procedures concerning State aid (EU atypical multilevel system).

compliance with it, AG Kokott noted that this method of transposition could be in breach of the Spanish constitutional system and would fail to acknowledge the legislative responsibility associated with the legislative competence of the Autonomous Communities. Through this 'argumentum ad adiuvandum', Kokott recognises that the right/duty of the Autonomous Communities to participate in the implementation of EU law in their areas of responsibility is an essential part of the constitutional identity of the Spanish State.[51]

Another important statement of the ECJ concerns the official languages in use in the territorial subdivisions of a Member State. In *Las*, the ECJ held that the national identity of the Member States 'includes protection of the official language or languages of those States'.[52] In the Opinion concerning the same case, Advocate General Jääskinen had argued that the notion of 'official language' embraces 'the official language or various official languages of the State and, where appropriate, the territorial subdivisions in which the various official languages are in use. The concept of 'national identity' therefore concerns the choices made as to the languages used at national or regional level'.[53] The protection of regional (or national) languages could even justify restrictions to the free movement of workers (Article 45 TFEU), provided that these are compliant with the principle of proportionality.[54]

3) The ECJ could be requested the correct interpretation of the concept (principle) of multilevel governance through a preliminary reference, when this concept is used in the EU secondary law (only Regulation (EU) No 1233/2010 on renewable energy sources and Regulation (EU) No 1303/2013 on the EU economic, social and cohesion policy have referred expressly to 'multilevel governance'; cf. supra Sect. B.4).

---

[51] Cf. Opinion of AG Kokott delivered on 30 May 2013 in Case C-151/12, *Commission v Spain* (cf. paras. 34–35).

[52] Judgment of the Court of Justice (Grand Chamber) of 16 April 2013, Case C-202/11, *Anton Las v PSA Antwerp NV*, not yet published (para. 26).

[53] Opinion of AG Jääskinen delivered on 12 July 2012 in Case C-202/11 (para. 59).

[54] The ECJ took AG Jääskinen's advice that restrictions to the free movement of workers based on linguistic reasons must be proportionate and decided that 'Article 45 TFEU must be interpreted as precluding legislation of a federated entity of a Member State, such as that in issue in the main proceedings, which requires all employers whose established place of business is located in that entity's territory to draft cross-border employment contracts exclusively in the official language of that federated entity, failing which the contracts are to be declared null and void by the national courts of their own motion'. Cf. Judgment of the Court of Justice (Grand Chamber) of 16 April 2013, Case C-202/11, *Anton Las v PSA Antwerp NV*, not yet published (para. 35). The Order of the General Court of 6 March 2012, Case T-453/10, *Northern Ireland Department of Agriculture and Rural Development v Commission*, ECR [2012], paras. 36–38, dismissed the argument advanced by the applicant that the lack of recognition of locus standi to Northern Ireland goes against the obligation for the EU (stemming from Art. 4(2) TEU) to respect the national identity of the UK, including its regional self-government (cf. supra Chap. 2).

C. The Making Phase of EU Law and Policy

1. The Notion of Legitimacy Used in This Study

In the context of this study, the term 'legitimacy' indicates the *acceptability*, albeit not necessarily the inner/psychological acceptance, of authoritative decision-making by the subjects to power and by all the players concerned. A distinction can be made between two types of 'legitimacy': one being 'output legitimacy', the second being 'input legitimacy'. 'Output legitimacy' is linked to the content of a decision. The fundamental output legitimacy alternative is between 'approval' and 'disapproval' of a decision by the subject (or, which is ultimately the same, between 'like' and 'dislike', 'good' and 'bad'). Such 'approval/disapproval', 'like/dislike', 'good/bad', or dichotomy is the result of a subjective evaluation, which is 'political' in nature. Being a political concept, 'output legitimacy' does not legitimise law and policy objectively, only subjectively. Different groups of subjects, political parties or even individuals may well have different opinions as to what amounts to 'good', 'not so good' or 'bad' governance. This study is only concerned with 'input legitimacy'.[55]

'Input legitimacy' conveys 'acceptance' of authoritative decisions not for their 'content' but for the *way* in which a decision is taken. In this way, it leads to the objective legitimacy of a decision, i.e., to the legitimacy of a decision *vis-à-vis* everybody, *objectively*, i.e., irrespective of whether a group or an individual agrees or disagrees with it. Legitimacy, here, derives from respect for certain objective procedural criteria; i.e., it results from compliance with a 'procedure'. Like for democracy, observance of a democratic procedure generates objective legitimacy, that is, objective acceptance. Every member of the community will (have to) accept a democratically taken decision, *or* a decision made in accordance with a previously agreed procedure, and could not challenge its (objective) legitimacy, even if he or

---

[55] The concept of 'legitimacy' used here is different from Max Weber's construction of legitimacy (*Legitimität*) in 'Economy and Society', where legitimacy is the foundation of validity of an entire system ('type') of power rather than of a single political decision or of an identified set of political decisions. Cf. Weber (1999 [1922]), pp. 207 ff. The input/output legitimacy distinction proposed by Fritz Scharpf is slightly different from that suggested here insofar as this scholar ascribes an objective legitimising effect also to 'output legitimacy', which he sees as a manifestation of the 'government for the people'. In Scharpf's view, 'output legitimacy' does not concern only 'what' is decided but also 'how' a decision is taken ('. . . output-oriented legitimacy depends on institutional norms and incentive mechanisms that must serve two potentially conflicting purposes. They should hinder the abuse of public power and they should facilitate effective problem-solving – which also implies that all interests should be considered in the definition of the public interest, and that the costs and benefits of measures serving the public interest should be allocated according to plausible norms of distributive justice'). Cf. Scharpf (1999), pp. 6 ff. (the quote can be found at p. 13).

she disagrees with the merit. A decision could be 'bad' or 'inexpedient' from an individual or group point of view but still be fully 'legitimate'.[56]

Legitimacy should not be mistaken for mere 'legality'. A decision can be *formally* adherent to 'procedural law' but still be in conflict with fundamental constitutional values, such as human dignity or, for what concerns this book, regional and local autonomy. Accordingly, a further distinction needs to be made between 'formal' and 'substantial' legitimacy. 'Formal legitimacy' means simple adherence to a procedure. 'Substantial legitimacy' includes respect for substantial constitutional requirements. Even a democratic regime should respect certain fundamental values to maintain its substantial legitimacy along with its formal legitimacy. At the same time, it needs to be taken into account that procedures are never 'neutral'. They facilitate the achievement of certain, previously identified, substantial objectives. For example, the right of the citizen to a hearing in an administrative procedure contributes to the 'fairness' of the decision-making activity. Other types of procedures serve different values; for example, judicial proceedings serve the principle of fairness and equality between the parties in the superior interest of justice. The question is not only whether the procedures in force in the single countries and in the EU for regional/local participation have been complied with but also *if* these procedures are coherent with, and fully satisfactory for, regional and local autonomy, which is a constitutive part of 'national identity' (cf. supra Sect. B.5; Article 4(2) TEU). Accordingly, legitimacy in the context of this study has a 'constitutional' foundation.[57]

Multilevel governance, by commanding the involvement of sub-national authorities in EU lawmaking and policymaking and in the implementation of EU law and policy, requires a 'procedure', which contributes legitimacy to the decision-making system of the EU.[58] There are three minimum conditions for (input) legitimacy through multilevel governance: *A)* openness, *B)* equality, *C)* effectiveness. *A)* 'Openness' implies that the decision-making process must be open and inclusive; more specifically, the decision-making process must involve *all* the players, and only those players, that in the light of each national constitution have to take part in it. This means that every exclusion or limitation of sub-national participation has to find its rational justification in the national constitution (for example, limitation of participation/involvement to regional authorities with legislative power). *B)*

---

[56] During a public roundtable with members of the European Affairs Committee of the *Land* parliament of Baden-Württemberg, Wolfgang Reinhart (CDU), remarked that 'Akzeptanz' and 'Legitimität' are a consequence of the appropriate involvement of the regional and local authorities in the EU decision-making process (11 February 2014, Stuttgart, Kuppelsaal, *Land* parliament of Baden-Württemberg). On the idea that procedures produce legitimacy of decisions see, from a perspective of sociology of law, Luhmann (2013 [1978]).

[57] Carl Schmitt creates a radical opposition between 'legality' and 'legitimacy'. Cf. Schmitt (2004 [1932]). On the antinomy between legality and legitimacy, but especially on the concept of 'substantial legitimacy', see also Martínez-Sicluna y Sepúlveda (2006 [1991]), pp. 220 ff.

[58] See also the reference to a 'transparent, open and inclusive policy-making process' in the Charter for Multilevel Governance in Europe (Point 1.1).

'Equality' requires that *all* the sub-national authorities that take part in the decision-making process (at least if they belong to the same tier of government) must be placed on an equal footing. This does not rule out a weighing of the political influence of each region (for instance, the weighed voting system in place within the German *Bundesrat*), *if* the method chosen to differentiate between the sub-national authorities is *rational* and not arbitrary or based on discriminatory criteria. *C)* 'Effectiveness' requires that *all* the sub-national participants in the decision-making process must be able to play an effective role. This does not necessarily imply that the final decision must be dictated by a level of government or by a single regional authority. However, participation must be 'real', not mere facade; it must be based on full information and on genuine 'dialogue' and 'negotiation' between all the players concerned.

2. Legitimacy in the Making Phase of EU Law and Policy

Regional/local participation in the promulgation of EU law and policy finds application in three fundamental ways: *A)* through coordination of national and sub-national authorities on the EU policy position of the Member State, *B)* through consultation of the sub-national authorities on EU law and policy, *C)* through informal contacts and lobbying and *D)* through forms of structured consultation and dialogue with the associations of the sub-national authorities.

A) Coordination of national and sub-national authorities on the EU policy position of the Member State—in a number of Member States, there are mechanisms coordinating the position of the national government and of the sub-national authorities for the formulation of the position of the Member State in EU decision-making fora (cf. Table 2.1). In this way, when an EU proposal or policy would have an impact on regional responsibilities or interests, the position of the Member State in these fora will incorporate, or at least take account of or be informed by, the point of view of the sub-national authorities. Coordination mechanisms produce legitimacy, because they protect the constitutional standing of the sub-national authorities, when EU initiatives or policies touch on matters falling within their responsibility. For example, in a typical federal state like Germany, when the Council agenda features items falling within the regional responsibility, the *Länder* can determine the Member State's position in the Council. In this way, the legitimacy of the EU decision-making process from a German perspective is guaranteed by the involvement of all the *Länder* (openness), on an equal basis (equality) and with the real opportunity to contribute to the formulation of the policy position of their Member State (effectiveness). In other Member States, such as Italy and the United Kingdom, with regional authorities (Italy) or devolved administrations with legislative powers (UK), coordination takes place through appropriate forms of dialogue and negotiation between the national government and the sub-state entities. In this way, the Member State's position will result from a coordination process in which the sub-state entities are involved on the basis of openness, equality and effectiveness. Once again, like for Germany, the structure and operation of the procedure aim to ensure the *legitimacy* of the Union decision-making process from a national perspective.

B) Consultation of the sub-national authorities on law and policy—sub-national participation in the EU is not only channelled by national institutions and filtered by national mechanisms. The EU multilevel system also consists of more direct participation channels at EU level. The most important of those channels is the Committee of the Regions (CoR). Alex Warleigh defines the CoR as the 'perfect embodiment of multilevel governance in the European Union'.[59] This definition might be too enthusiastic; however, there is no doubt that the CoR is a cornerstone of the EU multilevel system, in that it creates a direct relationship between the EU and the sub-national level. Furthermore, through their embedment in the CoR, the sub-national authorities are officially recognised as an integral part of the Union's institutional architecture. However, due to its mixed composition, including both regional and local authorities (and many different types of regional/local authorities), the CoR entails heterogeneous, potentially even conflicting, interests.[60] The consultative activity of the CoR embraces potentially all areas of the EU legislative responsibility. Accordingly, the impact of the regions on the EU lawmaking process could go beyond the boundaries of regional legislative responsibility and stretch into wider constitutional or macroeconomic matters.[61] However, due to its merely advisory role, it is uncertain and difficult to determine to what extent the CoR is really able to grant the

---

[59] Warleigh (1999), p. 57.

[60] Cf. Domorenok (2009), p. 146. See also Moore (2008): 'Devolution and decentralization across the EU's member states has not resulted in anything approaching a single 'third level' of constitutional actors. Significant variations in policy competences are identifiable across even the strongest tier of actors below the national level, limiting the extent to which these actors can lobby jointly on policy issues' (p. 524). The difficulty for the CoR to represent authentic sub-national interests is evidenced also by the creation of 'political groups' within the CoR. Cf. Ricci (2011), p. 115.

[61] Cf. Art. 304(1) TFEU: 'The Committee shall be consulted by the European Parliament, by the Council or by the Commission where the Treaties so provide. The Committee may be consulted by these institutions in all cases in which they consider it appropriate. It may issue an opinion on its own initiative in cases in which considers such action appropriate'. Accordingly, the field of intervention of the CoR is potentially unlimited. Cf. Ricci (2011), p. 118. The TFEU requires an opinion of the CoR for legislative proposals in the following policy areas: transport (Art. 91.1), including sea and air transport (Art. 100.2); employment (Arts. 148(2) and 149(1)); social policy (Art. 153(2)); education, vocational training, youth and sport (Arts. 165(4) and 166(4)); culture (Art. 167(5)); public health (Art. 168(4) and (5)), trans-European networks (Art. 172), economic, social and territorial cohesion (Arts. 175(3), 177(1), and 178(1)); environment (Art. 192(1), (2) and (3)), energy policy (Art. 194(2)). In all these fields, the Union acts in the exercise of shared powers. The principle of subsidiarity should therefore play a decisive role.

sub-national authorities an impact on the EU decision-making process.[62] The cooperation arrangements in place in the Member States, *if suitably structured*, could be more effective in providing opportunities for regional/local involvement in the EU decision-making. Yet this suggestion should not lead to neglect the important *symbolic* role of the CoR as the 'official' representative of the EU sub-national level, contributing inclusivity and legitimacy to the EU decision-making activity.[63]

C) Informal contacts and lobbying by individual sub-national authorities and by their associations—over the last 25 years, many regions and local authorities across the EU opened representation offices in Brussels. The main tasks of these liaison offices are the representation of the regional/local authority *vis-à-vis* the EU institutions (especially the Commission), the promotion of the image and interests of the regional or local authority on the EU level and networking with the EU institutions and other national or sub-national authorities.[64] It is hard to measure the influence of these offices on the EU decision-making process. However, their large number (at present, 338 liaison offices are operational in Brussels[65]) and the significant resources allocated to them by some regions, such as the German *Länder*, suggest that the offices are often seen as a valuable investment. Alongside the liaison offices, there are a number of associations of regional and local authorities that engage in regular contacts with the EU institutions in the interest of their members.[66] Lobbying can be important for legitimacy purposes, in that it creates a direct link between local/regional level and the EU and insofar as it may facilitate a positive result for a region or a group of regions (output legitimacy), in this way also fostering a feeling of European

---

[62] On the difficulty to determine the direct impact of the CoR on the decision-making process, cf. Domorenok (2009), p. 154. The CoR itself monitors its influence on EU lawmaking and policymaking and publishes the findings in its periodic impact assessment reports. Cf., for example, the document METIS GmbH, *Impact Assessment at the CoR: methodology and its implementation* (published 2010). See also Hönnige and Panke (2013), pp. 452 ff., who highlight the overall little influence of the CoR.

[63] Cf. Ricci (2011): 'All the activities which form the real core of the CoR's action pursue the goal to provide the decision of the institutions with the broadest possible degree of inclusion and legitimacy' (at p. 128). On the 'symbolic' function of the CoR, cf. Christiansen (1996), pp. 93 ff.; more recently, cf. Carroll (2011), pp. 348–350.

[64] On the regional liaison offices, cf. Rowe (2011), passim. On the activity of the liaison offices of the German *Länder*, cf. Knodt et al. (2009), pp. 123 ff. A very interesting, albeit dated, UK–Germany comparison can be found in Jeffery (1997), pp. 183 ff.

[65] Cf. the list of regional offices based in Brussels published by the Committee of the Regions (update: 16 September 2013). Some sub-national parliaments (e.g., the Welsh National Assembly, the *Landtag* of Bavaria, the *Landtag* of Baden-Württemberg, etc.) opened their representation offices in Brussels alongside those of the respective governments. Cf. Moore (2008), pp. 529–530.

[66] The principal Europe-wide associations of regional and local entities are the Council of European Municipalities and Regions (CEMR), the Assembly of the European Regions (AER), the Conference of European Regions with Legislative Power (REGLEG) and the Conference of European Regional Legislative Assemblies (CALRE). On the structure and activity of these associations, cf. Domenichelli (2007), pp. 28 ff.

loyalty among regional/local authorities. However, lobbying by individual regions or groups cannot create objective 'input legitimacy', i.e. *objective* acceptance of a decision, in that it does not comply with the principle of *equality*. The different resources (funding, personnel, equipment, etc.) available to each sub-national player are likely to allow each player to have larger or smaller influence on the EU. A player who is able to spend significant resources in lobbying, networking, etc., is likely to make its voice heard in Brussels better and louder than smaller, weaker and especially 'poorer' players. Lobbying, moreover, is typically carried out through informal contacts, outside of formal 'procedures' and with little or no transparency. Accordingly, despite the practical importance of such direct contacts between sub-national authorities and EU institutions, the *objective* 'legitimising effect' of these activities on the EU decision-making process is negligible in comparison to other participation and legitimisation mechanisms. Through the creation at national level of appropriate consultation channels that facilitate the involvement of *all* the authorities concerned on an in principle equal footing, the equality concern can be addressed effectively.[67]

D) Structured consultation and dialogue with the associations of the sub-national authorities—consultation with the sub-national authorities outside the CoR can create objective legitimacy only if the consultation process is 'structured' in an objective manner and the openness, equality and effectiveness concerns are addressed satisfactorily.[68] The Union should identify and develop adequate communication channels with the sub-national authorities, for example by selecting for the Structured Dialogue, and for any other form of consultation, truly representative regional and/or local authorities' associations whose internal life is organised *democratically*.[69] Appropriate pre-legislative 'dialogue' and/or 'consultation' can contribute legitimacy to the EU lawmaking process. This conclusion is corroborated by the case *UEAPME*, where the Court of First Instance held that whenever the European Parliament does not participate in the enactment of a legislative act, the principle of democracy requires an

---

[67] Surprisingly a recent study challenges the idea that greater lobbying resources would necessarily lead to a greater share of structural funding for a region. At the same time, according to the same research, regions with stronger participation rights in national decision-making processes ('shared-rule') are more likely to receive greater structural funding than regions with more autonomy ('self-rule') and less participation rights ('shared-rule'). Cf. Chalmers (2013), pp. 815 ff.

[68] On the importance of consultation in EU lawmaking, cf. Interinstitutional Agreement on Better Lawmaking, OJ C 321, 31 December 2003, pp. 1–5 (Point 26).

[69] The Commission Communication of 19 December 2003 and the Decision of the Bureau of the CoR of 19 March 2004 establish that participation in the Structured Dialogue is open to political representatives at the highest level of national and European associations of local and regional authorities. The participant associations are selected by the Commission with the help of the CoR and have to match certain criteria, including 'a wide basis of territorial and democratic representation' and 'the need to keep a fair balance among associations representing different categories of regional and local authorities'. On the challenge arising from the Structured Dialogue to the role of the CoR, cf. Ricci (2011), p. 122.

alternative form of participation of the people. If such participation takes the form of 'social dialogue', the Commission and the Council have the obligation to verify that the social partners involved are 'sufficiently representative'. Only in this way can the democratic legitimacy of the lawmaking process be maintained.[70]

3. Partnership and Loyal Cooperation

The Committee of the Regions' *White Paper* defines multilevel governance as 'coordinated action by the European Union, the Member States and local and regional authorities, based on *partnership* and aimed at drawing up and implementing EU policies' (emphasis added).[71] The concept of 'partnership' indicates that multilevel governance should be based on 'negotiation' and 'dialogue', rather than on 'hierarchy'.[72] The idea of 'partnership' between levels of government (Commission-Member State-sub-national players) on an in principle equal footing is one of the cornerstones of the EU social and cohesion policy.[73] According to the vision of the Committee of the Regions, partnership should apply potentially to the entire sphere of action of the Union. However, in the Member States, significant hierarchical elements survive both in the making and in the implementation of EU law and policy. For example, in Italy and in the UK, the national

---

[70] See the Case T-135/96, *UEAPME v Council* [1998] ECR II-2335 (paras. 88–89). On this point, cf. Popelier (2011), p. 567. See also Smismans (2004), pp. 340 ff.

[71] Committee of the Regions (2009), at front page. In the *White Paper* the term 'partnership' or 'partner' appears 51 times in 40 pp.

[72] The Commission converges to the same position when it argues that 'the delivery system developed for the structural funds is characterized by multi-level governance, i.e., the Commission, national governments, and regional and local governments are formally autonomous, but there is a high level of shared responsibility at each stage of the decision making process. The relationship between these is, accordingly, one of partnership and negotiation, rather than being a hierarchical one'. Cf. the *Sixth Periodic Report on the Social and Economic Situation and Development of the Regions of the EU*, published in 1999, p. 143. Here, for the first time, the Commission used the expression multilevel governance in an official document.
See also Hooghe and Marks (2001), p. 114: 'Partnership is a variation on the theme of subsidiarity. Instead of compartmentalizing decision making so that each level of government is uniquely responsible for particular policies, it envisages shared decision making across territorial levels'.

[73] Cf. Regulation (EU) No 1303/2013 of the European Parliament and of the Council of 17 December 2013 laying down common provisions on the European Regional Development Fund, the European Social Fund, the Cohesion Fund, the European Agricultural Fund for Rural Development and the European Maritime and Fisheries Fund and laying down general provisions on the European Regional Development Fund, the European Social Fund, the Cohesion Fund and the European Maritime and Fisheries fund and repealing Council Regulation (EC) No 1083/2006. Cf. also Commission Delegated Regulation (EU) No 240/2014 of 7 January 2014 on the European code of conduct on partnership in the framework of the European Structural and Investment Funds. On the role of the principle of partnership in the context of structural funding before Regulation (EU) No 1303/2013 see Bovis (2011), pp. 86–87.

government emerges as a 'primus inter pares' *vis-à-vis* the regional authorities and, in case of an insurmountable disagreement, could impose its view in the formulation of the national position in EU decision-making fora (cf. supra Sect. C.2). Even in federal states like Austria and Germany, in exceptional circumstances the national government may impose its position on the *Länder* for the pursuit of the superior 'national interest'.[74] The exercise of substitute powers of implementation of EU law and policy by the central governments are another example of the survival of considerable hierarchical elements. In reality, rather than a complete renouncement to 'hierarchy', the proper functioning of multilevel governance arrangements at national and EU levels requires a high degree of loyal cooperation (both 'vertical' and 'horizontal') between the different tiers of government. Loyal cooperation commands mutual respect for and attention to the *other*'s point of view, role and interests by *all* the tiers of government. An explicit reference to cooperation can be found both in EU primary law (cf. Article 4(3) TEU, 'sincere cooperation') and in the constitutional laws of the Member States. In Germany and in Italy, the principles of 'federal loyalty' (*Bundestreue*) and 'loyal collaboration' (*leale collaborazione*), respectively, are the foundation of the Federation–*Länder* and State–Regions relationships.[75] In order to respect the maximum possible extent of the role and constitutional status of the sub-national authorities, hierarchical powers are to be construed in the light of loyal cooperation (for example, the substitute powers need to be exercised in 'dialogical' rather than strictly 'hierarchical' manner and in conformity with the principle of proportionality). Only in this way, i.e. *if* the point of view of the sub-state entities is taken seriously into account, can the participation mechanisms created at State level contribute *legitimacy* to the Member State's participation in the EU and, as a result, to Union's action.[76]

---

[74] In Austria, when the *Länder* reach a common position in relation to a matter falling within their responsibility, the Federal Government is bound to uphold this stance in the Council. The Federal Government can depart from this common position only 'for compelling reasons of European integration policy and of foreign policy' (*aus zwingenden integrations- und außenpolitischen Gründen*). The existence of such 'compelling reasons' is determined politically by the Federal Government and is not justiciable. Cf. Art. 23d para. 2 B-VG (*Bundes-Verfassungsgesetz*, Federal Constitutional Law). In the literature, see Eberhard (2011), p. 223. As to Germany, when an EU proposal focuses on a matter falling within the legislative competence of the *Länder*, the Federal Government must pay 'the greatest possible respect' (*maßgeblich zu berücksichtigen*) to the *Bundesrat*'s position. This expression probably means that the Federal Government has to defend the position of the *Bundesrat* in the Council, unless this goes against the interest of Germany as a Member State or unless compelling reasons of foreign policy or European integration justify departure from that position. Cf. Art. 23(5) Basic Law.

[75] Cf. Woelk (1999), passim.

[76] Also, Wessels highlights the key role of loyal cooperation in the context of regional participation: 'In diesem Szenarium sind die Beziehungen Land-Bund-Europäische Gemeinschaften durch eine Bundes- und Gemeinschaftstreue gekennzeichnet, die die Akteure aller Ebenen Gemeinschaftspolitik auch in Konfliktfällen im Geiste gegenseitiger Rücksichtnahme gestalten läßt'. Cf. Wessels (1986), p. 187.
The EU legislator too sees multilevel governance as a form of cooperation among different tiers of government. The Regulation (EU) No 1233/2010 of the European Parliament and of the Council of

4. The Role of the Domestic Courts for the Definition and Enforcement of Multilevel Governance

With the exception of the UK, where the coordination of EU policy issues is regulated by instruments that are 'binding in honour only', national courts, especially constitutional courts, play a key role for the definition and enforcement of multilevel governance arrangements established by domestic law. There are three fundamental routes through which domestic courts can play a role: *1)* through the enforcement of national multilevel governance arrangements, *2)* through the constitutional review of these arrangements and *3)* (also in the UK) through the definition of key concepts, such as 'national identity', 'fundamental structures, political and constitutional', and 'regional and local self-government' (cf. Art. 4 (2) TEU).

1) With the exception of the UK, if multilevel governance arrangements established by domestic law are not observed, sub-national (or national) authorities could require a court to decide the matter. For example, the constitutional participation rights of the German *Länder* are judicially enforceable before the Federal Constitutional Court.[77] In 1995, the Court declared the Federal Government's behaviour as illegal for not respecting the participation rights of the *Bundesrat* on the occasion of the adoption of Directive 89/522/EEC on television. The Court held that this behaviour was in breach of the principle of 'federal loyalty'.[78] However, this declaration has not resulted, nor could it result, in the invalidity of the directive. The lack of invalidity of the final EU act could undermine the effectiveness of the judicial enforcement. This situation corroborates the submission of this book that the sanction in case of non-compliance with multilevel governance requirements is principally the loss of legitimacy, not the invalidity, of the Union's action.[79]

---

15 December 2010 amending Regulation (EC) No 663/2009 establishing a programme to aid economic recovery by granting Community financial assistance to projects in the field of energy says that 'Cooperation among the various tiers of government (multi-level governance) is essential in th[e] context [of the development of further renewable energy sources and the promotion of energy efficiency]' (Point 3 of the Preamble).

The close link between multilevel governance and loyal cooperation is highlighted also in the Preamble to the Charter for Multilevel Governance in Europe: '[While promoting multilevel governance in the EU] we fully respect the equal legitimacy and accountability of each level of government within their respective competences and the principle of loyal cooperation'. See also Point 2.2 of the Charter: 'We commit ourselves to cooperate closely with other public authorities by thinking beyond traditional administrative borders, procedures and hurdles'.

[77] See Article 93(1), No. 1 and No. 3, of the Basic Law. On this point, see Streinz (2009), p. 924 (Rn. 120).

[78] Cf. Ruling of the Federal Constitutional Court of 22 March 1995, published in *BVerfGE*, Vol. 92, pp. 203 ff.

[79] Popelier ascribes a key role to the courts as 'regulatory watchdogs' over the legitimacy of regulatory instruments. Yet the same author admits that the European Courts' response until now

2) When assessing the constitutionality of the arrangements created by the Member States to protect the autonomy of the sub-national authorities in the context of the EU, constitutional courts can judge whether these arrangements and tools are consistent with the constitutional concept of regional and local autonomy. Examples of intervention by national constitutional courts include the creation by the Austrian Constitutional Court of a right/duty of the sub-national units to comply with EU obligations,[80] the statement by the Spanish Constitutional Court that the central government can exercise substitute powers only ex post (i.e., only after a non-fulfilment of an EU obligation by an Autonomous Community has taken place),[81] the 'Lisbon Ruling' of the German Federal Constitutional Court, which contains reference to the protection of the federal structure of the German State and especially to the role to be played by the *Bundesrat* (the house of the *Länder*) in EU affairs.[82]

3) The concept of 'national identity' (which embraces those of 'fundamental structures, political and constitutional' and of 'regional and local self-government'; cf. Art. 4(2) TEU) is a notion of EU law, and as such its content can be further specified by the CJEU. However, the specific content of the notion of 'national identity' results from the 'self-understanding' of the own identity by each Member State. Accordingly, the CJEU will have to rely necessarily on the national law and on the jurisprudence of domestic courts.[83]

D. Concluding Remarks

Multilevel governance has a 'legal' as well as a 'political' dimension. More specifically, it is a legal concept emerging from the EU 'constitutional composite'. Evidence of this is that it is constitutionally required by the Member States' constitutions to protect regional/local autonomy as an essential part of their 'constitutional identity'. Multilevel governance is required also by the EU primary law, since the EU must respect the 'national identity', to be intended as the 'constitutional identity' of the Member States (cf. Art. 4(2) TEU). Multilevel governance is a general concept. It commands participation and involvement of sub-national authorities in EU lawmaking and policymaking and in the implementation phase of EU law/policy. Accordingly, it is a 'principle' resulting from the EU constitutional composite, and more precisely, it is a 'procedural' principle because it

---

has been 'equivocal'. Cf. Popelier (2011), pp. 565–566. Popelier does not analyse the possible role of domestic courts as legitimacy watchdogs.

[80] Cf. the rulings of the Austrian Constitutional Court published in the official collection *Erkenntnisse und Beschlüsse des Verfassungsgerichtshofes* (*VfSlg.*) 14.863/1997 and 17.022/2003.

[81] Cf. Ruling of the Spanish Constitutional Court No. 80 of 8 March 1993.

[82] Cf. Judgment of the Second Senate of the Federal Constitutional Court of 30 June 2009 ('Lisbon Ruling').

[83] Cf. von Bogdandy and Schill (2010), pp. 8 ff. (Rn. 20 ff.); Streinz (2012), p. 28 (Rn. 14).

Table 3.1 Sub-national participation mechanisms and contribution to objective 'input' legitimacy

Participation at national level	CoR	Structured consultation (consultation on the basis of a formal/ structured procedure)	Lobbying and unstructured consultation (consultation without a formal/structured procedure)
High objective legitimising effect if compliant with openness, equality and effectiveness	Important for symbolic and objective legitimacy but limited effectiveness due to composition and advisory role of the CoR	Consultation of regional/local associations by Union institutions, if it is structured properly (openness, equality, effectiveness), may lead to objective (input) legitimacy	No objective 'input' legitimacy due to lack of equality and little or no transparency, but it could be fruitful for single regions or groups of regions (subjective 'output legitimacy')

commands a 'method' of governance. Multilevel governance is an *asymmetrical* concept. There is a common basis for it in the EU primary law, along with 28 different national conjugations of it in accordance with the single national systems. The raison d'être of multilevel governance is to contribute *legitimacy* to the participation of the Member States in the EU and to the EU decision-making activity. *Legitimacy* (in the form of objective 'input legitimacy') is conveyed by participation procedures at national and EU levels (structured participation), provided that they meet certain criteria (openness, equality, effectiveness). Mere lobbying by single regions and/or collective entities can be fruitful for these regions and lead to subjective 'output legitimacy', but it does not achieve full and objective legitimacy (input legitimacy) (Table 3.1).[84]

References

I. Bache, Multi-level governance and European Union regional policy, in *Multi-Level Governance*, ed. by I. Bache, M. Flinders (OUP, Oxford, 2004). pp. 165 ff

M.W. Bauer, T.A. Börzel, Regions and the European Union, in *Handbook on Multi-Level Governance*, ed. by H. Enderlein et al. (Edward Elgar, Cheltenham, 2010), pp. 253 ff

D. Benson, A. Jordan, Exploring the tool-kit of European integration theory: what role for cooperative federalism? J. Eur. Integr. **33**(1), 1 f. (2011)

G. Bognetti, Federalismo, in *Digesto delle discipline pubblicistiche*, vol. VI. (UTET, Torino, 1994), pp. 273 ff

---

[84] See Table 3.1. Respect for 'national identity' by the EU (cf. Art. 4(2) TEU), and therefore 'legitimacy' is ensured *not only* by participation in multilevel governance but also by the recognition of the role of regional/local authorities in other sectors, such as 'locus standi', ex Article 263 TFEU; adequate defence/participation mechanisms in case of substitution powers of the State and of infraction proceedings; appropriate involvement in the implementation of EU law/policy (cf. supra Chap. 2).

C. Bovis, The role and function of structural and cohesion funds and the interaction of the EU regional policy with the internal market policies, in *The Role of the Regions in EU Governance*, ed. by C. Panara, A. De Becker (Springer, Heidelberg, 2011). pp. 81 ff

W.E. Carroll, The Committee of the Regions: a functional analysis of the CoR's institutional capacity. Reg. Fed. Stud. **21**(3) (2011). pp. 341 ff

A.W. Chalmers, Regional authority, transnational lobbying and the allocation of structural funds in the European Union. J. Common Mark. Stud. **51**(5) (2013). pp. 815 ff

T. Christiansen, Second thoughts on Europe's 'Third Level': the European Union's Committee of the Regions. Publius **26**, 93 f. (1996)

Commission of the European Union, *Sixth Periodic Report on the Social and Economic Situation and Development of the Regions of the EU* (1999)

Commission of the European Union, *European Governance – A White Paper*, COM(2001)428, 25 July 2001

Commission of the European Union, Communication 'A framework for target-based tripartite contracts and agreements between the Community, the States and regional and local authorities' COM (2002) 709 final

Commission of the European Union, Communication of the Commission COM (2003)811 final of 19 December 2003 on 'Structured Dialogue'

Commission of the European Union, Communication to the Council, the European Parliament, the Committee of the Regions and the Economic and Social Committee, *Green Paper on Territorial Cohesion. Turning Territorial Diversity into Strength*, 6 October 2008, COM(2008) 616 final

Committee of the Regions, Bureau Decision CoR 380/2003 part II of 19 March 2004 on 'Structured Dialogue'

Committee of the Regions, *White Paper on Multilevel Governance*, CdR 89/2009, 17–18 June 2009

Committee of the Regions, *Scoreboard for Monitoring Multilevel Governance (MLG) at the European Level 2011* (research coordinated by Gracia Vara Arribas and Martin Unfried, published in December 2011)

Committee of the Regions, Opinion, *Building a European Culture of Multilevel Governance: Follow-Up from the Committee of the Regions' White Paper* (94th plenary session 15–16 February 2012)

A.V. Dicey, *Introduction to the Study of the Law of the Constitution*, 10th edn. (Macmillan, London, 1959)

L. Domenichelli, *Le regioni nella Costituzione europea* (Giuffrè, Milano, 2007)

E. Domorenok, The Committee of the Regions: in search of identity. Reg. Fed. Stud. **19**(1), 143 f. (2009)

H. Eberhard, Austria: the role of the Länder in a 'Centralised Federal State', in *The Role of the Regions in EU Governance*, ed. by C. Panara, A. De Becker (Springer, Heidelberg, 2011). pp. 215 ff

S. George, Multi-level governance and the European Union, in *Multi-Level Governance*, ed. by I. Bache, M. Flinders (OUP, Oxford, 2004). pp. 107 ff

C. Hönnige, D. Panke, The Committee of the Regions and the European Economic and Social Committee: how influential are consultative committees in the European Union? J. Common Mark. Stud. **51**(3), 452 f. (2013)

L. Hooghe, G. Marks, *Multi-Level Governance and European Integration* (Rowman & Littlefield, Lanham, 2001)

L. Hooghe, G. Marks, Unraveling the central state, but how? Types of multi-level governance. Am. Polit. Sci. Rev. **97**(2), 233 f. (2003)

L. Hooghe, G. Marks, Types of multi-level governance, in *Handbook on Multi-Level Governance*, ed. by H. Enderlein et al. (Edward Elgar, Cheltenham, 2010), pp. 17 ff

P.M. Huber, Offene Staatlichkeit: Vergleich, in *Handbuch Ius Publicum Europaeum*, ed. by A. von Bogdandy et al. (C.F. Müller, Heidelberg, 2008), pp. 403 ff

C. Jeffery, Regional Information Offices in Brussels and Multi-Level Governance in the EU: A UK-German Comparison, London, Frank Cass (1997), p. 183 ff

M. Knodt et al., Die Brüsseler Informationsbüros der deutschen Länder: Aktive Mitspieler im Mehrebenensystem der EU, in *Europapolitik und Europafähigkeit von Regionen*, ed. by K.-H. Lambertz, M. Große Hüttmann (Nomos, Baden-Baden, 2009), pp. 123 ff

A. Littoz-Monnet, *Dynamic Multi-Level Governance – Bringing the Study of Multi-Level Inter- actions into the Theorising of European Integration*, in European Integration online Papers [EIoP], vol. 14 (2010), http://eiop.or.at/eiop/index.php/eiop/article/view/2010_001a. Accessed Sept 2014

N. Luhmann, *Legitimation durch Verfahren* (Suhrkamp, Frankfurt a.M., 2013) (reprint of the third edition of 1978)

G. Marks, Structural policy in the European community, in *Europolitics: Institutions and Policymaking in the "New" European Community*, ed. by A. Sbragia (The Brooking Institute, Washington, DC, 1992). pp. 191 ff

G. Marks, Structural policy and multilevel governance in the EC, in *The State of the European Community*, ed. by A. Cafruny, G. Rosenthal, vol. 2 (Lynne Rienner, Boulder, 1993). pp. 391 ff

G. Marks, An actor-centred approach to multi-level governance, in *The Regional Dimension of the European Union. Towards a Third Level in Europe?* ed. by C. Jeffery (Cass, London, 1997). pp. 20 ff

G. Marks, L. Hooghe, Contrasting visions of multi-level governance, in *Multi-Level Governance*, ed. by I. Bache, M. Flinders (OUP, Oxford, 2004). pp. 15 ff

G. Marks et al., European integration from the 1980s: State Centric v. Multi-level Governance. J. Common Mark. Stud. **34**(3), 341 f. (1996)

C. Martínez-Sicluna y Sepúlveda, *Legalità e legittimità: la teoria del potere* (ESI, Napoli, 2006) [Italian translation of *Legalidad y legitimad: la teoría del poder*, Actas, Madrid, 1991]

M. Mazzoleni, The first Tripartite agreement in the EU. An actor-centred analysis of an experi- mental multi-level interaction. Reg. Fed. Stud. **16**(3), 263 f. (2006)

METIS GmbH, *Impact Assessment at the CoR: Methodology and Its Implementation* (2010)

C. Moore, A Europe of the Regions vs. the Regions in Europe: reflections on regional engagement in Brussels. Reg. Fed. Stud. **18**(5), 517 f. (2008)

A. Moravcsik, F. Schimmelfenning, Liberal intergovernmentalism, in *European Integration Theory*, ed. by A. Wiener, T. Diez, 2nd edn. (OUP, Oxford, 2009). pp. 67 ff

M. Nettesheim, *Subsidiarität durch politische Koordination*. Paper presented at the symposium "Grenzen Europäischer Normgebung – EU-Kompetenzen und Europäische Grundrechte", Frankfurt am Main, 19 March 2014

H. Neuhofer, Gemeindegebiet und Gemeindebewohner, in *Das österreichische Gemeinderecht*, ed. by F. Klug et al. (Manz, Wien, 2008), Rz. 45

I. Pernice, The Treaty of Lisbon: multilevel constitutionalism in action. Columbia J. Eur. Law **15** (3), 349 f. (2009)

V. Persson, Local government in Sweden: flexibility and independence in a unitary state, in *Local Government in Europe: The 'Fourth Level' in the EU Multi-Layered System of Governance*, ed. by C. Panara, M. Varney (Routledge, Oxford, 2013). pp. 305 ff

S. Piattoni, Multi-level governance: a historical and conceptual analysis. J. Eur. Integr. **31**(2), 163 f. (2009)

S. Piattoni, *The Theory of Multi-Level Governance. Conceptual, Empirical, and Normative Challenges* (OUP, Oxford, 2010)

R. Pomahač, Local government in the Czech Republic: history, current position, prospective evolution, in *Local Government in Europe: The 'Fourth Level' in the EU Multi-Layered System of Governance*, ed. by C. Panara, M. Varney (Routledge, Oxford, 2013). pp. 52 ff

P. Popelier, Governance and better regulation: dealing with the legitimacy paradox. Eur. Public Law **17**(3), 555 f. (2011)

A. Reposo, *Profili dello Stato autonomico Federalismo e regionalismo*, 2nd edn. (Giappichelli, Torino, 2005). pp. 119 ff

S. Ricci, The Committee of the Regions and the challenge of European governance, in *The Role of the Regions in EU Governance*, ed. by C. Panara, A. De Becker (Springer, Heidelberg, 2011). pp. 109 ff

C. Rowe, *Regional Representations in the EU: Between Diplomacy and Interest Mediation* (Palgrave-Macmillan, New York, 2011)

A. Sbragia, Multi-level governance and comparative regionalism, in *Handbook on Multi-Level Governance*, ed. by H. Enderlein et al. (Edward Elgar, Cheltenham, 2010), pp. 267 ff

F. Scharpf, *Governing in Europe Effective and Democratic?* (OUP, Oxford, 1999)

C. Schmitt, *Legality and Legitimacy* (Duke University Press, Durham, 2004) [English translation of *Legalität und Legimität*, 1932]

M. Smith, Toward a theory of EU foreign policy-making: multilevel governance, domestic politics, and national adaptation to Europe's common foreign and security policy. J. Eur. Public Policy **11**(4), 740 f. (2004)

S. Smismans, *Law, Legitimacy, and European Governance. Functional Participation in Social Regulation* (OUP, Oxford, 2004)

K.-P. Sommermann, Offene Staatlichkeit: Deutschland, in *Handbuch Ius Publicum Europaeum*, ed. by A. von Bogdandy et al. (C.F. Müller, Heidelberg, 2008), pp. 3 ff

P. Stephenson, Twenty years of multilevel governance: 'Where Does It Come From? What Is It? Where Is It Going?'. J. Eur. Public Policy **20**(6), 817 f. (2013)

R. Streinz, [Commentary to] *Art. 23 GG*, in *Grundgesetz. Kommentar*, 5th edn. ed. by M. Sachs (Beck, München, 2009), pp. 905 ff

R. Streinz, [Commentary to] *Art. 4 EUV*, in *EUV/AEUV*, 2nd edn. ed. by R. Streinz (C.H. Beck, München, 2012), pp. 20 ff

G. Vara Arribas, The changing dynamics of sub-state participation: the commission's proposals for increasing regional and local involvement in European policy processes. Eipascope **2**, 19 f. (2005)

S. Villamena, Organisation and responsibilities of the local authorities in Italy between unity and autonomy, in *Local Government in Europe: The 'Fourth Level' in the EU Multi-Layered System of Governance*, ed. by C. Panara, M. Varney (Routledge, Oxford, 2013). pp. 183 ff

A. von Bogdandy, S. Schill, [Commentary to] *Art. 4 EUV*, in *Das Recht der Europäischen Union*, vol. 1, ed. by E. Grabitz et al. (C.H. Beck, München, 2010 July), 36 p

A. von Bogdandy, S. Schill, Overcoming absolute primacy: respect for national identity under the Lisbon Treaty. Common Mark. Law Rev. **48**(5), 1417 f. (2011)

A. Warleigh, *The Committee of the Regions: Institutionalising Multi-Level Governance?* (Kogan Page, London, 1999)

M. Weber, *Economia e società*, vol. I. (Comunità, Milano, 1999) [Italian translation of *Wirtschaft und Gesellschaft*, Economy and Society, 1922]

J.H.H. Weiler, The community system: the dual character of supranationalism. Yearb. Eur. Law **1**, 267 f. (OUP, Oxford, 1981)

W. Wessels, Die deutschen Länder in der EG-Politik: Selbstblockierung oder pluralistische Dynamik? in *Die Deutschen Länder und die Europäischen Gemeinschaften*, ed. by R. Hrbek, U. Thaysen (Nomos, Baden-Baden, 1986). pp. 181 ff

J. Woelk, *Konfliktregelung und Kooperation im italienischen und deutschen Verfassungsrecht: "Leale collaborazione" und Bundestreue im Vergleich* (Nomos, Baden-Baden, 1999)

Chapter 4
The Principle of Subsidiarity

A. Introduction

The driving idea of subsidiarity is that public functions should be exercised as close as possible to the citizen. Only if the 'closest' authority is not in a position to perform a function or to do it effectively will this function be allocated to a 'higher' level of government. Subsidiarity is based on the assumption that 'closer' authorities are better suited to respond to certain social demands stemming from their community. Only those demands that are not limited to a given community or that require action on a wider scale or that can be better fulfilled by another authority shall be exercised by other (higher) tiers of government. Ideally, each, 'higher', tier of government should only perform a 'subsidiary function' in relation to other tiers of government 'closer' to the citizen.[1]

---

[1] Cf. Communication of the Commission to the Council and the European Parliament (1992), p. 1: 'The subsidiarity principle as applied in the institutional context is based on a simple concept: the powers that a state or a federation of states wields in the common interest are only those which individuals, families, companies and local or regional authorities cannot exercise in isolation. This commonsense principle therefore dictates that decisions should be taken at the level closest to the ordinary citizen and that action taken by the upper echelons of the body politic should be limited'. The concept of subsidiarity is usually traced back by commentators to the encyclical *Quadragesimo Anno: Encyclical of Pope Pius XI on Reconstruction of the Social Order* (1931) at §§ 79–81. This document uses the expression 'principle of subsidiary function' [in Latin: *'subsidiarii officii principio'*] (§80). Cf. Trnka (2007), pp. 242–243. Scholars distinguish 'vertical subsidiarity', which applies to the 'vertical' distribution of powers between the different tiers of government, from 'horizontal subsidiarity'. This is a principle governing the relationship between the state and private players in relation to the performance of activities of public interest (for example, in the field of education or transport). 'Horizontal subsidiarity' received an important recognition in Article 118(4) of the Italian Constitution: 'The State, regions, metropolitan cities, provinces and municipalities shall promote the autonomous initiatives of citizens, both as individuals and as members of associations, relating to activities of general interest, on the basis of the principle of subsidiarity' [provision introduced by Constitutional Law No. 3 of 18 October 2001]. Another reference to horizontal subsidiarity can be found in Article 4(3)(a) of Italian Law

© Springer International Publishing Switzerland 2015
C. Panara, *The Sub-national Dimension of the EU*,
DOI 10.1007/978-3-319-14589-1_4

The Committee of the Regions' *White Paper on Multilevel Governance* envisages a close link between multilevel governance and the principle of subsidiarity. According to the *White Paper*, subsidiarity fulfils two fundamental tasks: first, to prevent decisions from being restricted to a single tier of government and, second, to ensure that policies are decided and implemented at the most appropriate level. The *White Paper* further suggests that respect for subsidiarity and multilevel governance are 'indissociable'; one indicates the responsibilities of the different tiers of government, whilst the other emphasises their interaction.[2]

Subsidiarity presupposes coexistence and interaction between multiple tiers of government, which, in turn, is a feature of multilevel governance (cf. supra Chap. 3). At the same time, multilevel governance requires the protection of a degree of autonomy of state and sub-state entities without which the system would become 'centralised', i.e., the opposite of a 'multilevel polity'. However, the specific terms of the relationship between subsidiarity and multilevel governance need further exploration. To address this problem, it is necessary to remember that multilevel governance requires the involvement of the sub-national authorities in the EU decision-making process ('integrating the objectives of local and regional authorities within the strategies of the European Union (...) and encourage their participation in the coordination of European policy'[3]). This notion will be used as a conceptual foundation to link subsidiarity and multilevel governance.

This chapter will outline the concept and application of subsidiarity in the EU (Sect. B); will analyse the concept and judicial application of subsidiarity in Germany and in Italy, where the principle plays a key role (Sect. C); will deal with the 'procedural' approach to subsidiarity in the Lisbon Subsidiarity Protocol (Sect. D); and, finally, will put forward a sustainable concept of subsidiarity in the light of multilevel governance (Sect. E).

It will be argued that subsidiarity is not per se 'non-justiciable'. However 'justiciability' of this principle is not sustainable in the long run due to the practical and political implications of it. Accordingly, the only viable way to enforce subsidiarity is through 'procedural' arrangements during the lawmaking process. Subsidiarity emerges as a 'procedural principle' that pursues the same fundamental objective of multilevel governance to legitimise the Union's authoritative decision-making. In this way, it can be considered a manifestation of multilevel governance.

No. 59 of 15 March 1997. Cf. Camerlengo (2006), pp. 2350–2355. The focus of the present chapter is on the vertical dimension of subsidiarity.

[2] Cf. Committee of the Regions (2009), p. 7. See also the Charter for Multilevel Governance in Europe (2014), which includes 'subsidiarity' and 'proportionality' among its fundamental principles (Point 1.4).

[3] Cf. Committee of the Regions (2009), p. 7.

B. The Principle of Subsidiarity in the EU

1. The Origin of Subsidiarity in the EU

The principle of subsidiarity obtained the first important recognition in Community law in the Single European Act of 1986. In the field of environment, Article 130r EEC limited Community action to the objectives that could be attained better at Community than at Member State level.[4] With the Treaty of Maastricht, subsidiarity became a principle informing the entire Community action, beyond environmental law, with the exception of the areas falling within the exclusive Community competence.[5]

The Treaty of Lisbon enhanced the position of regional and local authorities in the EU through their explicit incorporation into the principle of subsidiarity. According to Article 5(3) TEU, '(...) the Union shall act only if and insofar as the objectives of the proposed action cannot be sufficiently achieved by the Member States, *either at central level or at regional and local level* (...)' (emphasis added).[6]

This amendment met a request that federal Member States and the Committee of the Regions had repeatedly put forward to have the Treaty to reflect the reality that Union objectives can be attained not only at national but also at regional or local level.[7] It would appear that the reference to the 'regional and local level' would imply that the Union shall be aware of the decentralised structure of the Member States. This is of great symbolic importance. However, already under the previous

---

[4] Art. 130r (4) EEC Treaty: 'The Community shall take action relating to the environment to the extent to which the objectives referred to in paragraph 1 can be attained better at Community level than at the level of the individual Member States'.

[5] Cf. Art. 3b of the EC Treaty (which became Art. 5 after the entry into effect of the Treaty of Amsterdam): 'In areas which do not fall within its exclusive competence, the Community shall take action, in accordance with the principle of subsidiarity, only if and in so far as the objectives of the proposed action cannot be sufficiently achieved by the Member States and can therefore, by reason of the scale or effects of the proposed action, be better achieved by the Community'. The Preamble to the Treaty Establishing the EU emphasised the role of the principle of subsidiarity in the new setting created by the Treaty of Maastricht: '[The High Contracting Parties are] RESOLVED to continue the process of creating an ever closer union among the peoples of Europe, in which decisions are taken as closely as possible to the citizen in accordance with the principle of subsidiarity[.]'

[6] This is the full text of Art. 5(3) TEU: 'Under the principle of subsidiarity, in areas which do not fall within its exclusive competence, the Union shall act only if and insofar as the objectives of the proposed action cannot be sufficiently achieved by the Member States, either at central level or at regional and local level, but can rather, by reason of the scale or effects of the proposed action, be better achieved at Union level'. Originally, this provision had been included in the Treaty Establishing a Constitution for Europe (cf. Art. I-11).

[7] Cf. Van Nuffel (2011), p. 59. See, for example, the proposals put forward in 1990 by the governments of the regional entities meeting as 'Europe of the Regions' in Brussels on 24 and 25 May 1990, as well as the proposals presented by the German *Bundesrat* in 1990 and 1995 and by the Federal Republic of Germany during the 1996 Intergovernmental Conference [all cited in Van Nuffel (2000), pp. 397–398]. See also the Opinions of the Committee of the Regions of 21 April 1995 (OJ 1996 C 100, pp. 6 and 10), 20 November 1997 (OJ 1998, C 64, p. 98) and 11 March 1999 (OJ 1999, C 198, p. 73).

definition of subsidiarity it was sufficiently clear that the capacity of the Member States to attain certain policy objectives had to be determined whilst taking account of possible action by each level of government at State or sub-national level.[8] The requirement for the Union legislator to bear in mind the role and the point of view of the 'regional and local level' is further confirmed by other provisions: for example, the Commission's duty to consult widely and 'take into account the regional and local dimension of the action envisaged',[9] the involvement of 'regional parliaments with legislative powers' in the early warning system,[10] the advisory role of the CoR in relation specifically to subsidiarity.[11]

2. The Court of Justice's Approach to Subsidiarity

Despite the importance attributed to subsidiarity, until now no Union act has ever been invalidated by the ECJ for a breach of this principle. It must be taken into account that only in very few cases subsidiarity has been put forward against an act and, also, that it has never been used as the first or principal plea.[12] Faced with subsidiarity challenges, the ECJ has systematically upheld Union action. This jurisprudence is explained by legal scholars in different ways. According to some, the ECJ's approach to subsidiarity is a 'light' or 'low intensity judicial review'.[13] For others, subsidiarity is a political or philosophical concept, therefore

---

[8] Cf. point 5(1) of the Amsterdam Subsidiarity Protocol ('... cannot be sufficiently achieved by Member States' action *in the framework of their national constitutional system* [...]', emphasis added). On this aspect, cf. Van Nuffel (2011), pp. 59–60. In *Belgium v Commission*, the claimant Member State submitted to the Court that Commission Regulation No. 2204/2002, by making measures favouring employment subject to the obligation to notify the Commission as possible State aid, did not take account of the regionalisation of some Member States and, as a result, infringed, inter alia, the principle of subsidiarity. The Court, without addressing this specific concern, simply noted that the Commission had acted within the powers conferred on it by the Treaty (Art. 87 TEC) and by Regulation No. 994/98. This case was decided before the entry into force of the new Article 5 TEU on subsidiarity ('either at central level or at regional and local level'); however, it is a clear testimony of the unwillingness of the ECJ to get involved in issues concerning the distribution of powers *within* the Member States. Cf. Case C-110/03 *Belgium v Commission* [2005] ECR I-2801, paras. 56–58.

[9] Cf. Art. 2 Lisbon Subsidiarity Protocol.

[10] Cf. Art. 6(1) Lisbon Subsidiarity Protocol.

[11] Cf. Art. 307 TFEU in relation to the role of the Committee of the Regions. Quite correctly, Bermann (1994), pp. 342–343, highlights that subsidiarity, by reducing the scope of Community action, also limits the erosion of the powers of the Member States' own component parts.

[12] Cf. Craig (2012), p. 80, who counted no more than ten real subsidiarity challenges in nearly 20 years, i.e., roughly only one every 2 years.

[13] Craig and De Búrca (2011), pp. 98–99. According to De Búrca (1998), p. 218, subsidiarity is 'a cloudy and ambiguous concept which is open to instrumental use. The principle is politically complex and legally uncertain'. Syrpis (2004), p. 334: '[Despite the lack of judicial enforcement] the principle of subsidiarity remains a useful device in that it directs attention to the "vertical" dimension of the European Union's legitimacy deficit and to the importance of diversity (alongside integration) as a value underpinning the European project'.

impossible (or very difficult) to enforce judicially.[14] More specifically, according to some, this principle would be perceived by the European Court as a 'threat to integration',[15] and for this reason its judicial enforcement would be in conflict with the 'broad ethos' of the Court.[16] Finally, there are those who argue that it would be wrong to describe the ECJ's approach to subsidiarity as an aprioristic refusal to engage with the complexities of the scrutiny; in reality, in all relevant cases landed before the ECJ, Union legislative intervention was perfectly lawful.[17]

Certainly, it is not true that the ECJ systematically accepts the position of the Union legislator without further scrutiny. This was probably the case in *UK v Council*, concerning the Working Time Directive, where the ECJ appeared to accept the point of view of the Council without an independent analysis of the subsidiarity question. According to the circular argument used by the ECJ on that occasion, if the Council found that it is necessary to achieve a certain objective 'to improve the existing level of protection as regards the health and safety of workers and to harmonize the conditions in this area', then 'achievement of that objective (. . .) necessarily presupposes Community-wide action'.[18]

By contrast, in other cases, the Court developed a more substantial reasoning in support of Union action. For example, in *Netherlands v Council*, concerning Directive 94/44/EC, albeit with a rather concise explanation, the Court held that the Directive's objective to harmonise legislation and practice in the area of protection of biotechnological inventions 'could not be achieved by action taken by the Member States alone'. In addition, according to the Court, as the scope of the

---

[14] Cf. Barber (2005a), pp. 308 ff. See also Toth (1994), pp. 282 ff., who argues that the question of whether an outcome would be better achieved by the Community or the Member States is not a purely legal question and therefore creates real difficulties when discussing the justiciability of the principle of subsidiarity. According to Toth, 'all that the Court may be expected to do in cases involving the application of Article 3b [current Art. 5 TEU] in areas of shared competence is to examine whether in arriving at its decision the Council has not committed a manifest error or a misuse of powers or has not patently exceeded the bounds of its discretion. These are the ultimate limits of justiciability of subsidiarity' (ibid. at p. 284). An interesting discussion of the political or legal nature of subsidiarity can be found in De Búrca (2000), pp. 95 ff. See also De Búrca (2001), pp. 131 ff. On the political nature of the principle of subsidiarity, see also Working Group I of the European Convention on the Principle of Subsidiarity, Brussels, 23 September 2002, CONV 286/02: 'The Group considered that as the principle of subsidiarity was a principle of an essentially political nature, implementation of which involved a considerable margin of discretion for the institutions (considering whether shared objectives could "better" be achieved at European level or at another level), monitoring of compliance with that principle should be of an essentially political nature and take place before the entry into force of the act in question' (p. 2).

[15] Estella (2002), p. 178.

[16] Barber (2005b), p. 199. Cf. also Toth (1992), p. 1079, who describes subsidiarity as 'totally alien' to the EU since it 'contradicts the logic, structure and wording of the founding treaties and the jurisprudence of the European Court of Justice'.

[17] Cf. Van Nuffel (2011), pp. 65–66. Van Nuffel criticises the opinion that depicts the ECJ as 'consistently unwilling to review Community legislation for alleged violations of subsidiarity' [cf., for example, Cooper (2006), p. 284]. See also Ziller (2007), pp. 377 ff.

[18] Case C-84/94 *UK v Council* [1996] ECR I-5755, para. 47.

protection had immediate effects on intra-Community trade, 'it is clear that, given the scale and effects of the proposed action, the objective in question could be better achieved by the Community'.[19]

The same argument, that harmonisation of laws is required in order to achieve common market objectives, arose also in later rulings. For example, in *British American Tobacco*, the ECJ held that 'the Directive's objective to eliminate the barriers raised by the differences which still exist between the Member States' laws (. . .) on the manufacture, presentation and sale of tobacco products' could not be sufficiently achieved by the Member States individually and called for action at Community level. 'It follows', according to the Court, that 'the objective of the proposed action could be better achieved at Community level'.[20]

Also in *Vodafone*, concerning EC Regulation No. 717/2007 on the 'Eurotariff' for roaming services, the Court engaged in a thorough analysis of the challenged act before accepting the explanation contained in the Regulation's Preamble,[21] i.e., that the interdependence between wholesale and retail roaming charges renders the choice to impose a 'ceiling' on both compliant with subsidiarity. Interestingly, the Court's reasoning in this case is similar to the German judicial doctrine of the *Annexkompetenzen*, according to which the Federation can extend its lawmaking activity to issues that are a necessary 'appendix' to the principal area of regulation. The regulation of the 'appendix' must be logical, necessary, corollary of the regulation of the main area.[22]

---

[19] Case C-377/98 *Netherlands v European Parliament and Council* [2001] ECR I-7079, para. 32: 'The objective pursued by the Directive, to ensure smooth operation of the internal market by preventing or eliminating differences between the legislation and practice of the various Member States in the area of the protection of biotechnological inventions, could not be achieved by action taken by the Member States alone. As the scope of that protection has immediate effects on trade, and, accordingly, on intra-Community trade, it is clear that, given the scale and effects of the proposed action, the objective in question could be better achieved by the Community'.

[20] Case C-491/01 *The Queen v Secretary of State for Health (ex parte British American Tobacco Ltd.)* [2002] ECR I-11453, paras. 181–183. A similar reasoning can be found in Joined Cases C-154/04 and C-155/04 *ANH v Secretary of State for Health* [2002] ECR I-6451, paras. 106–107, in relation to Directive 2002/46 on food supplements. Para 106 provides: 'To leave Member States the task of regulating trade in food supplements which do not comply with Directive 2002/46 would perpetuate the uncoordinated development of national rules and, consequently, obstacles to trade between Member States and distortions of competition so far as those products are concerned'. Cf. also Case C-103/01 *Commission v Germany* [2003] ECR I-5369, para. 47.

[21] Cf. Recital 14, Preamble, Regulation No. 717/2007: 'Regulatory obligations should be imposed at both retail and wholesale level to protect the interests of roaming customers, since experience has shown that reductions in wholesale prices for Community-wide roaming services may not be reflected in lower retail prices for roaming owing to the absence of incentives for this to happen. On the other hand, action to reduce the level of retail prices without addressing the level of the wholesale costs associated with the provision of these services could risk disrupting the orderly functioning of the Community-wide roaming market'.

[22] Case C-58/08 *The Queen v Secretary of State for Business (ex parte Vodafone)* [2010] ECR I-4999, para. 78: 'That interdependence [between wholesale and retail roaming charges] means that the Community legislature could legitimately take the view that it had to intervene at the level of retail charges as well. Thus, by reason of the effects of the common approach laid down in

The view depicting the ECJ's approach to subsidiarity as relaxed must be refuted also for another reason. The ECJ's judgments take into account the opinions of the Advocates General. In relation to subsidiarity, in no circumstance the Court came to a conclusion different from that envisaged by an Advocate General. Whilst admittedly some Advocates General's opinions entail a surface scrutiny of subsidiarity,[23] others are quite thorough when tackling the same issue.[24]

3. The Proportionality Test

Article 5 TEU allows for Union action not only 'if', but also 'insofar as', the objectives of the proposed action cannot be sufficiently achieved by the Member States and can be better achieved at Union level. The expression 'insofar as' refers to the proportionality requirement, according to which all Union action should not go beyond what is 'appropriate' and 'necessary' to achieve the proposed objective.[25] More specifically, proportionality demands that Union action be kept to the minimum necessary, i.e., as specified in Article 5(4) TEU, '. . . the content and form of Union action shall not exceed what is necessary to achieve the objectives of the Treaties'. Accordingly, the Amsterdam Subsidiarity Protocol required Union institutions to leave as much scope for national decision as possible, to prefer directives to regulations and framework directives to detailed measures and to minimise the burden, financial or administrative, of Union measures for, inter alia, national governments and local authorities.[26]

Some scholars argue that Member States' autonomy could be better protected through a judicial review of proportionality of Union action rather than through the

---

Regulation No 717/2007, the objective pursued by that regulation could best be achieved at Community level'. On the *Annexkompetenzen* and the implied powers in German federalism, cf. Panara (2008), pp. 425 ff.

[23] Cf., for example, AG Geelhoed Opinion in Joined Cases C-154/04 and C-155/04 *ANH v Secretary of State for Health*.

[24] See especially AG Poiares Maduro Opinion in Case C-58/08 *The Queen v Secretary of State for Business (ex parte Vodafone)*. See also AG Léger Opinion in Case C-84/94 *UK v Council* (Working Time Directive).

[25] Van Nuffel (2011), p. 58, explains that proportionality can be distinguished from subsidiarity, as it presupposes the legitimacy of a Union action and engages its intensity and scope. Cf. also AG Léger Opinion Case C-84/94, para. 125 ff. and Lenaerts and Van Nuffel (2011), pp. 144–145.

[26] Cf. Amsterdam Subsidiarity Protocol, points 6, 7, 9. These requirements are not portrayed in the Lisbon Subsidiarity Protocol. However, the new Protocol requires draft legislative acts to contain an assessment of the proposal's financial impact and, in the case of a directive, of its implications for the rules to be issued by Member States, including, where necessary, regional legislation (cf. Art. 5). Draft legislative acts should also take account of the need for any burden, whether financial or administrative, falling upon the Union, national governments, regional or local authorities, economic operators and citizens, to be minimised and commensurate with the objective to be achieved (ibid.).

traditional subsidiarity review.[27] This opinion pursues the noble aim of protecting Member States' autonomy through judicial review. However, it relies on the undemonstrated assumption that a focus on proportionality would favour Member States' autonomy.[28] In reality, there is no evidence that, by focusing on proportionality, the ECJ would be more likely to find in favour of the Member States.[29]

For example, in *UK v Council*, in relation to the Working Time Directive, the Court held that in order to establish whether a provision of Community law is compliant with proportionality, it must be ascertained 'whether the means which it employs are suitable for the purpose of achieving the desired objective' and 'whether they do not go beyond what is necessary to achieve it'.[30] In this case, the Court pointed out that judicial review of the exercise of discretionary powers of Community lawmaking institutions must be limited to examining 'whether [such exercise] has been vitiated by manifest error' or 'misuse of powers' or 'whether the institution concerned has manifestly exceeded the limits of its discretion'.[31] After comparing the content of the Working Time Directive with its objective (i.e., improving health and safety protection for workers), the Court concluded that '(...) the measures on the organization of working time (...) cannot (...) be regarded as unsuited to the purpose of achieving the objective pursued'.[32] Furthermore, the Court found that 'the Council did not commit any manifest error in concluding that the contested measures were necessary to achieve the objective'[33] or 'in taking the view that the objective of harmonizing national legislation on the health and safety of workers (...) could not be achieved by measures less restrictive'.[34] What seems to count, for the Court, is not whether an action is really 'necessary', or whether, in theory, less restrictive measures are 'possible', but whether there is a 'manifest error' vitiating the discretion of the Union legislature.[35]

---

[27] Cf. Schutze (2009), pp. 525–536, who differentiates 'federal proportionality', protecting Member States' autonomy, from 'liberal proportionality', protecting individual rights (ibid. p. 533). See also Davies (2006), pp. 63 ff.

[28] Davies (2006), pp. 81 ff., is very aware of the difficulties with the application of proportionality for the protection of Member States' autonomy.

[29] Cf. Craig (2012), pp. 82 ff.

[30] Case C-84/94 *UK v Council* [1996] ECR I-5755, para. 57, with reference to Case C-426/93 *Germany v Council* [1995] ECR I-3723, para. 42.

[31] Case C-84/94 *UK v Council* [1996] ECR I-5755, para. 58. Accordingly, Martinico (2011), pp. 649 ff., correctly describes the subsidiarity control by the ECJ as an 'extrema ratio'.

[32] Ibid., para. 59.

[33] Ibid., para. 60.

[34] Ibid., para. 66.

[35] See also Case C-58/08 *The Queen v Secretary of State for Business (ex parte Vodafone)* [2010] ECR I-4999, para 52: 'With regard to judicial review of compliance with [proportionality] the Court has accepted that in the exercise of the powers conferred on it the Community legislature must be allowed a broad discretion in areas in which its action involves political, economic and social choices and in which it is called upon to undertake complex assessments and evaluations. Thus the criterion to be applied is not whether a measure adopted in such an area was the only or the best possible measure, since its legality can be affected only if the measure is manifestly

The described approach does not promise more rigour than the typical subsidiarity reasoning.

This conclusion seems confirmed by the analysis of other cases. In *British American Tobacco*, for example, the boundary between subsidiarity and proportionality is blurred where the Court, judging on subsidiarity, made reference to the paragraphs of the same judgment examining and rejecting the plea on proportionality: '(. . .) the intensity of the action undertaken by the Community in this instance [as well as being in keeping with the requirements of proportionality] was also in keeping with the requirements of the principle of subsidiarity in that (. . .) it did not go beyond what was necessary to achieve the objective pursued'.[36] Accordingly, it appears unlikely that the Court may adopt a more rigorous approach to proportionality than to subsidiarity.

Another, greater, mistake in seeing proportionality as a possible panacea is that this view considers judicial enforcement as absolutely necessary for the proper functioning of subsidiarity. In reality, multilevel governance, by emphasising multilevel 'participation' and 'cooperation', pushes towards 'procedural subsidiarity', i.e., political consultation and negotiation rather than court action.[37] However, before explaining in further detail my understanding of subsidiarity in the light of multilevel governance, it is crucial to determine whether, to what extent and how subsidiarity can be judicially enforceable. This problem will be examined in relation to two national systems in which the principle plays a fundamental role: Germany (cf. infra Sects. C.1 and C.2) and Italy (cf. infra Sects. C.3 and C.4).

C. Comparative Analysis

1. Germany: The Long and Winding Road to the Judicial Enforcement of Subsidiarity

The introduction of a subsidiarity clause in Germany is the result of a vivid debate that took place during the approval of the *Grundgesetz* (acronym GG), the constitution of the Federal Republic of Germany.[38] Article 34 of the draft constitution approved on August 1948 by the Convention of Herrenchiemsee, a conference of

---

inappropriate having regard to the objective which the competent institution is seeking to pursue'. See also Case *Belgium v Commission* [2005] ECR I-2801, para. 68.

[36] Case C-491/01 *The Queen* v *Secretary of State for Health (ex parte British American Tobacco Ltd.)* [2002] ECR I-11453, para. 184. Also in Case C-176/09 *Luxembourg v European Parliament and Council*, not yet published in ECR, in relation to Directive 2009/12/EC on airport charges, the subsidiarity plea brought by Luxembourg seems to be concerned with proportionality rather than with subsidiarity strictly speaking. Cf. paras. 73–84.

[37] Contra cf. Sander (2006), pp. 517 ff., who regards judicial review of subsidiarity as both possible and desirable.

[38] The German term *Grundgesetz* can be translated into the English 'Basic Law'.

regional delegates endowed with the task of preparing a constitutional draft, stipulated that 'In the fields [in which the Federation has] the right to pass legislation with primacy [*Vorranggesetzgebung*] ... The Federation shall only regulate what must be uniformly regulated'.[39] Article 34 of the draft constitution was strongly criticised by the Allied Military Governors, who wished to see the reinforcement of the *Länder* vis-à-vis the central government. In their Memorandum of 2 March 1949, they proposed that 'the *Länder* shall retain the right to legislate in the fields hereinafter enumerated except where it is clearly impossible for a single *Land* to enact effective legislation or where the legislation if enacted would be detrimental to the rights or interests of other *Länder*; in such cases [...] the Federation shall have the right to enact such legislation as may be necessary or appropriate [...]'.[40] In the view of the occupying authorities, a more robust vertical division of powers between the Federation and the *Länder* would reduce the risk for Germany to fall again into totalitarianism.[41] At the same time, a weaker central government would prevent the reconstituted German state from becoming a threat for its neighbours. Following the Memorandum, the Parliamentary Council in Bonn (the body entrusted with the task of passing the constitution[42]) replaced the 'right [of the Federation] to legislate with primacy' with the 'concurrent legislative power' (*konkurrierende Gesetzgebung*) of Article 72 GG:

> (1) On the matters falling within the concurrent legislative power the *Länder* shall have the right to legislate so long as and to the extent that the Federation has not used its legislative power by enacting a law.
> (2) The Federation has the right to legislate in this field to the extent that there is a need for regulation through federal law[.]
> [Such need arises when]:
> 1. An issue cannot be effectively regulated by the legislation of a single *Land*, or
> 2. The regulation of an issue by a single *Land* through a *Land* law may compromise the interests of other *Länder* or of the whole [State], or

---

[39] This is the full German text of Article 34: 'Im Bereich der Vorranggesetzgebung behalten die Länder das Recht der Gesetzgebung, solange und soweit der Bund von seinem Gesetzgebungsrecht keinen Gebrauch gemacht hat. *Der Bund soll nur das regeln, was einheitlich geregelt werden muß*' (emphasis added). The right to pass legislation with primacy (*Vorranggesetzgebung*) echoed the 'concurrent competence of the *Reich*' (*konkurrierende Reichskompetenz*) of the Weimar Constitution. In the areas subjected to this type of competence, the *Länder* could only legislate as long as, and to the extent, that the *Reich* (i.e., the central authority) had not used its right to legislate (cf. Art. 12(1) Weimar Constitution).

[40] The Memorandum was sent by the Military Governors of the United States, the United Kingdom and France, the three occupying powers in the West part of Germany.

[41] The idea that vertical separation of powers is an antidote against tyranny is traditionally embedded in federalist thinking. Cf. Madison (1788), passim. See also Schenke (1989), pp. 698 ff. According to Neumann, there is no ultimate evidence that a federal state is more resistant to an autocratic involution than a centralised state: cf. Neumann (1957), pp. 216–232.

[42] After being passed by the Parliamentary Council (8 May 1949) and after being approved by the occupying powers (12 May 1949), the *Grundgesetz* was ratified by the parliaments of all the *Länder* (with the sole exception of Bavaria, which however declared its acceptance of the new constitution). The *Grundgesetz* came into effect on 24 May 1949.

3. It is required for the creation of legal or economic unity and especially for the maintenance of uniform living conditions within the federal territory beyond the territory of a
single *Land*.[43]

The *Bedürfnisklausel* (need clause) of Article 72(2) GG incorporated quite
clearly the idea of subsidiarity. Certainly, in comparison with the original
Herrenchiemsee proposal, it set stricter conditions to the intervention of the federal
legislator. From the wording of the 'need clause', it is apparent that in the fields of
concurrent legislation (including key areas such as 'civil law', 'criminal law',
'economic law', 'employment/labour law'[44]), the Federation had only a 'subsidiary' right to legislate; i.e. it could only legislate if certain issues could not be
effectively regulated by the *Länder* and, consequently, needed to be regulated by
the Federation. However, despite the clear wording and purpose of Article 72
(2) GG, the Federal Constitutional Court consistently construed it to a large extent
as a non-justiciable provision. Since its first judgment on the matter (Ruling of
30 April 1952[45]), the Court considered the assessment of whether a legislative
intervention was 'needed' as a 'non justiciable question falling within the discretion
of the legislator' (*nicht-justiziable Frage des gesetzgeberischen Ermessens*). The
only exception envisaged by the Court was the 'abuse of discretion' by the
legislator (*Ermessensmißbrauch*),[46] provided that, as specified in a later case, the
infringement of the 'need clause' was 'unequivocal and manifest' (*eindeutig und
evident*).[47] The self-restraint (or 'light touch' approach) of the Court on this matter
emasculated the 'need clause' and rendered it unable to limit the legislative
intervention of the Federation.[48] As a result, the Federal Republic of Germany

---

[43] This is the original German text of the key provision of Art. 72(2) GG: 'Der Bund hat in diesem
Bereich das Gesetzgebungsrecht, wenn und soweit ein Bedürfnis nach bundesgesetzlicher
Regelung besteht, weil: 1. eine Angelegenheit durch die Gesetzgebung einzelner Länder nicht
wirksam geregelt werden kann oder 2. die Regelung einer Angelegenheit durch ein Landesgesetz
die Interessen anderer Länder oder die Gesamtheit beeinträchtigen könnte oder 3. die Herstellung
der Rechts- oder Wirtschaftseinheit, insbesondere die Wahrung der Einheitlichkeit der Lebensverhältnisse im Bundesgebiet über das Gebiet eines Landes hinaus sie erfordert'.

[44] Cf. Art. 74 No. 1, 11, 12 GG.

[45] This case dealt with the Federal Law of 22 January 1952 laying down rules on the age limit for
the chimney sweep profession. The case is published in *Entscheidungen des Bundesverfassungsgerichts* (hereafter *BVerfGE*) Vol. 1 pp. 264 ff.

[46] Ibid. p. 273 para. 26.

[47] Cf. *BVerfGE* Vol. 34 pp. 9 ff. (at p. 39). In the same wavelength ('light touch' approach),
cf. *BVerfGE* Vol. 2 pp. 213 ff. (at p. 224); Vol. 4 pp. 115 ff. (at p. 127); Vol. 10 pp. 234 ff.
(at p. 245); Vol. 13 pp. 230 ff. (at p. 233); Vol. 26 pp. 338 ff. (at p. 382); Vol. 33 pp. 224 ff.
(at p. 229); Vol. 39 pp. 96 ff. (at p. 114); Vol. 65 pp. 1 ff. (at p. 63); Vol. 65 pp. 283 ff. (at p. 289);
Vol. 67 pp. 299 ff. (at p. 327); Vol. 78 pp. 249 ff. (at p. 270).

[48] The position of the Court has been criticised by many legal scholars. Cf., for example, Scholz
(1976), p. 262; Rengeling (1999), pp. 723 ff. (Rn. 121 ff.). By contrast, the 'light touch' approach
met the approval of, among others, Vogel (1995), pp. 1039 ff. (Rn. 64 ff.).

could be defined as a 'unitary federal state' (*unitarische Bundestaat*), i.e., a centralised federation.[49]

The position of the Federal Constitutional Court can be better understood if one considers that the 'need clause', having been imposed by the occupying powers during the post-war military occupation, had no roots in German constitutional history.[50] Probably for this reason the Court chose to construe the 'need clause' in terms similar to the *Bedarfsgesetzgebung* (need legislation) of Article 9 of the Weimar Constitution ('If there is a need for passing uniform regulations, the Reich [the central government] has the right to legislate [...]').[51] During the Republic of Weimar (1919–1933), the question of whether there was such 'need for passing uniform regulations' was generally considered as a non-justiciable matter falling entirely within the discretion of the legislator. Another important element to better understand the Court's approach is the participation of the *Länder* in the federal legislative process through the *Bundesrat*, the federal lawmaking body in which the *Länder* are represented. Where a federal law has received the approval of the *Bundesrat*, it becomes *politically* difficult for the Court to annul that law with the argument that it is not 'needed' and, therefore, it is in breach of the prerogatives of the *Länder*. This point is clearly sketched out in the Ruling of 30 April 1952, in which the Federal Constitutional Court held that the approval of the contested federal law by the *Bundesrat* revealed that the majority of *Länder* had approved a federal regulation in that field.[52]

With a view to limiting federal legislative action and to overcoming the lack of judicial enforcement of the 'need clause', in 1994 a constitutional amendment modified Article 72(2) GG and set more compelling conditions for federal intervention in the areas subject to concurrent legislation.[53] The amendment replaced the 'need clause' with a more rigorous 'necessity clause' (*Erforderlichkeitsklausel*):

> The Federation shall have the right to legislate in this field if and to the extent that the federal legislative regulation is necessary [A] for the creation of equivalent standards of living within the federal territory or [B] for the maintenance of legal or [C] economic unity in the interest of the whole state.[54]

---

[49] Cf. Hesse (1962), passim. The position of the Federal Constitutional Court generated a marginalisation of the role of the *Länder* in almost all the areas falling within the concurrent legislation. The Court made a significant contribution to the creation of a centralised setting also through its jurisprudence on implied powers of the Federation and through its broad construction of the federal competences.

[50] Cf. Rüfner (2007), p. 390.

[51] Cf. Ruling of 30 April 1952, in *BVerfGE* Vol. 1 p. 272 para. 26. This is the German text of Article 9 Weimar Constitution: 'Soweit ein Bedürfnis für den Erlaß einheitlicher Vorschriften vorhanden ist, hat das Reich die Gesetzgebung über: 1. die Wohlfahrtspflege; 2. den Schutz der öffentlichen Ordnung und Sicherheit'.

[52] Ibid. p. 273 para. 26.

[53] Law of 27 October 1994 Amending the GG (published in *Bundesgesetzblatt*, BGBl., Federal Law Gazette, I 1994 p. 3146).

[54] On the shift from the 'need clause' to the 'necessity clause', cf. Deimann (1996), pp. 110 ff. This is the original German text of Art. 72(2) GG after the 1994 constitutional amendment: 'Der Bund

The term 'necessary' translates the German *erforderlich*. The meaning of *erforderlich* is deemed to be more stringent than that of *Bedürfnis* (need) of the previous 'need clause'.[55]

Eight years after the constitutional amendment, in the Ruling of 24 October 2002 on the Geriatric Nursing Act (*Altenpflegegesetz*), for the first time the Federal Constitutional Court held the 'necessity clause' to be justiciable.[56] In the ruling, the following statement is key: 'In the constitutional scrutiny of a federal law under Art. 72(2) GG the following aspects shall be covered [...]: the prognosis [made by the federal legislator in relation to the existence of the conditions for federal intervention] must rely on factual assumptions, which are carefully determined or which at least can find confirmation in the context of a court scrutiny [...]. The prognosis must be supported by an appropriate prognostic method and this [method] must have been followed consistently (in the sense of the "reliability" of the prognosis [...]). The result of the prognosis has to be controlled [by the Court] to determine whether the fundamental aspects of the prognostic assessment have been disclosed with sufficient clarity or at least their disclosure is possible in the procedure for the control [of the constitutionality] of legal rules [before the Court] and whether any irrelevant considerations have been incorporated into the prognosis'.[57] In even clearer terms in the later Ruling of 27 July 2004 (case *Juniorprofessur*, junior professorship), the Court held that 'In order to determine whether the justification grounds of Art. 72(2) GG are fulfilled, the legislator has a margin of appreciation. The decision of the legislator, which shall be assessed in each specific area in the context of an overall view, can however be scrutinised with regard to its methodological foundations and its conclusiveness by the Federal

---

hat in diesem Bereich das Gesetzgebungsrecht, wenn und soweit die Herstellung gleichwertiger Lebensverhältnisse im Bundesgebiet oder die Wahrung der Rechts- oder Wirtschaftseinheit im gesamtstaatlichen Interesse eine bundesgesetzliche Regelung erforderlich macht'.

[55] In order to render the 'necessity clause' even more clearly justiciable, the 1994 constitutional amendment introduced a specific provision in the *Grundgesetz*; cf. Art. 93(1) 2a GG: '[The Federal Constitutional Court shall rule] In the event of disagreements on whether a law meets the requirements of Article 72(2) on application of the *Bundesrat* or of the Government or the Legislature of a *Land*'.

[56] *BVerfGE* Vol. 106 pp. 62 et seq. On this landmark case, cf. Rau (2003), pp. 223 ff. See also Taylor (2006), pp. 115 ff.

[57] Cf. para. 347 of the judgment: 'In die verfassungsgerichtliche Prüfung eines Bundesgesetzes am Maßstab des Art. 72 Abs. 2 GG sind folgende Aspekte einzubeziehen (vgl. Tettinger, DVBl 1982, S. 421 <427>; Breuer, Der Staat 1977, S. 21 <39 ff.>; ähnlich Ladeur, NuR 1985, S. 81 ff.): Der Prognose müssen Sachverhaltsannahmen zu Grunde liegen, die sorgfältig ermittelt sind oder sich jedenfalls im Rahmen der gerichtlichen Prüfung bestätigen lassen (vgl. Burghart, Die Pflicht zum guten Gesetz, 1996, S. 124 ff.). Die Prognose muss sich methodisch auf ein angemessenes Prognoseverfahren stützen lassen, und dieses muss konsequent verfolgt worden sein (im Sinne der "Verlässlichkeit" der Prognosen, von der auch BVerfGE 88, 203 <262> spricht). Das Prognoseergebnis ist daraufhin zu kontrollieren, ob die die prognostische Einschätzung tragenden Gesichtspunkte mit hinreichender Deutlichkeit offen gelegt worden sind oder ihre Offenlegung jedenfalls im Normenkontrollverfahren möglich ist und ob in die Prognose keine sachfremden Erwägungen eingeflossen sind'.

Constitutional Court'.[58] These two excerpts highlight that the Court sees the scrutiny in accordance with Article 72(2) GG as an examination of the *rationality* of the law, i.e., as a scrutiny aimed to determine whether the legislator exercised its discretion properly, in a methodologically appropriate way ('the prognosis must rely on factual assumptions, which are carefully determined'; 'The prognosis must be supported by an appropriate prognostic method'; 'this [method] must have been followed consistently'; '[it needs to be checked] whether any irrelevant considerations have been incorporated into the prognosis'; 'The decision of the legislator [...] can [...] be scrutinised from the point of view of its methodological foundations and of its conclusiveness').

In the Ruling on the Geriatric Nursing Act, the Court outlined its interpretation of the criteria established in Article 72(2) GG. In this way, it laid down a general theory of the constitutional scrutiny on subsidiarity. In relation to 'the creation of equivalent standards of living within the federal territory', the Court explained that this requirement is not fulfilled where, in addition to uniformity, there is no other added value in a federal legislative intervention. Likewise, a mere improvement of the existing standards of living is not enough in order to justify a federal intervention, which can be allowed only 'where the standards of living in the *Länder* of the Federal Republic have developed in significantly different ways, in this way jeopardizing the social cohesion of the Federal Republic, or such a development is concretely emerging'.[59]

In relation to the 'maintenance of legal unity', the Court is of the opinion that legal differences shall be acceptable in a federation and, accordingly, legal unity, as such, would not be jeopardised simply by varying laws across the *Länder*. A federal law is required only where there is a problematic fragmentation of the regulatory framework and, accordingly, a situation that clashes with the interests of both the Federation and the *Länder*.[60] In relation to the 'maintenance of economic unity', the Court argued that a federal intervention must ensure the correct functioning of the economic space of the Federal Republic. The enactment of federal laws is required only where different regional regulations or inaction by the *Länder* would cause major disadvantages to the national economy.[61]

---

[58] Cf. para. 102 of the judgment: 'Bei der Beurteilung, ob die Rechtfertigungsgründe nach Art. 72 Abs. 2 GG vorliegen, steht dem Gesetzgeber eine Einschätzungsprärogative zu. Dieser Entscheidungsraum des Gesetzgebers, der sachbereichsbezogen im Wege einer Gesamtbetrachtung zu ermitteln ist, kann jedoch verfassungsgerichtlich auf seine methodischen Grundlagen und seine Schlüssigkeit hin überprüft werden'.

[59] Cf. Ruling of 24 October 2002 (*'Altenpflegegesetz'*), paras. 320–321.

[60] Ibid., paras. 324–325. At para. 325, the Court offered a few theoretical examples of situations in which a federal law would be justified by the 'legal unity' requirement: (1) different regional regulations on marriage and divorce, (2) fundamentally different regulations on the constitution of the courts as they could prevent individuals and companies from receiving an equal legal protection in all the *Länder*, (3) different court procedural rules as they could make access to federal courts more difficult.

[61] Ibid., paras. 327–328.

The judgment on the *Altenpflegegesetz* paved a way to a new course in the jurisprudence of the Court in relation to Article 72(2) GG. In the Ruling of 16 March 2004, the Court held the Law on the Prevention of Vicious Dogs (*Gesetz zur Bekämpfung gefährlicher Hunde*) in conflict with Article 72(2) GG. This federal law introduced penalties for breaches of the regional laws on vicious dogs. However, given that the regional laws were not uniform (more specifically, the notion of 'vicious dog' and the outlawed behaviours were not identical in all the *Länder*), the federal law failed to produce a uniform system of penalties at national level. Accordingly, the Court concluded that the federal legislative intervention did not meet the 'legal unity' and the other criteria of Article 72(2) GG ('equivalent standards of living', 'economic unity').[62]

In the later Ruling of 9 June 2004 on the Shops Trading Hours Act (*Ladenschlussgesetz*), the Court held a federal law deciding the trading hours of shops on Saturdays and Sundays non-compliant with Article 72(2) GG. The Court found that the 'equivalent standards of living', along with the 'economic' and 'legal unity' of the Federal Republic, would not be jeopardised if shops were to have different opening times in the different *Länder*.[63]

In the Ruling of 27 July 2004 (case *Juniorprofessur*, junior professorship), the Court held the federal law modifying the recruitment of university professors to be in breach of Article 72(2) GG. The contested law allowed for the appointment to 'junior professorships' of candidates with a doctorate (*Promotion*) but with no *Habilitation*, i.e., the second doctorate normally required for the bestowing of a chair at German universities. In relation to 'legal unity', the Court observed that different regional regulations are a normal feature in a federal system. A uniform regulation is required only where different legal regimes for the same facts of life may generate substantial legal uncertainties and, in this manner, unreasonable obstacles to legal relations across the country (i.e., beyond *Länder* borders). In the view of the Court, the contested federal law had no justification under Article 72(2) GG, both from the perspective of the 'legal unity' and of the 'equivalent standards of living'. The federal law did not appear 'necessary' to overcome a 'risk situation' (*Gefahrenlage*) arising from legal fragmentation or to prevent the living conditions among the *Länder* from diverging in an unsustainable way or to remove the obstacles preventing an academic worker from moving from one *Land* to another or making such move more difficult. The Court also found that the federal law did not contribute to the maintenance of 'economic unity', given that its objective was to improve the quality of university teaching and/or research, whilst

---

[62] Cf. *BVerfGE* Vol. 110 pp. 141 et seq. (at §§ 120–121) concerning the Law on the Prevention of Vicious Dogs, *Gesetz zur Bekämpfung gefährlicher Hunde*, of 12 April 2001 (Federal Law Gazette I p. 630).

[63] Cf. *BVerfGE* Vol. 111 pp. 10 ff. (at para. 102). Despite its non-compliance with Art. 72(2) GG, the Court rescued the contested federal law in accordance with the transitional provision of para. 2 of Art. 125a GG: 'Law that was enacted pursuant to para. 2 of Art. 72 as it stood up to 15 November 1994 but which, because of the amendment of para. 2 of Art. 72, could no longer be enacted as federal law shall remain in force as federal law'.

the 'economic unity' of the Federal Republic remained relegated to the background.[64]

In the Ruling of 26 January 2005 (case *Studiengebühren*, tuition fees) concerning the federal law prohibiting the introduction by the *Länder* of tuition fees for first degrees, the Court found the law to be unjustified under Article 72 (2) GG. The Court held that there was no sufficient evidence that the prohibition of tuition fees was 'necessary' for the creation of 'equivalent living conditions' in the territory of the Federal Republic. The Court also held that the fee element (€500 per semester) would be probably outweighed by other elements in the students' evaluation, including variations in the living costs across the country. Admittedly, according to the Court, some people (those who are least well off) may be particularly affected by the introduction of tuition fees, yet 'The non quantified possibility of such cases does not justify, at least currently, an intervention by the federal legislator for establishing equal living conditions in accordance with Art. 72, para. 2, GG'. In relation to 'economic unity', the Court took the view that different fee arrangements in the *Länder* would not jeopardise the single economic area. Quite the opposite, by levying the fees, the *Länder* could improve the educational offer and make a valuable contribution to the national economy.[65]

So far, the federal law on tuition fees is the last federal law to have been found by the Court in breach of Article 72(2) GG. In later cases concerning the 'necessity clause', the Court always rejected the claims against the contested federal acts.[66] It is interesting to note the Ruling 14 October 2008 concerning the federal law implementing EC Regulation No. 1782/2003. The Court held the contested federal law to be justified against Article 72(2) GG since the correct implementation of the regulation required the enactment of uniform legal provisions at federal level. Accordingly, the 'necessity' of a federal law found justification, albeit indirectly, in EU law.[67]

---

[64] Cf. *BVerfGE* Vol. 111 pp. 226 et seq. (at paras. 99, 128, 132–135).

[65] Cf. Ruling of 26 January 2005 (*'Studiengebühren'*, in: *BVerfGE* Vol. 112 pp. 226 et seq.) 8 at paras. 71–72, 74–75, 77, 81–82. The original of the quote in the text can be found at para. 72: 'Die nicht näher quantifizierte Möglichkeit derartiger Fälle rechtfertigt zumindest derzeit kein Eingreifen des Bundesgesetzgebers unter dem Aspekt der Herstellung gleichwertiger Lebensverhältnisse gemäß Art. 72 Abs. 2 GG'. In the same decision, the Court also invalidated a provision on the compulsory creation of student unions on grounds of a breach of Art. 72(2) GG (paras. 85–92).

[66] Cf. Ruling of 18 July 2005 (in *BVerfGE* Vol. 113 pp. 167 et seq.) on the right of the Federation to legislate on the risk adjustment scheme (*'Risikostrukturausgleich'*), Ruling of 13 September 2005 on the federal law regulating the contribution rates to the health insurers operating in the field of health insurance (*'Krankenkassen'*), Ruling of 3 July 2007 on the federal law regulating the training of farriers, Ruling of 27 January 2010 on the Trade Tax Act (federal law obliging the Municipalities to levy a trade tax and to set not less than a minimum rate), Ruling of 21 July 2010 on the federal law modifying the Compensation Act (regarding issues arising after the German Reunification), Ruling of 24 November 2010 on the Genetically Modified Organisms Act (*'Gentechnikgesetz'*), Ruling of 28 January 2014 on the Law Supporting the German Film Industry (*'Filmförderungsgesetz'*).

[67] Cf. Ruling of 14 October 2008, paras. 88–89.

In 2006, an important constitutional reform came into effect (the *Föderalismusreform*, 'reform of the federal system'[68]). An aspect of the reform concerned specifically the 'necessity clause'. The wording of the clause was not modified, but its sphere of application was reduced dramatically. The 'necessity clause' does no longer apply to legislative activity in areas of key importance, including civil and criminal laws, employment/labour law, land law, but only to a limited number of, according to some, 'randomly selected' areas of secondary importance.[69] Most areas previously subjected to the 'necessity clause' fall now within the 'core' lawmaking power of the Federation (for example, 'civil law', 'criminal law') or, more rarely, within the lawmaking power of the *Länder* (for example, 'shops' trading hours', 'university'). The intended, and fully achieved, result of the 2006 reform was a dramatic fall in the number of cases concerning the 'necessity clause'. It would appear that the proactive approach of the Court in the period 2002–2006 had generated uncertainty and dissatisfaction by the federal legislator. The 2006 reform addressed this concern by taking power away from the Court in relation to the enforcement of subsidiarity and by returning it to the political players at federal and local levels, who are free to decide 'whether', 'when' and 'how' to regulate a given matter in conformity with the Basic Law.[70]

2. Lessons from the German Pattern

A few lessons can be learnt by contrasting the German experience with the jurisprudence of the ECJ on subsidiarity. In Germany, since 2002, the Federal Constitutional Court has recognised the 'necessity clause' of Article 72(2) GG as justiciable. Between 2004 and 2005, the Court invalidated four federal laws for

---

[68] Law of 11 September 2006 Amending the *Grundgesetz* (in Federal Law Gazette, I 2006 p. 2098). On the 2006 reform, cf. Hrbek (2007), pp. 225 ff.; Gunlicks (2008), pp. 111 ff.; Burkhart (2009), pp. 341 ff.

[69] Law relating to residence and establishment of foreign nationals; public welfare (with the exception of social care homes); law relating to economic matters (with the exception of the law on shop closing hours, restaurants, game halls, display of individual persons, trade fairs, exhibitions and markets); regulation of educational and training grants and promotion of research; expropriation for public purposes; economic viability of hospitals and hospital charges; food law, law on alcohol and tobacco; road traffic, motor transport, highways; state liability; medically assisted generation of human life, analysis and modification of genetic information; regulation of transplantation. Cf. Art. 74(1) Nos. 4, 7, 11, 13, 15, 19a, 20, 22, 25, 26. To this list should be added the provision of Article 105(2) GG, under which the Federation has concurrent legislative power over taxes if it is entitled to all or part of the proceeds or if the test laid down in Art. 72(2) GG is satisfied. Cf. Taylor (2009), p. 149: 'German constitutional law on subsidiarity is in an odd state. What purports to be a fully justiciable requirement of subsidiarity remains, but it applies only to what appears to be a randomly selected set of concurrent federal powers'.

[70] Cf. Taylor (2009), p. 142.

nonconformity with that constitutional provision. What are the main differences with the EU?

The 'necessity clause' is much more specific and compelling than the EU definition of subsidiarity, even though the Amsterdam Subsidiarity Protocol had tried to specify the notion of subsidiarity. The 'necessity clause' does not contain a generic formula ('if an objective cannot be sufficiently achieved', 'if an objective can be better achieved') but contains more specific criteria ('legal unity', 'economic unity', 'equivalent standards of living'). However, it must be highlighted that, whilst this aspect (specificity) may have contributed to the justiciability of the 'necessity clause', for a few years the 'necessity clause' remained only on paper (1994–2002). Therefore, the judicial enforcement of the 'necessity clause' seems first and foremost due to a change in the approach by the Court. A similar change is yet to occur for the ECJ.

In the case *Altenpflegegesetz*, the Federal Constitutional Court laid down in sufficiently clear terms its interpretation of the criteria of Article 72(2) GG. In this way, it further specified the content of the 'necessity clause'. So far, the ECJ has failed to develop a similar 'doctrine' in relation to subsidiarity.

The Federal Constitutional Court understands the scrutiny required by Article 72 (2) GG as an evaluation of the *rationality* of the law, i.e., of whether the federal legislator exercised its discretion correctly. The Court also specified the criteria of such scrutiny ('the prognosis must rely on factual assumptions, which are carefully determined'; 'The prognosis must be supported by an appropriate prognostic method'; 'this [method] must have been followed consistently'; '[it needs to be checked] whether any irrelevant considerations have been incorporated into the prognosis'; 'The decision of the legislature [. . .] can [. . .] be scrutinised from the point of view of its methodological foundations and of its conclusiveness').[71] By contrast, the ECJ has never been as specific in relation to subsidiarity. For example, in the Working Time Directive case, the ECJ stated that judicial review of the exercise of legislative discretion must be limited to 'whether [such exercise] has been vitiated by manifest error' or 'misuse of powers' or 'whether the institution concerned has manifestly exceeded the limits of its discretion'.[72] It is interesting to note a similarity of language between the ECJ and the Federal Constitutional Court prior to the *Altenpflegegesetz* case, when the Court required (albeit with reference to

---

[71] See also the Ruling of 28 January 2014 on the Law Supporting the German Film Industry (*'Filmförderungsgesetz'*): 'Dem Gesetzgeber steht insoweit zwar eine Einschätzungsprärogative zu; die verfassungsgerichtliche Kontrolle ist hier jedoch nicht auf eine bloße Vertretbarkeitskontrolle beschränkt (vgl. BVerfGE 106, 62 <148>; 110, 141 <174 f.>; 125, 141 <153>). Die verfassungsrechtliche Beurteilung hängt von der objektiven Rechtfertigungsfähigkeit der Einschätzung des Gesetzgebers ab (vgl. BVerfGE 106, 62 <150, 152>; s. auch BVerfGE 111, 226 <255>)' (para. 115). In English: 'To this purpose a discretionary evaluation prerogative belongs indeed to the [federal] legislator; however here the constitutional review is not limited to a mere control of the tenability [Vertretbarkeitskontrolle]. The constitutional law judgment depends on the objective justifiability of the evaluation of the legislator'.

[72] Case C-84/94 *UK v Council* [1996] ECR I-5755, para. 58.

Table 4.1 Summary of the comparison between Germany and the EU in relation to subsidiarity

Subsidiarity in Germany, Federal Constitutional Court	Subsidiarity in the EU, ECJ
Since 2002 justiciable, four federal laws invalidated (2004–2005); historically, Art. 72 (2) GG has not prevented centralisation of powers	Theoretically justiciable, no act invalidated so far, even though ECJ does not passively marry the legislator's view
Slightly more specific criteria in Art. 72(2) GG, 'necessity clause'	Generic definition of subsidiarity in Art. 5 TEU (however, some specification in Amsterdam Subsidiarity Protocol)
Further specification of criteria by the Court (cf. *Altenpflegegesetz* ruling); in later cases, the Court has applied the *Altenpflegegesetz* pattern consistently	No further specification of subsidiarity clause by the ECJ
Scrutiny of rationality of the law, specific criteria for scrutiny determined by the Court	Scrutiny of exercise of discretion (cf. Working Time Directive case), but judicial self-restraint (manifest error, misuse of powers, etc.) similar to Germany under the 'need clause', unlikely declaration of invalidity of an act

the old 'need clause') an 'unequivocal and manifest abuse of discretion' by the legislator.[73]

In summary, the opinion that subsidiarity is intrinsically unsuited for judicial enforcement emerges defeated from the analysis of the German case law. What also clearly emerges is that, albeit engaging with subsidiarity, the ECJ has not equipped itself with an armamentarium comparable to the *Altenpflegegesetz* doctrine of the German Court. The impression is that the ECJ is anchored to judicial self-restraint. However, the interventionist approach of the German Court caused a reaction from political players, in that it limited too powerfully the discretion of the federal legislator. The 2006 constitutional reform confined the 'necessity clause' to a small 'reservation'. It would appear that even a consolidated multilevel system like the Federal Republic of Germany could hardly cope with judicially enforceable subsidiarity. This explains why the legislator has chosen to return to less controversial constitutional pathways for the allocation of lawmaking authority (Table 4.1).

3. Italy: From Subsidiarity to Loyal Cooperation

(i) Subsidiarity in Administration

Despite the clear reference to subsidiarity in the European Charter of Local Self-Government (1985) ('Public responsibilities shall generally be exercised, in

---

[73] Cf., in particular, *BVerfGE* Vol. 34 pp. 9 ff. (at p. 39).

preference, by those authorities which are closest to the citizen. Allocation of responsibility to another authority should weigh up the extent and nature of the task and requirements of efficiency and economy'[74]), until 1997, the impact of the principle of subsidiarity in Italy remained limited.[75]

Law No. 59 of 15 March 1997 (known as 'legge Bassanini', 'Bassanini Law', named after Franco Bassanini, the then Minister of the Public Function) initiated an extensive transfer of administrative tasks and functions from the central government to regional and local authorities. This process is often referred to in Italian legal literature as 'administrative federalism'.[76] The 'Bassanini Law' and the following Legislative Decree No. 112 of 31 March 1998 (known as 'Decree on Administrative Federalism') started the transfer to the regions and the local authorities of all administrative tasks, with the sole exception of those expressly reserved for the central government (for example, 'foreign affairs', 'defence', 'scientific research'[77]). The 'Bassanini Law' enumerates the areas belonging to the exclusive responsibility of the central government and allows for the transfer of powers to the regions and the local authorities in all the remaining areas. This technique ('enumerated powers' to the central government and 'residuary powers' to the sub-state authorities) is similar to the typical method for the distribution of powers in federal systems and explains why the reform is indicated as 'administrative federalism'.[78]

In conformity with the subsidiarity principle, the objective of the 'Bassanini Law' is to bring administrative tasks and functions closer to the citizen. The 'Bassanini Law' stipulates that the 'generality' of administrative tasks and functions must be transferred to local authorities and that *only* those that cannot be effectively exercised by local authorities shall not be subject to transfer.[79] However, after 17 years, the system outlined by the 'Bassanini Law' has yet to be fully implemented.[80]

Four years after the 'Bassanini Law', a constitutional amendment[81] specifically entrenched the principle of subsidiarity in the Constitution as the basic rule,

---

[74] Art. 4(3) of the European Charter of Local Self-Government. The Charter was incorporated into domestic law by Law No. 439 of 30 December 1989.

[75] Sabino Cassese observes that Article 4(3) of the Charter only covers the 'positive' aspect of subsidiarity (public responsibilities shall be exercised, in preference, by those authorities that are closest to the citizen) and not the 'negative' aspect of it (no authority shall deal with any matter that could be better dealt with by those authorities that are closer to the citizen). Cf. Cassese (1997), p. 83.

[76] Cf., for example, Serra (1999), pp. 55 ff.; Torchia (2001), pp. 257 ff.; Pajno (2001), pp. 667 ff.

[77] Art. 1.3 (a), (b), and (p) 'Bassanini Law'.

[78] Cf., for example, the US Constitution (X Amendment), the Swiss Constitution (Art. 3), the Australian Constitution (Art. 107), the Austrian Constitution (Art. 15.1) and the Belgian Constitution (Art. 35.1).

[79] Art. 4(1) 'Bassanini Law'.

[80] Cf. D'Alessio and Di Lascio (2009), passim.

[81] Law Amending the Constitution No. 3 of 18 October 2001.

together with the principles of differentiation and adequacy, for the allocation of administrative responsibilities between the different tiers of government:

> Administrative functions are attributed to the municipalities, unless they are attributed to the provinces, the metropolitan cities, the regions or to the State with the aim to ensure their uniform exercise pursuant to the principles of subsidiarity, differentiation and adequacy.[82]

According to this constitutional provision, subsidiarity must be considered jointly with differentiation and adequacy. Accordingly, the allocation of an administrative function to a local authority depends also on its capacity for performing that function (adequacy). Compliance with the Constitution requires something more than mere 'proximity' to the citizen; it requires that an authority must be capable of achieving a certain result.[83] The lack of 'adequacy' may even determine the exercise of a competence, by way of 'subsidium', by a 'lower' tier of government, in case of failure to act by a 'higher' authority. For example, in 2005, an administrative court found that subsidiarity allowed a Municipality to issue a bylaw on the use of organic fertilisers, given that the Province (normally responsible for that matter) had failed to take action.[84]

Local authorities are far from being a homogeneous group. Ideally, a 'good' allocation of administrative functions would require a 'case-by-case' approach. This is the role assigned to 'differentiation', which implies that the State or the Regions, when allocating administrative responsibilities, have to take into account the characteristics of the recipient authorities. Due consideration must be given to aspects such as population and territorial size, type of organisation, performance of administrative activities in association with other authorities. This is to ensure that an administrative function is allocated to an authority that is capable of performing it in the most efficient and economic way.[85]

---

[82] Art. 118(1) Const. The principle of subsidiarity is also mentioned at Art. 118(4) Const. concerning 'horizontal subsidiarity' (cf. supra Sect. A) and at Art. 120(2) Const. concerning the central government's power to act for the regions or the local authorities, for example, in the case of failure by a region or a local authority to comply with international rules and treaties or EU law. An interesting application of this constitutional provision can be seen in Ruling No. 370 of 23 December 2003, where the Constitutional Court held that the principle of subsidiarity requires that the administrative responsibilities concerning nursery schools are exercised by municipalities and regions (cf. para. 5 of the judgment).

[83] Cf. Vandelli (2007), p. 131. The principle of adequacy is defined at Art. 4(3)(g) 'Bassanini Law'. See also Pernthaler (2007), p. 26, who says: 'Die geltende Kompetenzverteilung der meisten föderalen Systeme ist starr und schematisch, d.h. im Gegensatz zum Subsidiaritätsprinzip kaum auf die Bedürfnisse und Kapazitäten der einzelnen Subsysteme abgestimmt' [The distribution of competences in force in most federal systems is rigid and schematic, i.e. in contrast to the principle of subsidiarity, it is not suited at all to the needs and capabilities of the single subsystems].

[84] Cf. Regional Administrative Court [Tribunale Amministrativo Regionale, TAR in acronym], Puglia, Lecce, Second Division, Ruling No. 484 of 8 February 2005.

[85] The principle of differentiation is defined at Art. 4(3)(h) 'Bassanini Law'.

(ii) Subsidiarity in Legislation

Until the 2001 constitutional amendment,[86] the Italian Constitution gave the Regions the power to pass legislation only in a few enumerated subject matters (for example, 'fairs and markets', 'town planning', 'tourism', 'quarries and peat bogs', 'hunting', 'agriculture', etc.). Laws passed by the Regions in these areas had to be consistent with fundamental principles established by State law and had to comply with the national interest and the interests of the other Regions. This type of regional legislative power was known as 'shared' or 'concurrent' legislation ('legislazione ripartita' or 'concorrente'). All non-enumerated legislative powers belonged to the State.

Until 2001, the Italian Constitution followed the 'principle of parallelism' (*principio del parallelismo*) for the allocation of administrative responsibilities to the State and the Regions. According to this principle, administrative functions and legislative powers were 'parallel'. In principle, the Regions had the right to perform administrative tasks in the same subject matters in which they enjoyed legislative power (for example, 'town planning' or 'agriculture'). However, despite this clear theoretical framework, the central government retained the power to interfere with the exercise of a number of regional administrative functions. Just to mention only two examples, the 'permission to release a licence for opening a travel agency', in the area of 'tourism', and 'agricultural market regulation', in the area of 'agriculture', were reserved to the central government.[87]

The 2001 constitutional amendment changed the Italian regional system fundamentally. In the new regime, the State retains exclusive legislative powers only in those subject matters enumerated by the Constitution (enumerated powers),[88] whilst the Regions have the right to pass laws in all areas not enumerated by the

---

[86] Law Amending the Constitution No. 3 of 18 October 2001.

[87] Cf. Art. 58 and Art. 71 of the Decree of the President of Republic No. 616 of 24 July 1977.

[88] Art. 117(2) Const.: 'The State has exclusive legislative powers in the following matters: a) foreign policy and international relations of the State; relations between the State and the European Union; right of asylum and legal status of non-EU citizens; b) immigration; c) relations between the Republic and religious denominations; d) defence and armed forces; State security; armaments, ammunition and explosives; e) the currency, savings protection and financial markets; competition protection; foreign exchange system; State taxation and accounting systems; equalisation of financial resources; f) State bodies and relevant electoral laws; State referenda; elections of the European Parliament; g) legal and administrative organisation of the State and of national public agencies; h) public order and security, with the exception of local administrative police; i) citizenship, civil status and register offices; l) jurisdiction and procedural law; civil and criminal law; administrative judicial system; m) determination of the basic level of benefits relating to civil and social entitlements to be guaranteed throughout the national territory; n) general provisions on education; o) social security; p) electoral legislation, governing bodies and fundamental functions of the Municipalities, Provinces and Metropolitan Cities; q) customs, protection of national borders and International prophylaxis; r) weights and measures; standard time; statistical and computerised coordination of data of State, regional and local administrations; works of the intellect; s) protection of the environment, the ecosystem and cultural heritage'.

Constitution (residuary powers).[89] In addition, the Constitution lays down a list of subject matters in which the legislative power is 'shared' by the State and the Regions (concurrent legislative power). In these areas, the State dictates 'fundamental principles', i.e., it shall lay down the regulatory framework, whilst the Regions shall implement the principles through a detailed regulation.[90]

A second 'revolution' was introduced by the landmark Ruling No. 303 of 1 October 2003. In this case, the Court held that the principle of subsidiarity may justify 'a departure from the normal distribution of [legislative] powers'. The Court stated that this principle (like the 'konkurrierende Gesetzgebung' in Germany or the 'Supremacy Clause' in the United States) brings an 'element of flexibility' into what would otherwise be a too rigid distribution of powers. According to the Court, a State law can assign administrative tasks to the central government in areas belonging to the legislative power of the Regions and can also regulate the exercise of these tasks. A State law can do so provided that certain criteria are fulfilled: there must be a need for uniform action by the central government (principle of subsidiarity and principle of adequacy), the evaluation of the public interest underlying the allocation of regional responsibilities to the central government must be 'proportionate' (principle of proportionality), such evaluation must not be 'unreasonable' in the light of a 'strict scrutiny' (reasonableness) and, finally, the State law allocating an administrative function to the central government must provide for the involvement of the Regions in the exercise of that function in the form of an 'agreement' (*intesa*) between the Regions and the central government (principle of loyal cooperation). In summary, the key finding of Ruling No. 303 of 1 October 2003 is that the State, in addition to the areas laid down in the Constitution, can also legislate in other areas, if the principle of subsidiarity requires that a specific responsibility has to be exercised by the centre. This construction of subsidiarity paved the way to a (re-)centralisation of lawmaking power rather than to the

---

[89] Art. 117(4) Const.: 'The Regions have legislative powers in all subject matters that are not expressly reserved for State legislation'.

[90] Art. 117(3) Const.: 'The concurrent legislative power applies to the following subject matters: international and EU relations of the Regions; foreign trade; job protection and safety; education, subject to the autonomy of educational institutions and with the exception of vocational education and training; professions; scientific and technological research and innovation support for productive sectors; health protection; nutrition; sports; disaster relief; land-use planning; civil ports and airports; large transport and navigation networks; communications; national production, transport and distribution of energy; complementary and supplementary social security; harmonisation of public budgeting and co-ordination of public finance and taxation system; enhancement of the [Italian] cultural and environmental heritage, including the promotion and organisation of cultural activities; savings banks, rural banks, regional credit institutions; regional land and agricultural credit institutions. In the subject-matters falling within the concurrent legislative power, the Regions have the right to legislate, except for the determination of the fundamental principles, which are laid down in State legislation'. On the distribution of legislative competences in Italy after the 2001 constitutional reform, cf. Caravita (2009), pp. 16 ff. See also Cartei and Ferraro (2002), pp. 445 ff.

protection of regional autonomy in conformity with the idea of 'proximity' to the citizen.[91]

In the wake of this landmark judgment, in a number of rulings, the Constitutional Court upheld the existence of State 'subsidiary lawmaking powers'. In a first group of cases, the Court adopted a notion of subsidiarity similar to that emerging from the European Treaty (even though the Court has never made an open reference to the Treaty). In these cases, the reasoning of the Court is the following: an action of the central government is required, and therefore justified, where an objective cannot be sufficiently achieved by lower levels of government. For example, in Ruling No. 6 of 13 January 2004, the Court held that the central government can authorise the construction of new power plants and the enlargement of existing ones in order to satisfy the national demand of energy. This result, in the view of the Court, can be achieved only by the centre since the single Regions are not in a position to determine the national energy demand, nor can they cover it in full on their own.[92]

In a second group of cases, the reasoning of the Court in support of the need for uniform State action and the logic underpinning its judgment are reminiscent of the 'legal or economic unity' or of the 'equivalent standards of living' criteria of Article 72(2) GG (cf. supra Sect. C.1). For example, in Ruling No. 151 of 12 April 2005, the Court held that the payment of an €150 State subvention for the purchase or the hire of a decoder is a task that needs to be performed by the State. According to the

---

[91] On the Ruling No. 303 of 1 October 2003, cf. Groppi and Scattone (2006), pp. 131 ff. In the actual case, the Court found that it was lawful for the central government to perform, and for the State law to regulate, administrative tasks concerning planning and authorising large-scale infrastructures. It can be observed that, despite the abolition of the 'principle of parallelism' by the 2001 constitutional amendment, this ruling de facto restored that principle to new life.

[92] Cf. para. 7 of the judgment. A number of other rulings are on the same wavelength: cf. Ruling No. 62 of 29 January 2005 (choice of the location of the national deposit of radioactive waste), Ruling No. 242 of 24 June 2005 (creation and administration of a national fund supporting medium and large-size companies), Ruling No. 285 of 19 July 2005 (financial support of cinematographic industry), Ruling No. 383 of 14 October 2005 (licensing for building and/or enlarging and/or operating electricity transmission lines), Ruling No. 213 of 1 June 2006 (subvention of fisheries and approval of the 2004 National Plan for Fisheries and Aquaculture), Ruling No. 214 of 1 June 2006 (establishment of a national agency with responsibility for the promotion of tourism), Ruling No. 88 of 16 March 2007 (approval of plans for high-quality touristic infrastructures in publicly owned coastal areas), Ruling No. 165 of 11 May 2007 (creation of industrial districts and of a national agency for the dissemination of new technologies), Ruling No. 339 of 12 October 2007 (promotion of Italian agritourism on the national and the international levels), Ruling No. 63 of 14 March 2008 (creation and administration of a national fund for the bailout and the restructuring of companies facing financial difficulties), Ruling No. 76 of 20 March 2009 (measures aimed at supporting undertakings operating in the touristic sector and support of national and international players investing in the touristic sector in Italy), Ruling No. 79 of 11 March 2011 (establishment and administration of a national fund for infrastructures in seaports of national significance). See also Ruling No. 168 of 29 May 2009 concerning the allocation of financial resources to families, with the aim of supporting the permanence of the elderly within their family as an alternative to old people's homes. Here, the Court held that this type of public intervention can be classed as 'social welfare' and that, by nature, it goes beyond a merely regional dimension.

Court, this action is actually aimed to implement a constitutional principle, 'pluralism of information', and it must be carried out uniformly within the national territory.[93] More similar to the 'equivalent standards of living' approach is the reasoning displayed in Ruling No. 166 of 23 May 2008 concerning the national plan for social housing, where the Court held that a national plan is required in order to prevent strong regional differences in relation to the standards of social housing.[94]

In a third group of cases, the Court embraced a purely 'procedural' concept of subsidiarity. When following 'procedural subsidiarity', the Court does not question, or more precisely it takes as a given, the underpinning need for uniform State action. The Court only examines whether some procedural requirements are fulfilled (for example, the inclusion of an infrastructure in a national plan approved by the State-Regions Conference and/or the approval of the infrastructure by the territorially competent Region). If such procedural criteria are fulfilled, the Court accepts that subsidiarity has been respected. All the rulings within this group concern the regulation and/or authorisation and/or funding of infrastructures of national relevance. For example, in Ruling No. 303 of 1 October 2003, regarding large-scale infrastructure projects, the Court held that, when reviewing legislation, it is not part of the Court's role to decide whether a given infrastructure is 'strategic' or 'of preeminent national interest'. The Court attached an exclusively procedural meaning to subsidiarity. It required only that the law had to provide the involvement of the Regions in the form of an 'agreement' on the classification of an infrastructure as 'strategic' or 'of preeminent national interest'.[95] A further example of this approach can be seen in Ruling No. 79 of 11 March 2011 concerning Parma subway development. The Court held that, given the consent of the relevant Region (Emilia–Romagna), the inclusion of Parma subway in the national Plan of Strategic

---

[93] See also the earlier Ruling No. 31 of 26 January 2005, where the Court held that, pursuant to the principle of subsidiarity, it is a State's responsibility to create and manage a national funding body supporting research projects of remarkable scientific value. In this judgment, the principle of subsidiarity, as such, is only one of the possible justifications for State action, the main legal basis being the implementation of the constitutional objective to promote scientific research (cf. Art. 9 and Art. 33 Const.). Another remarkable example of 'legal/economic unity' reasoning is the Ruling No. 270 of 23 June 2005, where the Court found that the State had the right to transform certain public healthcare institutions into foundations and that such transformation process needed to abide by uniform national rules. On the same wavelength, cf. Ruling No. 339 of 12 October 2007, where the Court affirmed that the State had the right to lay down uniform criteria to classify a business as 'agriturismo' (agritourism). Here, again, the underpinning aim of the Court is apparently the 'maintenance of legal or economic unity' throughout the national territory (to use once again an expression borrowed from Art. 72(2) GG).

[94] See also Ruling No. 16 of 21 January 2010, where the Court held that the ongoing economic crisis required the creation, at State level, of a national fund for infrastructures. Additionally, the Court held that the need for uniform State action derived also from EC law. More specifically, it originated from the Community aim to reduce the social, economic and territorial disparities that have arisen particularly in countries and regions whose development is lagging behind (cf. para. 2.1 of the judgment).

[95] Cf. paras. 2.1 and 2.2 of the judgment.

Infrastructures justified the exercise by the State of legislative and administrative powers relating to this infrastructure.[96]

In a smaller number of cases, the Court refused to grant 'subsidiary lawmaking powers' to the State. In some rulings, the Court found that there existed no need for uniform action by the central government. For example, in Ruling No. 219 of 8 June 2005 on the 'lavori socialmente utili' (socially useful jobs[97]), the Court found that administrative tasks concerning those jobs have an exclusively local dimension and, accordingly, should be handled by the Municipalities. Another interesting example is Ruling No. 148 of 7 June 2012, where the Court held that the need to tackle the economic recession, alone, did not justify a temporary exception to the distribution of responsibilities between the central government and the Regions.[98]

In another group of cases involving the principle of subsidiarity, the Court carried out the proportionality test.[99] From the case law it emerges that when testing proportionality, the Court will look at the 'breadth' and/or the 'intensity' of regulation. For example, in Ruling No. 214 of 1 June 2006, the Court focused on the range of tasks assigned to a certain public body (breadth). The Court held that the law establishing the National Committee for Tourism had gone beyond what is strictly necessary for the promotion of tourism. The law in question, instead of specifying and delimiting the remit of the Committee, had entrusted it with an all-embracing activity of policy coordination for the entire touristic sector. Accordingly, in the Court's view, the scale of the State intervention was disproportionate.[100] When checking proportionality, the Court may also look at the 'intensity' of

---

[96] Cf. paras. 3–5 of the judgment. See also Ruling No. 121 of 26 March 2010 (national plan for public housing; cf. para. 6.1 of the judgment). It needs to be pointed out that this judgment relies on earlier cases decided by the Court on 'neighbouring' issues (see, for example, Ruling No. 166 of 23 May 2008 on social housing). In the Ruling No. 94 of 11 April 2008 concerning funding made available by the central government for the development of tourism, the Court did not analyse the need for uniform State action. This is probably due to the fact that the claimant Region failed to challenge the State's right to legislate on the issue. The Region only submitted to the Court an infringement of the principle of loyal cooperation. It also needs to be taken into account that prior to this judgment, the Court had already granted considerable powers to the State in the area of tourism on grounds of subsidiarity (cf. Ruling No. 214 of 1 June 2006 and Ruling No. 88 of 16 March 2007).

[97] These are jobs offered by local authorities to unemployed people in order to give them a source of income.

[98] See also Ruling No. 285 of 19 July 2005, where the Court held that the Region is the adequate level of government in relation to licensing multiplex movie theatres; Ruling No. 168 of 23 May 2008, where the Court held that the promotion of energy-saving initiatives is not such as to require uniform State action; and, finally, Ruling No. 215 of 17 June 2010, where the Court found that the urgency of creating infrastructures in the energy sector did not justify the allocation to the central government of the responsibility for planning and building such infrastructures.

[99] However, in most cases, the Court failed to analyse, or even to mention, the principle of proportionality and focused exclusively on subsidiarity.

[100] Cf. para. 8 of the judgment. By contrast, in the same ruling, the Court came to a different conclusion in relation to the establishment of a national agency with responsibility for the promotion of tourism. The agency was held compliant with proportionality since the tasks of the

regulation. For example, in Ruling No. 166 of 23 May 2008, it held the national plan on social housing compliant with the principle because the plan consisted of general guidelines leaving sufficient scope for regional implementation.

(iii) The Relationship Between Subsidiarity and Loyal Cooperation

In Italy, unlike in Germany, there is no national lawmaking body that represents the Regions in the legislative process. Therefore, since the landmark Ruling No. 303 of 1 October 2003, the Constitutional Court has maintained that *any* State law taking a function away from the Regions and allocating it to the central government in accordance with subsidiarity must provide adequate cooperation mechanisms. This means that the Regions need to be involved in the exercise of that function. In this way, by its jurisprudence on subsidiarity, the Court clearly enforces a 'procedural' and 'cooperative' pattern.[101]

Every time a 'subsidiary power' of the central government entails a decision on policy, or a decision affecting all the Regions, an 'understanding' (*intesa*), perhaps better defined as an 'agreement', with the (majority of the) Regions within the State-Regions Conference is required.[102] For example, in Ruling No. 6 of

---

agency were confined to the promotion of tourism (cf. para. 9 of the judgment). Only a few rulings dealt with proportionality in the context of subsidiarity. For example, in the Ruling No. 165 of 11 May 2007, in relation to the national agency for the dissemination of new technologies, the Court held that the principle of proportionality had been respected as the responsibilities of the national agency are limited to the strictly necessary (cf. para. 4.4 of the judgment). In the Ruling No. 215 of 17 June 2010, the Court held that it was disproportionate, in addition to the task of planning infrastructures in the energy sector, to grant the central government the task of completing such infrastructures, a task that, in the view of the Court, could be effectively performed by the Regions (cf. para. 4). In the Ruling No. 232 of 22 July 2011, the Court invalidated another all-embracing State provision concerning the creation of 'no bureaucracy areas' in the South of Italy (i.e., areas in which companies and businesses may obtain the required licences and permissions directly from a supervisor appointed by the central government). The Court pointed to the lack of justification for the State provision against the subsidiarity, proportionality and rationality criteria (cf. para. 5.5 of the judgment). On the same wavelength concerning the 'no bureaucracy areas', see also the Ruling No. 144 of 28 May 2014.

[101] The Constitutional Court has consistently applied the loyal cooperation requirement. Only in a limited number of cases did the Court fail to impose loyal cooperation mechanisms on the central government. This happened with the Rulings No. 31 of 26 January 2005 (on funding of research projects of considerable scientific significance) and No. 151 of 12 April 2005 (on the introduction of €150 state subvention for the purchase or the hire of a decoder). However, it needs to be highlighted that in both circumstances, the Court held that State uniform action was primarily justified by the need to implement a constitutional objective (promotion of scientific research, Ruling No. 31 of 2005) or a constitutional principle (pluralism of information, Ruling No. 151 of 2005).

[102] According to Art. 12(2) of Act No. 400 of 23 August 1988, the State-Regions Conference (*Conferenza Stato-Regioni*) is composed of the President of the Council of Ministers (chair), the presidents of the Regions and the presidents of the Autonomous Provinces of Trent and Bolzano. On the powers of the State-Regions Conference, cf. also Legislative Decree No. 281 of 28 August

13 January 2004, on the creation of new power plants and the enlargement of existing ones, the Court stated that the national plan concerning the power plants needed to be agreed within the State-Regions Conference.[103] Similarly, in Ruling No. 242 of 24 June 2005, concerning a national fund supporting medium and large-size enterprises, the Court held that the criteria for the administration of the fund had to be agreed within the Conference.[104] An agreement with an *individual* Region is required where a decision of the central government has a specific impact on that Region. For example, in Ruling No. 6 of 13 January 2004, the Court held that a power plant may be built in the territory of a Region only with the consent of the Region concerned.[105]

In Ruling No. 6 of 13 January 2004, the Court held that the opposition of a Region to the building of a power plant on its territory is an 'insuperable obstacle'. However, elsewhere the Court accepted that the regional opposition can be overcome through a special procedure inspired by loyal cooperation. For example, in Ruling No. 121 of 26 March 2010, the Court dealt with the opposition of the Unified Conference to the implementation of the national plan on public housing. The Court held that such opposition could be overcome only through a special procedure involving further negotiations. Accordingly, it invalidated a provision that established that, in case of failure to reach an agreement within 90 days, the central government could *unilaterally* decide on public housing. In fact, the invalidated provision downgraded the position of the Regions and of the local authorities to mere consultation.[106]

In Ruling No. 33 of 2 February 2011 (permission to build nuclear power plants), the Court held that failure to reach an agreement with an individual Region on the identification of sites suitable for building and operating nuclear power plants can

---

1997. In the view of the Constitutional Court, the State-Regions Conference is the principal forum for discussion and negotiation of policy between the State and the Regions (cf. Ruling No. 116 of 31 March 1994).

[103] Cf. para. 7 of the judgment.

[104] Cf. para. 7 of the judgment. On the same wavelength, cf. Ruling No. 163 of 27 June 2012 concerning a national strategic plan on broadband infrastructures (para. 2.2). When a function allocated to the central government also affects the position of the local authorities, as well as that of the Regions, the agreement has to take place within the Unified Conference (*Conferenza Unificata*, a forum merging the State-Regions Conference and the State–Cities–Local Authorities Conference). The Unified Conference (established by Legislative Decree No. 281 of 28 August 1997) is a forum for discussion of political issues affecting all tiers of government: national, regional and local levels. In Ruling No. 33 of 2 February 2011, concerning the authorisation to build nuclear power plants, the Court held that the ministerial decree identifying the locations suitable for such plants required an agreement within the Unified Conference (cf. para. 6.2.2 of the judgment).

[105] In the same wavelength, cf. Ruling No. 163 of 27 June 2012 concerning a national strategic plan on broadband infrastructures (at para. 2.2) and Ruling No. 179 of 11 July 2012 concerning administrative cooperation between different public authorities and tiers of government (at para. 5.2.1).

[106] Cf. para. 9 of the judgment.

be overcome only through a procedure requiring further negotiations with the Region concerned. The negotiations have to take place within a committee comprising an equal number of representatives of the central government and of the Region concerned. If, after 60 days, no agreement is achieved, the central government will be entitled to decide where to build the plants, but the president of the Region will be involved in the decision by taking part in the relevant session of the Council of Ministers.[107]

No agreement but mere consultation within the State-Regions Conference is required when a decision is not 'political' but merely 'technical' (i.e., it is based on the application of standards and methods derived from science). For example, in Ruling No. 278 of 22 July 2010 (licence to build and operate nuclear power plants), the Court found that a decision of the central government identifying the types of nuclear power plants that are considered to be suitable for the Italian territory does not require an agreement with the Regions. Such decision is not 'political' but merely 'technical'. Accordingly, simple consultation with the Regions within the State-Regions Conference would be enough for complying with the principle of loyal cooperation and for legitimising the lawmaking activity of the State.[108]

4. Lessons from the Italian Pattern

A few lessons can be learnt from the jurisprudence of the Italian Constitutional Court. Since its introduction in the Constitution in 2001, subsidiarity has been construed by the Court as a justiciable legal principle. A few State laws have been invalidated by the Court for being in breach of that principle. However, more often, subsidiarity has been used as an 'elevator' for lifting legislative and administrative responsibilities up to the central government. Even though this appears somewhat in conflict with the very idea of subsidiarity as 'proximity' to the citizen, it must be noted that subsidiarity clauses, despite their different structures, have generated a comparable outcome in Germany and on the EU level.

Unlike the German 'necessity clause' of Article 72(2) GG, the Italian Constitution contains reference to subsidiarity without further specifying or defining its content. However, Article 118(1) Const. includes 'adequacy' and 'differentiation',

---

[107] Cf. para. 7 of the judgment. In the same wavelength, cf. Ruling No. 39 of 15 March 2013 and Ruling No. 239 of 11 October 2013.

[108] Cf. para. 16 of the judgment. On the contribution of a balanced expert consultation process to legitimacy of the EU lawmaking activity, cf. Popelier (2011), p. 562. See also Schiek (2007), p. 456.

together with 'subsidiarity', among the criteria for the allocation of administrative responsibilities to the different tiers of government. Furthermore, in the landmark Ruling No. 303 of 1 October 2003, the Constitutional Court outlined its approach to the application of the principle of subsidiarity, by laying down a number of criteria: the State can act only if there is a need for uniform State action ('subsidiarity' and 'adequacy'); State action must be proportionate, i.e., limited to what is necessary for the achievement of an objective (proportionality); State legislation must undergo a 'strict scrutiny' by the Constitutional Court in relation to its 'reasonableness'; and, where subsidiarity pushes for 'lifting' a responsibility up to State, State action must abide by 'loyal cooperation'. The emphasis on loyal cooperation led, in some cases, to a merely 'procedural' approach to subsidiarity.

Whilst the German Federal Constitutional Court has followed consistently the original *Leitmotiv* outlined in the *Altenpflegegesetz* Ruling, the Italian Constitutional Court has sometimes departed from the theme designed in Ruling No. 303 of 1 October 2003. For example, in two cases, the Court failed to require loyal cooperation. In other cases, the Court took the need for uniform State action as a given and checked only whether loyal cooperation had been fulfilled.

'Loyal cooperation' plays a fundamental role in the application of the principle of subsidiarity in Italy. Cooperation between State and Regions, typically consisting in an 'agreement' between the two, is the most original feature in relation to subsidiarity in Italy. As noted above, in this way, subsidiarity pushes towards 'cooperation' and 'cooperative regionalism', i.e., it requires the involvement of the 'lower' echelons of government in governance in certain fields (energy, economic recovery, etc.). This idea of 'involvement' is a good example of multilevel governance at work, in that one of the implications of multilevel governance is the participation of sub-national entities in lawmaking and policymaking.

A comparable emphasis on 'loyal cooperation' does not emerge from the 'necessity clause' case law of the German Federal Constitutional Court and from the subsidiarity case law of the ECJ. This is probably due to the fact that in these systems loyal cooperation in the lawmaking process, i.e. the involvement of *Länder* or Member States, is guaranteed by the *Bundesrat* and the Council, respectively. By contrast, in Italy, there is no chamber representing the Regions at national level, and the only possible form of regional involvement is the 'agreement' with a single Region or within the State-Regions Conference or the Unified Conference (Table 4.2).

Table 4.2 Comparison between the Italian Constitutional Court, the German Federal Constitutional Court and the ECJ

Subsidiarity in Italy, Constitutional Court	Subsidiarity in Germany, Federal Constitutional Court	Subsidiarity in the EU, ECJ
In Italy, subsidiarity has a double function: it presides over the allocation of administrative responsibilities (cf. Art. 118(1) Const.), and it authorises a departure from the 'normal' distribution of legislative powers potentially in any area	Subsidiarity (necessity clause, Art. 72(2) GG) finds application in certain areas of concurrent legislation, where the Federation can legislate only if necessity clause criteria are met	Subsidiarity finds application in areas of non-exclusive competence of the EU, where the EU can act only if subsidiarity criteria are met
Since 2001, subsidiarity in Constitution, justiciable, a few State laws invalidated for breach of subsidiarity, more often used to give additional powers to central government	Since 2002 justiciable, 4 federal laws invalidated (2004–2005); however, historically, Art. 72(2) GG has not prevented centralisation of powers	Theoretically justiciable, no act invalidated so far, even though ECJ does not passively defer to the legislator's view
Generic reference to subsidiarity in Art. 118(1) Const.	Comparatively specific criteria in Art. 72(2) GG, 'necessity clause'	Generic subsidiarity definition in Art. 5 TEU
Further specification of criteria by the Court in Ruling No. 303 of 2003; in later cases, the Court has departed from that pattern only occasionally (e.g., merely procedural concept of subsidiarity)	Further specification of criteria by the Court (cf. *Altenpflegegesetz* Ruling); in later cases, the Court applied the *Altenpflegegesetz* pattern consistently	No further specification of subsidiarity clause by the ECJ (however, some specification to the benefit of the legislator in Amsterdam Subsidiarity Protocol)
Scrutiny of conformity with principle of subsidiarity/adequacy, principle of proportionality, reasonableness, principle of loyal cooperation	Scrutiny of rationality of the law, specific criteria for scrutiny determined by the Court	Scrutiny of exercise of discretion (cf. Working Time Directive case), but judicial self-restraint (manifest error, misuse of powers, etc.) similar to Germany under the 'need clause', unlikely declaration of invalidity of an act

D. The Enforcement of Subsidiarity in the Post-Lisbon Era

1. The Shift Towards a 'Procedural' Approach to Subsidiarity

The Amsterdam Subsidiarity Protocol of 1997 followed both a 'substantive' and a 'procedural' approach to subsidiarity. It laid down substantive guidelines in order to assess whether the conditions of Article 3b of the EC Treaty were fulfilled. Such guidelines referred, inter alia, to situations where 'the issue under consideration has transnational aspects which cannot be satisfactorily regulated by action by Member States' or where 'actions by Member States alone… would conflict with the requirements of the Treaty (such as the need... to avoid disguised restrictions on trade...)'.[109] Interestingly, the Lisbon Subsidiarity Protocol of 2007,[110] which replaced the Amsterdam Protocol, does not contain similar guidelines, apparently preferring to focus on 'procedural' rather than on 'substantive' aspects of the subsidiarity principle.

In addition to 'substantive' criteria, the Amsterdam Subsidiarity Protocol also laid down procedural requirements, ensuring that subsidiarity received due consideration by the Union legislator during the lawmaking process. Point 4 of the Protocol established that 'For any proposed Community legislation, the reasons on which it is based shall be stated with a view to justifying its compliance with the principles of subsidiarity and proportionality; the reasons for concluding that a Community objective can be better achieved by the Community must be substantiated by qualitative or, wherever possible, quantitative indicators'. This obligation received further specification in relation to the Commission, which had to 'justify the relevance of its proposals with regard to the principle of subsidiarity' (cf. Point 9), as well as in relation to the Parliament and the Council, which had to 'consider their consistency with Article 3b of the Treaty' (cf. Point 11). Similar obligations have remained in the new Protocol annexed to the Treaty of Lisbon.[111]

---

[109] Amsterdam Subsidiarity Protocol, point 5: 'For Community action to be justified, both aspects of the subsidiarity principle shall be met: the objectives of the proposed action cannot be sufficiently achieved by Member States' action in the framework of their national constitutional system and can therefore be better achieved by action on the part of the Community.

The following guidelines should be used in examining whether the abovementioned condition is fulfilled:

– the issue under consideration has transnational aspects which cannot be satisfactorily regulated by action by Member States;
– actions by Member States alone or lack of Community action would conflict with the requirements of the Treaty (such as the need to correct distortion of competition or avoid disguised restrictions on trade or strengthen economic and social cohesion) or would otherwise significantly damage Member States' interests;
– action at Community level would produce clear benefits by reason of its scale or effects compared with action at the level of the Member States'.

[110] This is the 'new' Subsidiarity Protocol replacing the previous (old) Subsidiarity Protocol annexed to Treaty of Amsterdam (1997). The new Protocol on Subsidiarity was originally drafted by the European Convention (Working Group I on the Principle of Subsidiarity) and annexed to the Treaty Establishing A Constitution for Europe.

[111] Cf. Art. 5 Lisbon Subsidiarity Protocol: 'Draft [Union] legislative acts shall be justified with regard to the principles of subsidiarity and proportionality. Any draft legislative act should contain a detailed statement making it possible to appraise compliance with the principles of subsidiarity and proportionality. This statement should contain some assessment of the proposal's financial impact and, in the case of a directive, of its implications for the rules to be put in place by Member States, including, where necessary, the regional legislation. The reasons for concluding that a Union objective can be better achieved at Union level shall be substantiated by qualitative and, wherever possible, quantitative indicators. Draft legislative acts shall take account of the need for any burden, whether financial or administrative, falling upon the Union, national governments, regional or local authorities, economic operators and citizens, to be minimised and commensurate with the objective to be achieved'. On the concept of 'procedural subsidiarity', cf. D'Atena (2010),

However, the most important 'procedural' innovation introduced by the new Protocol is the 'early warning system', a mechanism aiming to create a 'dialogue' between Union legislator and national and, where applicable, regional parliaments. According to the new Protocol, any national parliament, or chamber thereof, is entitled, within 8 weeks from transmission of a draft EU legislative act, to submit to the European Parliament, the Council and the Commission a reasoned opinion stating why it considers the draft in question non-compliant with subsidiarity. It is for each national parliament, or chamber thereof, to consult, where appropriate, regional parliaments with legislative powers (Art. 6(1) Protocol). The reasoned opinions will have to be taken into account by Union lawmaking institutions and the proponent of the act (cf. Art. 7(1) Protocol).

Within the framework of the 'early warning system', each parliament has two votes and each chamber of a bicameral parliament has one vote (cf. Art. 7(2) Protocol). Where reasoned opinions viewing a draft act as non-compliant with subsidiarity represent at least one-third of the total number of votes allocated to national parliaments, the draft needs to be reconsidered but not necessarily amended (this is the 'yellow card').[112] After such review, the Commission, or any other proponent of an act, will decide whether to maintain, amend or withdraw the proposal, giving reasons for its choice (cf. Art. 7(2) Protocol).

The 'early warning' could be more influential in the framework of the 'ordinary legislative procedure' (i.e., the old co-decision procedure). In this scenario, if reasoned opinions pointing out a non-compliance of a legislative proposal with the principle of subsidiarity represent at least a simple majority of the votes allocated to national parliaments, then the proposal must be reviewed by the Commission (this is the 'orange card'). After such review, if the Commission decides to maintain the proposal, it will have to justify, in a reasoned opinion, why it considers it to be compliant with subsidiarity. The Commission's reasoned opinion, together with those of the national parliaments, will be submitted to the Parliament and the Council to be considered during the decision-making process (Art. 7(3) Protocol). In this way, the 'multilevel dialogue' between national parliaments and the Commission is *officially* brought to the attention of the EU

---

p. 183. In relation to the duty to state reasons, in the Case C-233/94 *Germany v European Parliament and Council* [1997] ECR I-2405, paras. 25–29, the Court of Justice stressed that, so long as the subsidiarity aspect has been considered by the lawmaking institutions, there does not exist a duty to make express reference to subsidiarity in the act. Along the same lines, in the Case C-377/98 *Netherlands v Parliament and Council* [2001] ECR I-7079, para. 33, the Court dismissed the argument brought forward by the Netherlands, according to which the Directive on the legal protection of biotechnological inventions did not state sufficient reasons. The Court found the Directive to be sufficiently reasoned as 'Compliance with the principle of subsidiarity is necessarily implicit in the fifth, sixth and seventh recitals of the preamble to the Directive, which state that, in the absence of action at Community level, the development of the laws and practices of the different Member States impedes the proper functioning of the internal market'.

[112] The threshold is of only 1/4 of all the votes in the case of a draft legislative act submitted under Art. 76 TFEU in the area of freedom, security and justice (cf. Art. 7(2) Protocol).

lawmaking institutions, and it will need to be taken into account by the institutions when making their final decision.[113]

The early warning system's rationale in the legislative process is to ensure appropriate consideration of subsidiarity by the initiator of a draft legislative act and by the Union legislator. At the same time, the 'early warning system' aims to tackle the EU democratic deficit by involving the national (and, where appropriate, the regional) parliaments in the EU lawmaking process.[114] In addition to the Commission's duty to consult widely before making a legislative proposal and to justify each legislative proposal against subsidiarity (cf. Art. 2 Lisbon Subsidiarity Protocol[115]), in the early warning system there is also a fully fledged dialogue between national (and regional) parliaments and Union institutions and, at the same time, a production of evidence, in the form of reasoned statements, concerning compliance with subsidiarity.[116]

---

[113] According to Philipp Kiiver, the early warning system resembles formalised advice procedures as provided by councils of state in relation to national legislation: cf. Kiiver (2011), pp. 102–103. See also Kiiver (2012), pp. 126 ff. In his talk at the fifth Subsidiarity Conference (Bilbao, Spain, 21 March 2011), Jens Nymand Christensen, at the time Director for Parliamentary and Interinstitutional Issues of the European Commission, assured that during the first year of operation of the 'early warning system', even where the 'yellow card' threshold was not reached, the reasoned opinions did not fail to receive attention from the Commission and most of the concerns were later addressed by the European Parliament and the Council. According to Van Nuffel (2011), p. 72, the refusal by the Union legislator to further consider a proposal may appear more radical than it really is; where such majority would be found to vote against the proposal, its chances for being adopted would anyway have been rather reduced. See also Kiiver (2008), p. 81.

[114] Cf. Cooper (2006), p. 292, argues that whilst the early warning system does not necessarily erase the democratic deficit, it does modestly alleviate it. Along the same lines, Van Nuffel (2011), pp. 73–74, observes: 'If concrete results are to be expected from the introduction of the early warning procedure, they will . . . be found in the democratic control exercised within the Member States on the position taken by the national government acting within the Council, rather than in the sphere of the legal protection of Member States' freedom of action vis-à-vis the Union legislator'. Barber (2005b), p. 203, is critical of the restrictions imposed on the involvement of national parliaments, stating that their ability to act should be broadened to allow them to register an objection based on proportionality, human rights or any other possible consideration. See also Cooper (2006), p. 290, who highlights that the rationale for limiting to subsidiarity the right of national parliaments to intervene through the early warning system is that national parliaments should not become 'co-legislators' in the EU and should not delay or block the EU lawmaking activity.

[115] Such a duty had been introduced already by the Amsterdam Subsidiarity Protocol (Point 9).

[116] It is difficult to reach the minimum number of votes for putting the 'yellow' or 'orange' card mechanism into operation. So far, only two yellow cards have been issued. The first was issued on 7 July 2012 in relation to the Proposal for a Council regulation on the exercise of the right to take collective action within the context of the freedom of establishment and the freedom to provide services (cf. COM(2012)130). As a result, the Commission decided to withdraw the proposal. The second yellow card was issued on 28 October 2013 in relation to the Commission's proposal on the establishment of the European Public Prosecutor's Office ('EPPO proposal'; cf. COM(2013)514 final). These are two important precedents showing the potential effectiveness of the 'early warning mechanism' and the willingness of the Commission to take yellow cards seriously. In the European Convention, some members had proposed to introduce also the 'red card', according

At least in theory, the early warning system could also offer a contribution to modify the ECJ's 'light touch' approach to subsidiarity, especially if one considers that any national parliament or chamber thereof may require its respective Member State to notify on its behalf an action of direct annulment on grounds of subsidiarity against an EU legislative act.[117] The supporting evidence contained in the reasoned opinions of the national parliaments could be taken into account by the ECJ when dealing with subsidiarity. However, multilevel governance, demanding additional involvement and participation in the EU lawmaking/policymaking would not be fulfilled *only* through judicial review of subsidiarity.[118] When dealing with subsidiarity, both German and Italian constitutional courts have generally favoured an increase in the power of the central government. In both systems, the principal route to the recognition of the constitutional role of the regional level is the cooperation taking place between the central and the regional levels. In Germany, such cooperation takes place mainly within the *Bundesrat*, where the *Länder* can input to the lawmaking process of the Federation. In Italy, cooperation takes the shape of 'loyal cooperation', i.e., 'co-governance' of a certain field by the State and the Regions through involvement and negotiation.

2. The Role of the Sub-national Authorities in the Enforcement of Subsidiarity After the Lisbon Treaty

(i) The Early Warning Mechanism

The early warning mechanism allows each national parliament (or chamber thereof) to submit to the EU lawmaking institutions reasoned opinions concerning compliance of a legislative proposal with the principle of subsidiarity. It is up to each national parliament (or chamber thereof) to consult, where appropriate, regional parliaments with legislative powers (Art. 6(1) Subsidiarity Protocol). The functioning of the early warning mechanism and the role played in it by the sub-national authorities depend on each individual Member State, namely *A)* on whether the sub-national authorities are represented in one of the legislative chambers of the

---

to which a two-third majority of the national parliaments would have forced the Commission to amend or even withdraw its proposal. However, this proposal failed to obtain sufficient support. Against the introduction of the 'red card', cf. Louis (2008), p. 438, since with no 'red card' the prerogatives of the Commission are preserved. In favour of the 'red card', cf. Bermann (2008), p. 454.

[117] Cf. Art. 8(1) Lisbon Subsidiarity Protocol.

[118] So far, no direct challenge under Article 8(1) has been lodged. This could be seen as a sign of little interest or little confidence of national parliaments in using the judicial route to enforce the principle of subsidiarity.

national parliament and *B)* on whether regional parliaments with legislative powers are consulted by the national parliament.[119]

A) There are three patterns of sub-national representation in the national parliament.

(1) The regional authorities are represented within a national legislative house performing the role of 'chamber of the regions' (Austria[120] and Germany[121]).
(2) There is a national chamber that includes sub-national representatives without being a proper 'chamber of the regions'. This is the case of the French Senate[122] and of the Spanish Senate.[123] The Belgian Senate comprises representatives of the Communities, whilst the majority of its members are directly elected by the citizens.[124]

---

[119] There is another important element whose analysis will be carried out in Chap. 5, whether/how the regional parliaments have equipped themselves for carrying out the subsidiarity scrutiny in the context of the early warning mechanism and whether they engage with it regularly and effectively. On this aspect, see the Committee of the Regions' research report (2010). See also Alonso de León (2012), pp. 305 ff. According to Cygan (2013), pp. 187–188, the new Subsidiarity Protocol has failed to deliver an identifiable shift of regulatory power in favour of the regions.

[120] The Austrian parliament consists of two chambers: the National Council (*Nationalrat*, directly elected by the people) and the Federal Council (*Bundesrat*, in which the *Länder* are represented). According to Article 23g para. 1 B-VG (*Bundes-Verfassungsgesetz*, Federal Constitutional Law, the 'core' constitutional document of Austria), the two chambers of the Austrian parliament can send a reasoned opinion stating why they consider that a legislative draft of the EU does not comply with subsidiarity. This provision is part of the Chapter 'European Union' of the Federal Constitutional Law, which dates back to the beginning of the Austrian membership in the EU (1995). This chapter has been amended several times since. Following the entry into force of the Treaty of Lisbon, it has been amended by the 'Lissabon-Begleitnovelle' (i.e., the constitutional amendment accompanying the entry into force of the Lisbon Treaty, published in *Bundesge-setzblatt*, Federal Law Gazette, in acronym *BGBl.* I 2010/57).

[121] In Germany, there are two legislative chambers on the national level. One is the Federal Diet (*Bundestag*, directly elected by the people); the other is the Federal Council (*Bundesrat*, representing the *Länder*).

[122] The French parliament consists of two houses: the National Assembly (directly elected) and the Senate. The 348 members of the Senate are elected by indirect suffrage by approximately 150,000 elected officials (*grands électeurs*), including regional councillors, department councillors, mayors, city councillors and their delegates in large towns, members of the National Assembly.

[123] Cf. Art. 69(5) of the Spanish Constitution. At present, only 58 out of 266 senators are appointed by the Autonomous Communities. Two-hundred eight members are directly elected by popular vote.

[124] The Belgian Senate cannot be considered a 'chamber of the regions'. A total of 21 of the 74 senators are elected by the Parliaments of the Communities; 40 Senators are directly elected in federal elections; 10 are appointed by the 61 elected senators; three are the 'royal' senators (Princes Philip and Laurent and Princess Astrid). Some proposals have been made to transform the Senate into a 'chamber of the regions', but they have not been carried forward.

(3) There is no representation of sub-national authorities in the national parliament (Italy,[125] Finland,[126] Portugal,[127] UK[128]).

The early warning mechanism was designed primarily as a tool for parliamentary involvement in the EU decision-making, not as a tool for promoting sub-national participation. However, by looking at the use that the mechanism has been made until now, it would appear that also the sub-national authorities have contributed to operating this tool through the chambers of the respective national parliaments. In the first 4 years and a half since the entry into force of the Treaty of Lisbon (period 1 December 2009–1 June 2014), the Commission received a total of 309 reasoned opinions. Of these, 24 (7.7 % of total) came from the 'chambers of the regions' of Austria and Germany (14 from the Austrian Federal Council, 10 from the German *Bundesrat*). Whilst these two chambers have not been hyperactive in drafting reasoned opinions if compared to the Swedish Parliament (50), the Dutch House of Representatives (20), the Luxembourgish Chamber of Deputies (15), the Polish Sejm (14), none of which is a 'regional' or 'territorial' chamber, their activity appears quite significant if compared to the number of reasoned opinions issued by the Austrian National Council (2) and by the German *Bundestag* (3). A similar tendency can be seen in relation to the French Senate (20 reasoned opinions as opposed to only three from the French National Assembly).[129]

So far, only two yellow cards have been issued: the first on 7 July 2012 in relation to the right to strike, the second on 28 October 2013 in relation to the

---

[125] The Italian Senate is elected on a regional basis (i.e., in regional constituencies), with the exception of the seats assigned to the overseas constituency (cf. Art. 57(1) Italian Const.). However, this does not imply a representation of the Regions in the Senate; it only means that the electoral constituencies coincide with the regional territory.

[126] The Finnish parliament (Eduskunta) is unicameral. Art. 25(2) of the Finnish Constitution guarantees that Åland always has a representative in parliament. However, this representative is a member of parliament elected in Åland and not a delegate of the Åland region.

[127] The Portuguese parliament (Assembleia da República, Assembly of the Republic) is unicameral. Both Autonomous Regions (Azores and Madeira) are electoral constituencies on their own (five members of parliament are elected in Azores and six in Madeira). Like for Finland (cf. previous footnote), all members of parliament elected in the constituencies in the Autonomous Regions are not delegates of the Autonomous Regions.

[128] The UK parliament consists of two houses: the House of Commons, which is directly elected by voters, and the House of Lords. The House of Lords consists of Lords Temporal and Lords Spiritual, and it is not a chamber of the regions, nor does it represent the devolved administrations.

[129] In this context, the position of Belgium and Spain is peculiar. As previously stated, the Belgian Senate (only two reasoned opinions, against four from the Belgian Chamber of Representatives) does not include representatives of the Regions (only of the Communities). From this point of view, the Belgian Senate cannot be seen as a proper tool for regional involvement in the early warning system. In Spain (where a limited number of representatives of the Autonomous Communities are members of the Senate), the reasoned opinions are issued by both houses of the Spanish parliament. To date (September 2014), the Spanish parliament (Cortes Generales) has issued 15 reasoned opinions, none of which seems to relate to a legislative proposal of primary relevance to the Autonomous Communities.

establishment of the European Public Prosecutor's Office. On both occasions, the sub-national authorities did not play a major role in achieving that result, probably because the subject matter of the legislative proposals was not of specific and immediate interest for these authorities. On both occasions, only the French Senate, among the chambers with territorial representatives, issued a reasoned opinion.[130]

B) In five Member States (Austria, Spain, Portugal, Finland, Italy), consultation of regional parliaments by national parliaments is expressly provided by law. In Austria, the Federal Council (*Bundesrat*, i.e., the house of national parliament representing the *Länder*) has to inform immediately the *Länder* parliaments about EU legislative proposals and has to give them the opportunity to make comments. The Federal Council has to consider these comments (*erwägen*) when deciding whether to oppose an EU proposal on grounds of subsidiarity.[131]

In Spain, the two houses of the national parliament (Congress and Senate) are obliged to forward all EU legislative proposals to the parliaments of the Autonomous Communities. Within 4 weeks from the day of receipt of a legislative draft, the regional parliaments have the opportunity to submit to the Joint Commission of the Congress and of the Senate for the EU a reasoned opinion on the infringement of the principle of subsidiarity.[132]

In Portugal, before issuing a reasoned opinion against an EU proposal falling within the remit of the Autonomous Regions of Azores and Madeira, the Assembly of the Republic shall consult the Legislative Assemblies of the Autonomous Regions.[133] In Finland, the Åland Parliament can submit an opinion to the Finnish Parliament on the impact of a legislative initiative of the EU on the principle of subsidiarity. The Åland Parliament's opinion has to be forwarded to the EU institutions.[134] In Italy, the chambers of parliament 'may' (*possono*) consult the regional councils and assemblies in accordance with Article 6(1) of the Protocol.[135]

Formally, Belgium does not belong to this group of States with a formal consultation procedure of the regional parliaments by the national parliament.

---

[130] On the first yellow card, cf. Fabbrini and Granat (2013), pp. 115 ff.; Goldoni (2014), pp. 90 ff.

[131] Cf. Art. 23g para. 3 B-VG.

[132] Article 6 of the Protocol has been implemented by Law 24/2009, published in *Boletín Oficial del Estado* (BOE) No. 308 of 23 December 2009. Law 24/2009 amended Law 8/1994 on the Joint Commission of the Congress and of the Senate for the European Union, in order to adapt it to the Treaty of Lisbon. On the implementation of the early warning system in Belgium and Spain, cf. Vandamme (2012), pp. 515 ff. Specifically on the Basque Country, cf. de Castro Ruano (2012), pp. 93 ff.

[133] Cf. Art. 3(3) Law No. 43/2006 of 25 August 2006 on monitoring, assessment and pronouncement by the Assembly of the Republic within the scope of the process of constructing the European Union, amended by Law No. 21/2012 of 17 May 2012.

[134] Cf. Art. 59 a Åland Autonomy Act (this provision was introduced on 4 November 2011).

[135] Cf. Art. 8(3) Law No. 234 of 24 December 2012. This provision is complemented by Article 25 of the same Law, which says that regional councils and assemblies 'may' (*possono*) file their 'observations' (*osservazioni*) to the chambers of Parliament before completion of the parliamentary examination of an EU legislative proposal.

However, a cooperation agreement between national parliament and regional parliaments had been signed on 19 December 2005 in order to guarantee the application of the Protocol on Subsidiarity and Proportionality annexed to the EU Constitutional Treaty.[136] This agreement has not been renewed yet, nor has it been replaced by an alternative one. However, the Belgian Constitutional Court has decided that this should not prevent the application of the Lisbon Protocol on Subsidiarity in Belgium.[137]

Even where there is no ad hoc legal provision or other arrangement in place (such as an agreement), the sub-national authorities are not necessarily 'cut off' and prevented from playing a role in the early warning system. Indeed, nothing would prevent them, individually or collectively, from making their position known to the national parliament in relation to an EU legislative proposal. At the same time, nothing would prevent the national parliament from consulting the sub-national parliaments on its own initiative. However, the position of the sub-national parliaments is certainly stronger in those Member States in which there are a legal basis for consultation and a procedural framework for their involvement in the constitution (see, for example, Austria) or in sub-constitutional law (see, for example, Spain). The concept of multilevel governance put forward in this study pushes towards the creation of an appropriate consultation procedure rather than towards a discretionary case-by-case-based arrangement and requires that regional opinions are taken into account by the national parliament. Failure to examine a regional opinion (especially if this concerns matters of regional legislative responsibility) would cause a considerable 'short circuit' in the system of involvement of the sub-national authorities in the EU legislative process and would undermine the *legitimacy* of the participation of the Member State in the EU (cf. supra Chap. 3).[138]

(ii) The Right to Challenge Union Acts

In the new Protocol on Subsidiarity, any national parliament or chamber thereof is entitled to make the respective Member State notify on its behalf a direct action for annulment against Union legislative acts on grounds of an infringement of the principle of subsidiarity.[139] A number of Member States have implemented this provision of the Protocol. In a first group of States, the national government has to lodge an action for direct annulment if this is requested by one of the chambers (Germany, Austria, Italy) or even by a minority within one of the chambers

---

[136] Co-Operation Agreement of 19 December 2005 between the Federal Legislative Chambers, the Parliaments of the Communities and the Regions in application of the Protocol on Subsidiarity and Proportionality attached to the Constitutional Treaty of the European Union.

[137] Constitutional Court Ruling No. 58/2009 of 19 March 2009.

[138] On the idea that participation of regional actors through the early warning system contributes legitimacy to the EU legislative process, cf. de Castro Ruano (2012), p. 99.

[139] Cf. Art. 8(1) Lisbon Subsidiarity Protocol.

Table 4.3 Implementation of Article 8(1) of the Subsidiarity Protocol

Austria	Article 23h of the Federal Constitutional Law stipulates that the National Council and the Federal Council (the two legislative chambers) can decide to bring an action against a legislative act of the Union on grounds of an infringement of the principle of subsidiarity. The Federal Chancellery (the national government) has the obligation to forward the action on to the ECJ.
Belgium	In Belgium, the implementation of Article 8(1) of the Protocol has been thoroughly debated. Declaration 51 annexed to the Treaty of Lisbon states: 'Belgium wishes to make clear that, in accordance with its constitutional law, not only the Chamber of Representatives and Senate of the Federal Parliament but also the parliamentary assemblies of the Communities and the Regions act, in terms of the competences exercised by the Union, as components of the national parliamentary system or chambers of the national parliament'. This statement can only be understood in the context of the Belgian constitutional framework, which endeavours to establish legal parity between the state and the sub-state entities. What is the legal impact of this declaration? Does it imply that the European Commission, the Parliament and the Council shall forward their legislative drafts and their amended drafts to the parliaments of the Belgian Communities and Regions? The Union may regard Declaration 51 as a unilateral declaration by a Member State that is not binding upon the Union (whilst being binding upon that Member State). Article 4 of the Protocol on Subsidiarity specifically limits the obligation to forward legislative drafts and amended drafts to 'national parliaments'. The Belgian standpoint that the parliamentary assemblies of the Communities and the Regions act as branches of the 'national parliamentary system' seems difficult to reconcile also with Article 6 of the Protocol. Indeed, this Article provides that 'it will be for each national parliament or each chamber of a national parliament to consult, where appropriate, regional parliaments with legislative power'. A Co-operation Agreement between the central authority and the sub-state parliaments seems to be the only viable solution to make Declaration 51 annexed to the Treaty of Lisbon applicable in Belgium. Such agreement has yet to be signed. It is reasonable to expect that it will provide both the chambers of the National Parliament and the sub-state parliaments with the right to compel Belgium to bring an action before the ECJ. They will be entitled to do so if they estimate that the principle of subsidiarity has been violated by a legislative act of the Union falling within their respective area of responsibility.
Germany	The Bundestag and/or the Bundesrat (the two legislative chambers) can initiate a direct claim for judicial review against an EU legislative act before the ECJ if it is believed that the act in question contains an infringement on the principle of subsidiarity. Cf. Art. 23(1a) of the Basic Law.
Spain	The Joint Commission of the Congress and of the Senate for the EU (a commission composed by members of both legislative chambers) and each legislative chamber may petition the Government for filing a direct action for annulment before the ECJ on grounds of an infringement of the principle of subsidiarity. The Government retains the right to disregard the petition, but it needs to explain the reasons for doing so. Cf. Art. 7 of the consolidated statute resulting from approval of Law 24/2009 of 22 December 2009. Law 24/2009 introduced in the Law 8/1994 of 19 May 1994 (the law regulating the participation of the chambers of national parliament in the EU lawmaking process) a new Chapter II on the principle of subsidiarity.
Italy	The Italian Government has to challenge without delay legislative acts of the Union on grounds of a breach of subsidiarity upon request from either house of the Italian Parliament. The rather imperative formulation used by the law ('Il Governo presenta senza ritardo alla Corte di giustizia dell'Unione europea i ricorsi . . .'; cf. Art. 42 (4) Law of 27 November 2012) leads to the conclusion that the Government is obliged to file the lawsuit.

(continued)

Table 4.3 (continued)

UK	In the UK, there is no legislative provision on this issue, and the recently passed European Union Act 2011 does not address it either. Some form of implementation seems to be necessary as it is unlikely that Article 8(1) of the Protocol could be seen as being self-executing in the UK. In accordance with British constitutional tradition, it is to be expected that implementation will be done through protocols and/or other non-legally binding instruments rather than through an act of Parliament. Cf. EU Committee of the House of Lords, *Strengthening national parliamentary scrutiny of the EU – the Constitution's subsidiarity early warning mechanism*, 14th Report of Session 2004–2005 (published on 14 April 2005).
France	Article 88-6 of the Constitution states that each House of Parliament may institute proceedings before the ECJ against an EU legislative act for non compliance with the principle of subsidiarity. Such proceedings shall be referred to the ECJ by the Government. Importantly, if at least 60 members of the National Assembly (out of total 577) or 60 senators (out of total 346) request such proceedings to be instituted, the Government is obliged to comply with such request.
Finland	N/A
Portugal	The Assembly of the Republic (the unicameral parliament) may, by means of a resolution, urge the Government to lodge an appeal before the Court of Justice of the European Union on the grounds that the principle of subsidiarity has been violated by a legislative act of the EU. The use of the term 'urge' (*instar*), rather than 'oblige' (*obrigar*) or 'compel' (*compelir*), fosters the interpretation that the Portuguese Government, like the Spanish, may dismiss the request. In Portugal, Article 8(1) of the Protocol has been implemented by Law 21/2012 of 17 May 2012 (which added a new Article 4(5) to Law 43/2006 of 25 August 2006).

(France). In a second group of States (Spain and Portugal), the national government may, albeit exceptionally, refuse to comply with the parliamentary request. In other Member States (Belgium, Finland, UK), no implementation measure has been passed yet. This may prevent Article 8(1) of the Subsidiarity Protocol from becoming fully operational. However, it needs to be taken into account that in all the Member States, the parliament could persuade the government to lodge a subsidiarity lawsuit by using its political weight and constitutional prerogatives.[140] The positions of the various Member States are summarised in Table 4.3.

It would appear that the position of the houses of the French Parliament in relation to the subsidiarity lawsuit is stronger than in any other analysed Member State. Indeed, in France, a minority of 60 members of the National Assembly or 60 senators may oblige the government to file a subsidiarity claim before the ECJ. By contrast, the position of the Spanish chambers and of the Portuguese parliament

---

[140] It must be taken into account that some Member States adopt a monist approach as regards the relationship between domestic law and international law. The same approach also applies to the relationship between domestic law and EU law. This is, for example, the case of Slovakia, where no specific implementation of Article 8(1) has taken place, nor is it likely to take place. In Slovakia, Article 8(1) can without any particular difficulty be considered self-executing and automatically operational.

seems weaker, given that the government could refuse to follow up the request by giving reasons for the refusal. With specific reference to the regional authorities, it would appear that their potential role can be stronger in those Member States in which there is a chamber representing them at national level (Austria, Germany). However, also the French system (requiring 60 senators only for a direct action to be lodged) may ensure a significant role for territorial communities in bringing a subsidiarity claim.

Over 4 years after the entry into force of the Protocol, no direct challenge under Article 8(1) has been lodged yet. Together with the lack of implementation of Article 8(1) in some Member States, this could be seen as a sign of little interest of national parliaments in using the judicial route to enforce the principle of subsidiarity. In theory, the Lisbon Protocol on Subsidiarity creates some new opportunities for sub-state entities to make their voice heard on the EU level. However, whilst the early warning mechanism has generated some substantial result (two yellow cards, regional participation through the 'chambers of the regions', consultation of regional parliaments by national parliaments), so far the request of a legal action before the ECJ has failed to produce *any* result (in the interest not only of the sub-national but also of the national levels). Also in the light of the previous history of judicial enforcement of subsidiarity in the EU (cf. supra Sect. B), it appears unlikely that the situation may change in the near future.[141]

(iii) Committee of the Regions

The Committee of the Regions (CoR) is involved in the implementation of subsidiarity on the EU level and sees itself as the 'custodian' or 'watchdog' of the principle.[142] When performing its consultative role, the CoR has the duty to express its point of view in relation to the conformity of a legislative proposal with the principle of subsidiarity.[143] In addition, the Lisbon Subsidiarity Protocol gave the

---

[141] My sceptical position in relation to the judicial enforcement of subsidiarity clashes with the views of those scholars who, also in recent time, have been trying to develop viable patterns for judicial application of subsidiarity. See, for example, Schütze (2009), pp. 525 ff.; Craig (2012), pp. 72 ff.

[142] Cf. Opinion of the Committee of the Regions of 11 March 1999 on the principle of subsidiarity (*Developing a genuine culture of subsidiarity. An appeal by the Committee of the Regions*) in: *OJ* 1999 C 198/73 (cf. point 1.1.4 and point 1.1.3: 'Since it first came into existence, the Committee has made defence of the application of the subsidiarity principle one of its primary objectives'). In 2005, the CoR created the Subsidiarity Monitoring Network (SMN). The SMN is a forum available to regional and local authorities. It gives them an opportunity for expressing their views prior to the adoption of any EU act potentially affecting them. On the CoR as 'subsidiarity watchdog', cf. Ricci (2011), pp. 123–126.

[143] Cf. Art. 55(2) of the CoR's Rules of Procedure.

CoR the right to challenge an EU legislative act on grounds of an infringement of this principle.[144]

The CoR does not appear overly confident that subsidiarity can be enforced through judicial review. Up to now, no challenge has been lodged by the CoR against an act for an infringement of subsidiarity. However, it cannot be excluded that the right to challenge, albeit not yet exploited, may have strengthened the force of the opinions of the CoR vis-à-vis the lawmaking institutions and that, accordingly, the CoR may be playing a stronger role in the lawmaking process. Still, one more time the enforcement of subsidiarity seems to follow from cooperation (i.e., 'dialogue', if not fully fledged negotiation, among levels of government) rather than from judicial review.

E. Concluding Remarks: Subsidiarity Between Justiciability and Cooperation

Subsidiarity is a fundamental constitutional principle in the EU, Germany and Italy. In all these systems, subsidiarity aims primarily to protect the *autonomy* of the lower echelons of government by favouring 'proximity' of power to the citizen. Judicial review is one way to enforce subsidiarity. However, the EU experience and the comparative analysis show the shortcomings of the judicial route. In Germany, when the Federal Constitutional Court began to enforce the 'necessity clause', the activism of the Court generated a short circuit with the political system and the legislator and led to a reform that reduced drastically the sphere of application of the 'necessity clause'. The role of the *Länder* in legislation is ensured more effectively through their cooperation to the federal legislative activity within the *Bundesrat*. In Italy, subsidiarity is used by the Constitutional Court to enlarge the legislative powers of the central government rather than to protect regional autonomy. The centralisation of legislative powers has been counterbalanced through cooperation mechanisms requiring the Regions to contribute to governance of a certain field. In the EU, the pattern is not fundamentally different. The ECJ has never annulled an act for an infringement of subsidiarity, and this seems unlikely to occur against an act that has been negotiated and agreed by the (majority of the) Member States in the Council. Like in Germany and in Italy, 'multilevel

---

[144] Cf. Art. 8(2) of the Protocol. This only applies to those acts for whose adoption the consultation of the CoR is mandatory. The TFEU requires an opinion of the CoR for legislative proposals in the following policy areas: transport (Art. 91(1)), including sea and air transport (Art. 100.2); employment (Arts. 148(2) and 149(1)); social policy (Art. 153(2)); education, vocational training, youth and sport (Arts. 165(4) and 166(4)); culture (Art. 167(5)); public health (Art. 168(4) and (5)); trans-European networks (Art. 172); economic, social and territorial cohesion (Arts. 175(3), 177(1), and 178(1)); environment (Art. 192 (1), (2) and (3)); energy policy (Art. 194(2)). In all these fields, the Union acts in the exercise of shared powers. Accordingly, the principle of subsidiarity should play a decisive role.

cooperation' and 'dialogue' rather than judicial enforcement of State autonomy seem to be the most viable and sustainable solution.

Multilevel governance is based on 'coexistence and interaction', i.e., autonomy of and coordinated action/cooperation between different layers of government. The enforcement of the principle of subsidiarity pursues both autonomy and cooperation. By contrast, subsidiarity embodies the idea of 'exception', i.e., that only exceptionally powers shall be exercised by higher layers of government, the rule being 'proximity' of governance to the citizen.[145] Subsidiarity became a judicially enforceable principle both in Germany and in Italy, even though, more often, judicial application upheld the 'exception' (i.e., action by the central authority) rather than 'proximity'. Subsidiarity typically became a tool justifying intervention by the central authority. The key role of multilevel governance in relation to subsidiarity is to promote a shift of focus from the negative ('exceptionality' of the intervention by the central authority) to the positive, 'inclusive', aspect of subsidiarity, i.e., that all the layers of government must contribute, for what belongs to their responsibility, to the achievement of the Union's objectives. In all the analysed multilevel systems, the appropriate locus for the enforcement of subsidiarity is not the courtroom but participation in the lawmaking and policymaking processes as required by the principles of 'partnership' and 'loyal cooperation'. Judicial enforcement plays a role only if there is a 'clear' or 'evident' abuse; i.e., where the attribution of a certain power to the central authority is totally illogical or untenable. Multilevel governance requires 'co-governance' by a plurality of levels of government of a field in which a power is exercised by a central authority but in which essential interests of the other levels are also at stake. In this way, cooperation also addresses the issue of *legitimacy* of authoritative decision-making. This is a fundamental feature and function of the 'early warning system', whose proper functioning requires the involvement of national parliaments and of regional parliaments with legislative powers. The early warning system 'proceduralises' the principle of subsidiarity, insofar as it creates a '2-way communication' channel and promotes 'multilevel dialogue'. This implies that the role of the CJEU for the enforcement of subsidiarity, apart from extreme and unlikely cases of 'clear' or 'evident' abuse of power by the EU, could be confined to the enforcement of a 'procedure'.[146]

---

[145] Swaine (2000), pp. 53–54, even suggests that the principle of subsidiarity entails a presumption of competence in favour of the Member States.

[146] Nettesheim has recently proposed the oxymoronic notion of 'politisches Recht' (political law), indicating those legal provisions that are only or principally enforceable through forms of political coordination (*politische Koordination*). The role of the courts in this field is limited to the enforcement of the 'procedures' of political coordination. Cf. Nettesheim (2014), passim.

References

S. Alonso de León, Regions and subsidiarity in the European Union: a look at the role of the Spanish and other regional parliaments in the monitoring of compliance with the principle of subsidiarity. Eur. Public Law **18**(2), 305 f. (2012)

N.W. Barber, The limited modesty of subsidiarity. Eur. Law J. **11**(3), 308 f. (2005a)

N.W. Barber, Subsidiarity in the draft constitution. Eur. Public Law **11**(2), 197 f. (2005b)

G. Bermann, Taking subsidiarity seriously: federalism in the European Community and the United States. Columbia Law Rev. **94**(2), 331 f. (1994)

G.A. Bermann, National parliaments and subsidiarity: an outsider's view. Eur. Const. Law Rev. **4**(3), 453 f. (2008)

S. Burkhart, Reforming federalism in Germany: incremental changes instead of the big deal. Publius **39**(2), 341 f. (2009)

Q. Camerlengo, [Commentary to] Article 118 of the Italian Constitution, in *Commentario alla Costituzione*, vol. III, ed. by R. Bifulco et al. (UTET, Torino, 2006), pp. 2333 ff

B. Caravita, Judge made federalism? The role of the Italian Constitutional Court in the interpretation and implementation of the recent constitutional reform, in *Judge Made Federalism? The Role of Courts in Federal Systems*, ed. by H.-P. Schneider et al. (Nomos, Baden-Baden, 2009), pp. 16 ff

G.F. Cartei, V. Ferraro, Reform of the fifth title of the Italian constitution. A first step towards a federal system? Eur. Public Law **8**(4), 445 f. (2002)

S. Cassese, L'aquila e le mosche. Principio di sussidiarietà e diritti amministrativi nell'area europea, in *Sussidiarietà e pubbliche amministrazioni*, ed. by F. Roversi Monaco (Maggioli, Rimini, 1997). pp. 73 ff

Commission of the European Communities, Communication to the Council and the European Parliament, *The Principle of Subsidiarity*, SEC(92) 1990 final, 27 October 1992

Committee of the Regions, Opinion of 11 March 1999 on the principle of subsidiarity (*Developing a Genuine Culture of Subsidiarity. An Appeal by the Committee of the Regions*) in: *OJ* 1999 C 198/73

Committee of the Regions, *White Paper on Multilevel Governance*, CdR 89/2009, 17–18 June 2009

Committee of the Regions, research report, *The Role of Regional Parliaments in the Process of Subsidiarity Analysis Within the Early Warning System of the Lisbon Treaty*, no date (but 2010)

Committee of the Regions, Charter for Multilevel Governance in Europe (April 2014)

I. Cooper, The watchdogs of subsidiarity: national parliaments and the logic of arguing in the EU. J. Common Mark. Stud. **44**(2), 281 f. (2006)

Council of Europe, *European Charter of Local Self-Government* (15 October 1985)

P. Craig, Subsidiarity: a political and legal analysis. J. Common Mark. Stud. **50**(S1), 72 f. (2012)

P. Craig, G. De Búrca, *EU Law. Text, Cases and Materials*, 4th edn. (OUP, Oxford, 2011)

A. Cygan, Regional governance, subsidiarity and accountability within the EU's multi-level polity. Eur. Public Law **19**(1), 161 f. (2013)

G. D'Alessio, F. Di Lascio (eds.), *Il sistema amministrativo a dieci anni dalla 'Riforma Bassanini'* (Giappichelli, Torino, 2009)

A. D'Atena, *Diritto regionale* (Giappichelli, Torino, 2010)

G. Davies, Subsidiarity: the wrong idea, in the wrong place, at the wrong time. Common Mark. Law Rev. **43**(1), 63 f. (2006)

G. De Búrca, The principle of subsidiarity and the court of justice as an institutional actor. J. Common Mark. Stud. **36**(2), 217 f. (1998)

G. De Búrca, Proportionality and subsidiarity as general principles of law, in *General Principles of European Community Law*, ed. by U. Bernitz et al. (Kluwer, London, 2000), pp. 95 ff

G. De Búrca, Legal principles as an instrument of differentiation? The principle of proportionality and subsidiarity, in *The Many Faces of Differentiation in EU Law*, ed. by B. de Witte et al. (Intersentia, Antwerpen, 2001), pp. 131 ff

J.L. de Castro Ruano, El Sistema de Alerta Temprana para el control de la subsidiariedad: su aplicación por el Parlamento vasco. Revista CIDOB d'afers internacionals, (99), 93 f. (2012)

S. Deimann, Re-federalising Germany: from 'Uniform' to 'Equivalent' living-conditions. Public Law Rev. **7**(2), 110 f. (1996)

A. Estella, *The EU Principle of Subsidiarity and Its Critique* (OUP, Oxford, 2002)

F. Fabbrini, K. Granat, "Yellow card, but no foul": the role of the national parliaments under the Subsidiarity Protocol and the Commission proposal for an EU regulation on the right to strike. Common Mark. Law Rev. **50**(1), 115 f. (2013)

M. Goldoni, The early warning system and the Monti II regulation: the case for political interpretation. Eur. Const. Law Rev. **10**(1), 90 f. (2014)

T. Groppi, N. Scattone, Italy: the subsidiarity principle. Int. J. Const. Law **4**(1), 131 f. (2006)

A. Gunlicks, German federalism reform: part one. German Law J. **8**(1), 111 f. (2008)

K. Hesse, *Der unitarische Bundesstaat* (C.F. Müller, Karlsruhe, 1962)

R. Hrbek, The reform of German federalism: part I. Eur. Const. Law Rev. **3**(2), 225 f. (2007)

P. Kiiver, The Treaty of Lisbon, the national parliaments and the principle of subsidiarity. Maastrich. J. Eur. Comp. Law **15**(1), 77 f. (2008)

P. Kiiver, The early-warning system for the principle of subsidiarity: the national parliament as a "Conseil d'État" for Europe. Eur. Public Law **36**(1), 98 f. (2011)

P. Kiiver, *The Early Warning System for the Principle of Subsidiarity. Constitutional Theory and Empirical Reality* (Routledge, London, 2012)

K. Lenaerts, P. Van Nuffel, *European Union Law*, 3rd edn. (Sweet & Maxwell, London, 2011)

J.-V. Louis, The Lisbon Treaty: the Irish 'No': national parliaments and the principle of subsidiarity – legal options and practical limits. Eur. Const. Law Rev. **4**(3), 429 f. (2008)

J. Madison, Federalist Paper No. 51 (The structure of the government must furnish the proper checks and balances between the different departments). Independent J. (1788)

G. Martinico, Dating Cinderella: on subsidiarity as a political safeguard of federalism in the European Union. Eur. Public Law **17**(4), 469 f. (2011)

M. Nettesheim, Subsidiarität durch politische Koordination. Paper presented at the symposium "Grenzen Europäischer Normgebung – EU-Kompetenzen und Europäische Grundrechte", Frankfurt am Main, 19 March 2014

F. Neumann, *The Democratic and the Authoritarian State* (The Free Press, Glencoe, 1957)

A. Pajno, L'attuazione del federalismo amministrativo. Le Regioni **29**(4), 667 f. (2001)

C. Panara, I poteri impliciti nel federalismo tedesco del Grundgesetz. Quaderni costituzionali **28** (2), 425 f. (2008)

P. Pernthaler, Differenzierter Föderalismus, in *Auf dem Weg zu asymmetrischem Föderalismus*, ed. by F. Palermo et al. (Nomos, Baden-Baden, 2007), pp. 22 ff

Pius XI, encyclical *Quadragesimo Anno: Encyclical of Pope Pius XI on Reconstruction of the Social Order* (1931)

P. Popelier, Governance and better regulation: dealing with the legitimacy paradox. Eur. Public Law **17**(3), 555 f. (2011)

M. Rau, Subsidiarity and judicial review in German federalism: the decision of the Federal Constitutional Court in the Geriatric Nursing Act Case. German Law J. **4**(3), 223 f. (2003)

H.-W. Rengeling, Gesetzgebungszuständigkeit, in *Handbuch des Staatsrechts*, vol. IV, 2nd edn. ed. by J. Isensee, P. Kirchhof (C.F. Müller, Heidelberg, 1999), pp. 723 ff

S. Ricci, The Committee of the Regions and the challenge of European governance, in *The Role of the Regions in EU Governance*, ed. by C. Panara, A. De Becker (Springer, Berlin/Heidelberg, 2011). pp. 109 ff

W. Rüfner, Art. 72 Abs. 2 GG in der Rechtsprechung des Bundesverfassungsgerichts, in *Staat im Wort. Festschrift für Josef Isensee*, ed. by O. Depenhauer et al. (C.F. Müller, Heidelberg, 2007), pp. 389 ff

F. Sander, Subsidiarity infringements before the European Court of Justice: futile interference with politics or a substantial step towards EU federalism? Columbia J. Eur. Law **12**(2), 517 f. (2006)

W.-R. Schenke, Föderalismus als Form der Gewaltenteilung. JuS **29**(9), 698 f. (1989)

D. Schiek, Private rule-making and European governance – issues of legitimacy. Eur. Law Rev. **32**(2), 443 f. (2007)

R. Scholz, Ausschliessliche und konkurrierende Gesetzgebungskompetenz von Bund und Ländern in der Rechtsprechung des Bundesverfassungsgerichts, in *Bundesverfassungsgericht und Grundgesetz*, ed. by C. Starck, vol. II (Mohr, Tübingen, 1976). pp. 252 ff

R. Schutze, Subsidiarity after Lisbon: reinforcing the safeguards of federalism? Cambridge Law J. **68**(3), 525 f. (2009)

M.T. Serra, Il c.d. federalismo amministrativo nella legge 59/97 e nella sua prima attuazione. Studi parlamentari e di politica costituzionale **32**(123), 55 f. (1999)

E.T. Swaine, Subsidiarity and self-interest: federalism at the European Court of Justice. Harv. Int. Law J. **41**(1), 1 f. (2000)

P. Syrpis, In defence of subsidiarity. Oxford J. Leg. Stud. **24**(2), 323 f. (2004)

G. Taylor, Germany: the subsidiarity principle. Int. J. Const. Law **4**(1), 115 f. (2006)

G. Taylor, Germany: a slow death for subsidiarity? Int. J. Const. Law **7**(1), 139 f. (2009)

L. Torchia, Regioni e "federalismo amministrativo". Le Regioni **29**(2), 257 f. (2001)

A.G. Toth, The principle of subsidiarity in the Maastricht Treaty. Common Mark. Law Rev. **29**(6), 1079 f. (1992)

A.G. Toth, Is subsidiarity justiciable? Eur. Law Rev. **19**(4), 268 f. (1994)

J.-P. Trnka, Subsidiarity: competence control or political masquerade? in *Unsolved Issues of the Constitution for Europe Rethinking the Crisis*, ed. by N. Neuwahl, S. Haack (Thémis, Montreal, 2007). pp. 239 ff

T. Vandamme, From federated federalism to converging federalism? The case of EU subsidiarity scrutiny in Spain and Belgium. Reg. Fed. Stud. **22**(5), 515 f. (2012)

L. Vandelli, *Il Sistema delle autonomie locali* (il Mulino, Bologna, 2007)

P. Van Nuffel, *De rechtsbescherming van nationale overheden in het Europees recht* (Kluwer, Deventer, 2000), pp. 397 ff

P. Van Nuffel, The protection of Member States' regions through the subsidiarity principle, in *The Role of the Regions in EU Governance*, ed. by C. Panara, A. De Becker (Springer, Heidelberg, 2011). pp. 55 ff

H.-J. Vogel, Die bundesstaatliche Ordnung des Grundgesetzes, in *Handbuch des Verfassungsrechts*, vol. II, 2nd edn. ed. by E. Benda et al. (de Gruyter, Berlin, 1995), pp. 1039 ff

Working Group I of the European Convention on the Principle of Subsidiarity, Brussels, 23 September 2002, CONV 286/02

J. Ziller, Le principe de subsidiarité, in *Droit Administratif Européen*, ed. by J.B. Auby, J. Dutheil de la Rochére (Bruylant, Bruxelles, 2007), pp. 377 ff

Chapter 5
The Regional Responsibility for European Integration: Baden-Württemberg (Germany), Lombardia (Italy), Merseyside (UK)

A. Introduction: Regional Responsibility for European Integration

In this chapter, I will address the constitutional problem of regional and local participation in EU lawmaking and policymaking from a different perspective. In the previous chapters, I followed the traditional 'top-down' approach consisting of looking at the constitutional duty of the EU and of the Member States to facilitate regional and local involvement in the EU lawmaking and policymaking. In this chapter, I will adopt a 'bottom-up' approach looking at what the sub-national authorities themselves are constitutionally required to do to perform a role in the EU.[1] A useful concept in this context is that of 'responsibility for European integration' (Integrationsverantwortung) created by the German Federal Constitutional Court, which refers to the necessary involvement of the national legislative bodies in all the decisions broadening the responsibilities of the EU.[2] The scope of the notion of 'responsibility for European integration', however, can be further

---

[1] A similar 'bottom-up' approach, albeit from a political science perspective, is adopted by Lindh et al. (2009), passim.

[2] Judgment of the Second Senate of the German Federal Constitutional Court of 30 June 2009, 'Lisbon Ruling' (BVerfG, 2 BvE 2/08). From the Headnotes of the Judgment: '(2) a) In so far as the Member States elaborate treaty law in such a way as to allow treaty amendment without a ratification procedure, whilst preserving the application of the principle of conferral, a special responsibility is incumbent on the legislative bodies, in addition to the Federal Government, within the context of participation which in Germany has to comply internally with the requirements of Article 23(1) of the Basic Law (responsibility for integration) and which may be invoked in any proceedings before the Federal Constitutional Court. (3) b) A law within the meaning of Article 23 (1) second sentence of the Basic Law is not required, in so far as special bridging clauses are limited to subject areas which are already sufficiently defined by the Treaty of Lisbon. However, in such cases it is incumbent on the Bundestag and, in so far as legislative competence of the Länder are affected, the Bundesrat, to assert its responsibility for integration in another appropriate manner'.

© Springer International Publishing Switzerland 2015   127
C. Panara, *The Sub-national Dimension of the EU*,
DOI 10.1007/978-3-319-14589-1_5

expanded. Martin Nettesheim suggests that this concept 'implies that the organs of an organisation whose self-rule is limited by supra-state decision-making, must engage in the exercise of supra-state authority in a manner which suits the democratic principle (idea of compensation)'.[3] In this way, he widens the scope of the concept both horizontally and vertically. On the one hand, 'responsibility for integration' is not limited to the transfer of powers to the EU and comes to embrace potentially the entire spectrum of Union action (horizontal dimension). On the other hand, the 'responsibility' is not confined to central organs of the state; it also applies to the Länder, the sub-national level (vertical dimension).

The validity of this submission (that the sub-national authorities have a responsibility for European integration) will be tested in relation to three case studies: Baden-Württemberg (Germany), Lombardia (Italy) and Liverpool City Region (England). Baden-Württemberg is a Land of a typical federal state; Lombardia is a region of a typical regional state; Liverpool City Region is an English combined authority, including Liverpool and a number of other local authorities. These 'regions' (in reality, the German Länder regard themselves as 'states') are good examples of 'European regions', in that Baden-Württemberg and Lombardia are among the most economically developed parts of Europe and among the motors of EU economy. Liverpool City Region is one of the areas of England that has benefited the most from EU funding and, for that reason, is a 'leader' in the UK's atypical system based on devolution (in Scotland, Wales and Northern Ireland) and local self-government (in England). The analysis of these three case studies will allow a comparison between three different regional pathways to European integration and the identification of the advantages and disadvantages of each model.[4]

B. Case Study 1: A Multilevel Constitutional Approach to Integration in the EU: Land Baden-Württemberg

Baden-Wurttemberg is one of the 16 federal states (Länder) constituting the Federal Republic of Germany. It is the third largest German Land by population (10.5 million in 2012) after North Rhine-Westphalia (17.5) and Bavaria (12.5). It is the third largest German Land also for GDP (14.33 % of total German 2013 GDP), again after North Rhine-Westphalia (21.91 %) and Bavaria (17.83 %).[5] Along with Catalonia, Lombardia and the Rhône-Alpes, it is one of the Four Motors for Europe, a network of four highly industrialised European regions. The strong engagement of

---

[3] See Nettesheim (30 July 2009), paragraph 3; Nettesheim (2010), pp. 177–178. On the 'responsibility for integration' of Länder parliaments, see Kluth (2010), pp. 289 ff.

[4] The following part of the study takes account of some semi-structured interviews of key members of the Brussels offices, the legislatures and the administrations of the selected local and regional authorities. The minutes of these interviews are on file with me.

[5] These figures are from the Federal Statistical Office of Germany (Statistisches Bundesamt).

the Land Baden-Württemberg in the EU is therefore a consequence of its important economic role within Germany and Europe. The responsibility of Baden-Württemberg for European integration, the right and duty to engage with the EU, however, has a more profound constitutional foundation both on the national level (Grundgesetz) and on the local level (Land Constitution). The second indention of the Preamble to the Grundgesetz (the federal constitution of 1949) says that 'inspired by the determination to promote world peace as an equal partner in a united Europe', the German people have adopted the Grundgesetz. The aspiration to the unity of Europe is therefore fundamental in the Grundgesetz. The same aspiration is reflected in the Constitution of the Land Baden-Württemberg of 1953, whose Preamble stipulates that this Land shall be a 'vital member of the Federal Republic of Germany in a united Europe, whose construction fulfils the federal principles and the principle of subsidiarity'. It shall also actively contribute to the creation of a 'Europe of the regions' and to 'cross-border cooperation'.[6] The aspiration to the creation of a united Europe is translated into more operational terms by Article 23 of the Grundgesetz (Europa-Artikel), which also regulates the participation of the Länder in matters concerning the EU.[7]

The right and duty of the Länder to engage with the EU and, more specifically, to defend the interests stemming from the regional community on the EU level derive in primis from their 'state quality' reflected in Article 30 of the Grundgesetz. As established by Article 30, in principle ('except as otherwise provided or permitted by the Grundgesetz'), 'the exercise of state powers and the discharge of state functions is a matter for the Länder'.[8] A further foundation of their engagement in the EU decision-making processes is identified by Nettesheim in the democratic self-governance of the Länder (cf. Art. 20(1) GG and Art. 79(3) GG). Indeed, the defence of a free and democratic self-governance of the Länder requires that these retain a right to participate in the formulation of EU law and policy.[9] Overall, there is a responsibility of the Länder for European integration that requires the Länder to play an active role in the EU, i.e., to actively engage in the EU level. Another element to take into account is that, in a case where a Land infringes an EU obligation (for example, for failure to implement a regulation), it has to bear the financial consequences towards the Bund, i.e., it must pay the fine (cf. Art. 104a

---

[6] See Preamble of the Constitution of the Land Baden-Württemberg of 11 November 1953.

[7] On the participation rights of the Länder, see Panara (2010), pp. 59 ff., and Panara (2011), pp. 133 ff. Nettesheim (2009), paragraph 4, highlights how Article 23(1) says that 'the Federal Republic of Germany' shall participate in the development of the EU. Accordingly, he argues, the democratic safeguarding of the integration process is a task not solely of the Federation (Bund) but also of the Länder, which are an integral part of the Federal Republic.

[8] Cf. Fastenrath (1986), p. 195. Pernice, by contrast, holds that the 'Reise- und Besuchsdiplomatie' (trips and visits diplomacy) of the Länder is based on a mere de facto tolerance by the Federal Government of the day. Cf. Pernice (2006), p. 789 (Rn. 38).

[9] See Nettesheim (30 July 2009), passim (especially paragraph 14).

(6) GG).[10] As a result, also from a practical point of view, it makes sense to involve the Länder in the promulgation of EU law and policy. Arguably, a learning process takes place during the making phase of EU law and policy, and the participation of the Länder in the EU decision-making process is likely to minimise the risk of infringements due to a lack of full understanding of EU legislation. An important task of the Land Representation to the EU is to inform the Land Government about any new EU law/policy development that is relevant to the Land and about the position of the various players, including partners of the Land (for example, the other 'motors'). In this way, the Land has time to prepare for the implementation of the EU law/policy and/or for working out a position.[11]

There are two channels through which the Land can play a role in matters concerning the EU: (1) the national route and (2) direct external engagement of the Land in the EU political arena.[12]

(1) National route—the national route, i.e. the involvement of the Länder in the EU decision-making process via national participation routes, is based on two participation channels: *A)* the Bundesrat and *B)* the Landtag (the parliament of the Land).

A) Participation through the Bundesrat[13]—the Länder shall participate in matters relating to the EU through the Bundesrat. Full and accurate flow of information on

---

[10] An infringement can result from legislative, administrative or jurisdictional State acts. This is established by § I(1) of the law on the division between the Federation and the Länder of costs resulting from the infringement of supranational and international obligations (Lastentragungsgesetz [LastG]) contained in Article 15 of the law accompanying the 2006 federalism reform (Föderalismusreform-Begleitgesetz): in *BGBl.*, I, 2006, p. 2098. A special regulation is provided by Article 109(5) GG for the violation of the parameters set by the 'European Stability and Growth Pact'. Under such circumstances, the Federation will carry 65 % and the *Länder* 35 % of the overall burden of the sanctions applied by the EU to the Federal Republic pursuant to Article 126 (11) TFEU (ex Art. 104 EC). Cf. Panara (2011), pp. 151 ff.

[11] Since 1959, the Länder have had a common observer (Länderbeobachter) in Brussels. He is appointed by the Conference of the Land ministers responsible for the EU (Europaministerkonferenz, EMK in acronym) and works closely with the Permanent Representation of the Federal Republic of Germany to the EU. The observer is entitled to attend the EU advisory and institutional bodies' meetings, but he is not allowed to participate in discussions or to vote. The observer's task is to pass all useful information to the Länder. The work of the Länderbeobachter is regulated in detail by the Erfurt Agreement of 24 October 1996 between the Länder (Abkommen über den Beobachter der Länder bei der Europäischen Union).

[12] On this summa divisio, cf. Panara and De Becker (2011), pp. 307 ff.

[13] The Bundesrat (lit. 'Federal Council') participates in federal legislation and administration and in matters related to the EU (cf. Art. 50 GG). It is a national (i.e., federal) constitutional body where the governments of the 16 German Länder are represented at federal level. The members of the Bundesrat are appointed by the Länder Governments. Each Land is allocated a number of votes (from a minimum of three to a maximum of six) on the basis of the size of the respective population (cf. Art. 51 GG). The involvement of the Bundesrat (and of the Bundestag) in affairs concerning the EU is consistent with the acknowledgement that European integration cannot be regarded merely as a matter of foreign policy. It is also an important matter of domestic policy. Cf. Streinz (2007), p. 918 (Rn. 91). This explains why the issue of the participation rights of the Länder was settled via constitutional rules and was not left to agreements between the Federation (Bund) and Länder or to sub-constitutional legislation.

EU affairs is therefore key to the pivotal role of the Bundesrat. To this purpose, the Federal Government has to inform the Bundesrat in an exhaustive and timely manner about all matters in which the Länder may have an interest.[14] The Bundesrat has to participate in EU affairs in two scenarios: first, when it has the right to intervene on a comparable domestic matter and, second, when an issue on the EU agenda falls within the responsibility of the Länder.[15]

The weight of the Bundesrat's opinions concerning EU matters varies in accordance with the topic. The first possible scenario is when the interests of the Länder are affected by an EU proposal falling within the exclusive competence of the Bund (including areas such as defence, air transport, federal railways, etc., cf. Art. 73 GG)[16] or falling within the federal legislative power (notably, for example, the concurrent legislative power of the Bund on economic matters, cf. Art. 74(1) No. 11 GG). In such a case, the position of the Bundesrat does not have a binding character and must be only taken into account (berücksichtigt) by the Federal Government. Consequently, the Federal Government may choose to depart from that position, if it deems it appropriate to do so.[17]

The second possible scenario is when legislative powers of the Länder, the structure of Land authorities or Land administrative procedures are *primarily* affected (im Schwerpunkt betroffen) by an issue on the EU agenda. In such a case, the position of the Bundesrat acquires a quasi-binding (if not a fully binding) value. The Grundgesetz stipulates that the Federal Government must pay to the position of the Bundesrat the greatest possible respect (maßgeblich zu berücksichtigen).[18] It is controversial whether this expression means that the position of the Bundesrat is binding. In practice, only a small minority of the positions of the Bundesrat (about 4 % of the total) are normally regarded as being due the greatest possible respect.[19] In principle, the position of the Bundesrat would have to be reflected in the vote cast by Germany in the Council.[20] An element that

---

[14] Cf. Art. 23(2) GG.

[15] Cf. Art. 23(4) GG. Article 23(4) GG does not set any limits to the cooperation of the Bundesrat on issues concerning the EU. However, § 11 of the EUZBLG excludes the Common Foreign and Security Policy (former Second Pillar) from that cooperation.

[16] The exclusive competence of the Federation includes the issues listed in Article 73 GG, the conduct of relations with foreign states (Art. 32(1) GG), the administration by the Länder on behalf of the Federation (Art. 85 GG), as well as the administration of the Federation (Art. 86 GG).

[17] Cf. Art. 23(5), first subparagraph, GG.

[18] Art. 23(5), second subparagraph, GG. No doubts remain about the non-binding character of the Bundesrat's position when increases in expenditures or reduced federal revenues could result from the approval of an EU proposal. In such events, the Federal Government shall keep the last say. See Art. 23(5), final subparagraph, GG, and § 5(2), sixth subparagraph, EUZBLG.

[19] Cf. Meyer (2008), p. 368.

[20] A conflict resolution mechanism is provided by § 5(2) EUZBLG. It establishes that in the case of an insuperable disagreement with the Federal Government, the Bundesrat can confirm its initial position by a two-thirds majority. The position would become 'decisive' (maßgebend), and in this context the expression is certainly to be intended as synonymous with binding. The conflict resolution mechanism of § 5(2) EUZBLG has found no application so far. There was only one

plays a huge role is also the political reality surrounding the negotiations on the EU level. When the position of the Länder is likely to obtain a majority within the Council, the Federal Government will normally defend that position and vote in accordance with it. When, however, the position of the Länder is clearly incapable of obtaining a majority, the Federal Government may decide to take a different, more realistic, approach and depart from that position in exchange for the support of other Member States on a different topic.[21]

The experience shows that there is normally unanimity between the Länder within the Bundesrat in relation to education. This subject is very controversial internally, within each Land, but when issues concerning education are on the EU agenda, the Länder always manage to find a unitary position to present to the Federal Government. Quite the opposite, protection of the environment and energy policy are topics where it is more difficult to achieve large majorities in the Bundesrat due to the different views of the Länder. An example of successful engagement of the Länder was their 'pressing' on the Federal Government in relation to the Europe 2020 targets (Smart Growth), one of which concerns specifically education (reducing the rate of early school leaving below 10 % and having at least 40 % of 30–34-year-olds completing third-level education). The German Länder obtained the inclusion in the final document setting the targets for the single Member States of a target for Germany of 42 % tertiary education by 2020, inclusive of ISCED 4 (International Standard Classification of Education Level 4).

An even more advanced form of participation, at least on paper, is provided for by Article 23(6) GG, which stipulates that when an EU proposal focuses primarily (im Schwerpunkt) on school education, culture or radio/TV broadcasting, which are key matters belonging to the exclusive legislative responsibility of the Länder, the rights of Germany in the relevant EU fora (Council, working groups of the Council, committees of the Commission) are exercised by a representative of the Länder delegated by the Bundesrat.[22] For what concerns the Council, such participation relies on Article 16(2) TEU, which allows for the representation of a Member State in the Council by a representative 'at ministerial level', including a Minister of a Land, 'who may commit the government of the Member State in question and cast its vote'. Yet, at least in the Council, this form of external representation of the Länder has remained mainly on paper, having been used only on very few occasions.

---

occasion, involving Directive 96/61/CE of 24 September 1996 on integrated pollution prevention and control, in which the conflict was so acute that the Bundesrat nearly confirmed its initial position by 2/3 majority. However, an agreement was ultimately achieved.

[21] The Bund actually remains responsible for the nation as a whole: cf. Art. 23(5), second subparagraph, GG.

[22] Art. 23(6), first subparagraph, GG. However, when Germany holds the Council presidency, chairing Council meetings remains always and invariably a responsibility of the Federal Government (cf. §6(3), first subparagraph, EUZBLG). In the Coreper and in the working groups of the Council, the Länder are represented by the representatives of two Länder, one ruled by the CDU and one ruled by the SPD.

At least in theory, the Bundesrat can play a role in the EU decision-making process also through the early warning system. However, the extreme difficulty to achieve the quorum for a yellow or an orange card explains why it does not use this tool very much. For this reason, the Länder prefer to use the political dialogue that has been launched by the Barroso Commission since 2006, albeit only on important issues (for example, the political dialogue on the added value tax directive in 2013).[23]

B) The role of the Landtag of Baden-Württemberg—in the context of the German executive federalism (Exekutivföderalismus), i.e. of the federal system centred on the pivotal role of the Federal Government and of the governments of the Länder (the members of the Bundesrat are appointed by the Land Governments), the ability of the Landtage (Land parliaments) to have a say on EU affairs is of crucial importance for the democratic legitimacy of the internal EU-related decisional processes. In 2006, the Landtag of Baden-Württemberg created the Europe Committee,[24] which is the leading committee for all the EU proposals that are cross-cutting, i.e., which touch upon more than one issue. The Committee performs a merely advisory role to other committees if only one issue, covered by an existing committee of the Landtag, is involved by an EU proposal. If a proposal, for example, is only about agriculture, it will be for the ad hoc Committee to deal with it. Whilst over the half of the EU proposals before the Landtag concern agriculture, the large majority of these are examined by the Europe Committee as the 'leader' because they involve more than a single issue. The Europe Committee is also the 'leader' on questions concerning the constitutional setting of the EU that affect Baden-Württemberg.[25]

The Land Minister for the Bundesrat, European and International Affairs (or a state secretary on his behalf) must attend the monthly sessions of the Europe Committee. In this way, it is ensured that the position of the Committee is known to the Minister and that there is permanent dialogue and exchange of information between the Landtag and the Land Government.[26]

When an EU proposal focuses primarily on an area of exclusive legislative responsibility of the Länder (education, culture, police law, radio/TV broadcasting), the Landtag may impose an imperative mandate on the Land Government. In such a scenario, the Land Government would be bound to follow the position of the Landtag and to defend that position in the Bundesrat, unless the position is in

---

[23] The new President of the EP Martin Schultz has announced the intention to create a political dialogue also between the EP and the national and regional parliaments.

[24] Since 2011, the Committee also has dealt with the international relations of the Land Baden-Württemberg. The full name of the Committee is Europe and International Committee (Auschuss für Europa und Internationales).

[25] The Europe Committee is convened once a month.

[26] The Land Government has the duty to pass all the relevant EU-related information to the Landtag; cf. Art. 34a (1) of the Constitution of the Land Baden-Württemberg (this article was introduced in 2011). See also §§ 1–7 Gesetz über die Beteiligung des Landtags in Angelegenheiten der Europäischen Union of 17 February 2011 (Law on the Involvement of the Landtag in Affairs of the European Union, EULG in acronym).

conflict with substantial Land interests. In this way, the democratic legitimacy of the Land (and indirectly of the whole internal, i.e., German) EU-related decision-making activity is enhanced.[27]

By contrast, the early warning system is an area of democratic legitimacy introduced by the Lisbon Treaty, which, due to practical realities, does not really seem to work in practice, at least in Baden-Württemberg. Six weeks is too little time for a reasoned opinion. The Europe Committee of the Landtag Baden-Württemberg meets once a month. Furthermore, there are summer holidays, bank holidays, etc. As a result, despite the great theoretical importance of the early warning system to promote multilevel-governance-driven cooperation and legitimacy in the EU (cf. supra Chap. 4), the deadlines are too tight for this instrument to work properly.[28]

The Europe committee can rely on a number of sources of support and expertise. There is a slim support structure with one assistant on a 50 % basis (shared with another committee). There is an advisor for EU affairs whose recommendation the Committee takes and often follows. The Committee can also count on advice from the Land Government, given that the Minister or his representative must participate in the sessions of the Committee. The Committee also has close relations and takes advice from the academia (for example, Tübingen University), but also with research centres (such as the Steinbeis-Europa-Zentrum in Stuttgart, funded by the Land, the cities of Baden-Württemberg and the EU Commission, and the Centre for European Economic Research in Mannheim).

Whilst there is no structured or formal consultation with the local (i.e., sub-regional) authorities (for example, the municipalities) of Baden-Württemberg in relation to EU matters, there is some informal dialogue between these authorities and the Landtag. An area where this type of consultation takes place is, for example, the EU Strategy for the Danube Region, which concerns in particular the towns of Ulm and Sigmaringen.[29]

(2) Direct external engagement of the Land in the EU political arena—there are two main direct participation channels for the Land Baden-Württemberg: A) the representation of the Land by the Land Representation in Brussels (Vertretung des Landes Baden-Württemberg bei der EU) and, but by far less significant, B) the membership of the Committee of the Regions (CoR).

---

[27] Cf. Art. 34a (2), second sentence, of the Constitution of the Land Baden-Württemberg. See also § 9(2) EULG. The Landtag uses this instrument cum grano salis (i.e., not too often). Also, other Länder (for example, Bavaria) feature similar mechanisms of parliamentary participation in EU matters. Baden-Württemberg and Bavaria are the leading Länder for parliament involvement in EU affairs.

[28] See the keynote speech delivered by Prof. Dr. Gabriele Abels at the conference 'Strengthening the role of regional parliaments in EU affairs: challenges, practices and perspectives', Committee of the Regions, Brussels, 2 July 2014.

[29] Strengthening the dialogue with the local authorities on EU matters is one of the key elements of the 2011–2016 Coalition Agreement between the Bündnis 90/Die Grünen (Green Party) and the SPD (p. 74). A priority of the Green–Red Coalition is to protect the public services provided by the Municipalities (e.g., electricity, water supply, local transport, savings banks, broadcasting, etc.) from being emptied by EU competition law (cf. ibidem, p. 74).

A) Land Representation in Brussels—the Land Baden-Württemberg operates an office ('Vertretung', i.e., 'representation') in Brussels with over 20 staff working there on a regular basis. The office, which is a department of the State Ministry (Staatsministerium), is key to the mini-foreign policy (kleine Außenpolitik) of the Land. The main role of the office is to carry out lobbying and networking in the interest of the Land.

Like all other German Länder offices in Brussels, the Land Representation is not in the list of lobbyists. Indeed, the mission of the Representation differs from those of lobbying organisations of big companies in that the Representation has the objective of representing the citizens of Baden-Württemberg on the EU level. Companies like, for example, Bosch or others carry out lobbying directly through their offices or through business organisations. They do not normally approach the Land Representation, though they may occasionally do so. Sometimes the interests of large companies from Baden-Württemberg and of the Representation collide. For example, the recent discussion around rules on car air-conditioning sees Bosch on one side and the Land Baden-Württemberg (ruled by a red–green coalition) on the other, along with organisations such as Greenpeace and other environmentalist groups.[30]

The lobbying activity of the Land Representation must reflect the general interest of the people of Baden-Württemberg, which is represented in the Landtag. To this purpose, the Landtag has one person at the Land Representation with the task of monitoring the activity of the Representation and of passing relevant information onto the Landtag. Also, members of the Landtag try to visit the Representation more and more often by taking part in travels (for example, visits to members of the Commission) and receptions in Brussels. However, the Landtag controls the Land Government, rather than directly and immediately the lobbying activity performed in Brussels. It is a control on the general direction of the Land in its relations with the EU, which is part of the general Landtag–Land Government relationship. The line manager *by law* for the Director of the Representation is the State Secretary General Manager. However, in practice, *politically*, the Director reports to the Minister of European Affairs. The Minister, in turn, gives instructions to the Director and, in particular, indicates the political priorities (i.e., for example, which European proposals need to be prioritised for lobbying purposes, etc.). The Minister ultimately reports to the Landtag. An important avenue of control for the Landtag lies in approval of the budget. By controlling the budget, the Landtag in fact decides on the allocation of resources to the Representation, and in this way it exercises considerable control on that department.

The Land Representation always uses multiple channels to lobby the institutions in the interest of the Land. One very important channel is the Permanent Representation of Germany to the EU, which has over 250 staff. Communication with this staff is essential because the German vote in the Council is cast by a

---

[30] On 25 September 2014, the Commission requested that Germany comply with the MAC (Mobile Air Conditioning) Directive 2006/40/EC aimed at limiting emissions of greenhouse gases.

Federal Government representative (with the very limited exception, which is more on paper than in real life, of Article 23(6) GG). Another key channel is direct contact with the Commission, especially Directors General and members of the Directorates General, especially if they are from Germany or from partner regions, such as the Four Motors or the Danube Macro-Region. To this purpose, the Land Representation organises receptions, events, etc., on a regular basis. These offer opportunities to meet with the relevant policymakers and to speak to them informally.[31] Last but not least, particularly in the post-Lisbon Treaty era, MEPs have become a very important channel. It is of key importance for the Land Representation to speak to rapporteurs and their staff, as well as to the chair of relevant EP committees, speakers and coordinators. Political allegiance (right/left) and nationality do not play a large role in the creation of coalitions. What really matters to the Representation is the position of a MEP on the issue at hand. The Director of the Land Representation regularly attends the meetings of the MEPs and of the European political parties irrespective of their political identity (left/right, etc.).

Whilst making the EU more local by helping to adjust EU policies to local needs, lobbying also raises a serious legitimacy problem, given that probably not all the Länder are necessarily able to spend the same amount of resources on lobbying as the Land Baden-Württemberg. This situation could favour richer and bigger Länder, like Baden-Württemberg vis-à-vis other (smaller and poorer) Länder. Whilst this theoretical legitimacy problem exists, in practice quite often the Länder lobby on different issues, which rules out competition. For example, Bremen (which is a small Land facing financial difficulties) is likely to lobby on issues concerning shipbuilding industry, which are irrelevant to Baden-Württemberg. Still, there might be fierce competition between the Länder for funding from the Commission. However, even there, whilst other Länder's bids may aim to convert the economy or to promote rural development (this is, for example, the case of Bavaria), the bids of Baden-Württemberg aim to reach different objectives (for example, enhancing the quality of products, promoting cooperation, etc.).

As to networking with other regional players, five or six times a year there is a meeting with the representations of the other German Länder and with the German Permanent Representation to the EU. This meeting is designed to facilitate the exchange of information and of best practice, rather than for the development of a common German-wide strategy, which would be in conflict with the very idea of federal autonomy of the Länder. There are working groups on various issues constituted by members of the different Länder. Baden-Württemberg is also a member of the Conference of European Regions with Legislative Power (REGLEG), a network including 73 regions from 8 Member States, of the 4 Motors for Europe (along with Catalonia, Lombardia and the Rhône-Alpes), and of the Danube Region, a macro-regional network involving 14 states.

---

[31] The office headquarters is located in the centre of Brussels. It is equipped for hosting conferences and receptions, including a wooden beer house similar to the typical Beerstuben of Baden-Württemberg.

B) CoR—Germany has 24 Members and 24 Alternates in the CoR. Each Land has at least one Member and an Alternate.[32] At present, Baden-Württemberg holds only one seat in the CoR.[33] This is a very limited representation, considering that Baden-Württemberg is bigger, both in terms of territory and of population, than some Member States. However, membership in the CoR does not seem to be of key strategic importance for Baden-Württemberg. Despite anecdotal evidence that the Commission and the other institutions take its opinions seriously, this general lack of interest on the part of the Land is due to the current lack of decisional power of the CoR (which is a merely advisory body). The CoR is mainly seen as a useful forum for networking, for exchange of information and knowledge, as well as for creating coalitions with other sub-national authorities from across the EU.[34]

Since 2012, there is another participation channel that is available to the EU citizens and, indirectly, to the sub-national players, including the German Länder. This is the European Citizens' Initiative (ECI). In 2013, the Land Baden-Württemberg played a key role in promoting the first successful ECI calling on the Commission to ensure affordable and non-privatised access to water for all EU citizens (Right2Water).

C. Case Study 2: Integration in the EU Through the Involvement of the 'System-Lombardia' in the EU Decision-Making

Like for Baden-Württemberg in Germany, also the position of Lombardia in the context of Italy is prominent due to a number of factors, including geographical location in the middle of Europe, size of the population (nearly ten million, one-sixth of the overall Italian population) and size of the economy (nearly a quarter of the overall Italian GDP).[35] The participation in EU integration and

---

[32] Three representatives are guaranteed for Municipalities and Associations of Municipalities, and a system of rotation among the different Länder is in place for the remaining five seats. See § 14 (2) EUZBLG.

[33] The Land Baden-Württemberg is currently represented by Land MP Wolfgang Reinhart (Member), CDU, who was elected in 2010, before the SPD-Green Party Coalition won the Land election, and by Peter Friedrich (Alternate), SPD, Minister of the Land.

[34] Due to the economic and other differences between the various regions of Germany, it is sometimes difficult to build a common strategy with other German Länder. Therefore, the CoR can be important in order to seek the support of the regions of other Member States.

[35] The 'EU dimension' of the Region Lombardia is apparent if one looks at the size of the EU programmes of the Region Lombardia for the 2014–2020 period: approximately, €970 million (half of which from the EU) in the context of the European Social Fund (ESF), €970 million (half of which from the EU) in the context of the European Regional Development Fund (ERDF), €499 million from the European Agricultural Fund for Rural Development (EAFRD). Cf. Session of the Regional Executive of Lombardia No. 73 of 11 July 2014.

decision-making is established as a duty of the Italian Region Lombardia in the regional Statute of autonomy (regional constitution).[36] In this way, the 'responsibility for EU integration' becomes a part of the institutional mission of the Region. This regional responsibility for EU integration is also embedded in the national Constitution in Article 117(5) ('The Regions ..., in the areas that fall within their responsibilities, take part in preparatory decision-making process of EU legislative acts'). At the same time, like the German Länder, the Italian Regions are responsible for the implementation and execution of Union measures in the fields falling within the regional remit (cf. Art. 117(5), final part, which specifies that the State can exercise substitute powers in the case of non-performance by the Region[37]). It is therefore of key importance to ensure that the regional level is given a say in relation to legal rules that are to be implemented within the regional territory and that may have a huge impact on the economy of this territory.

There are two channels through which the Lombardia Region can play a role in matters concerning the EU: (1) the national route, which is, however, quite weak if compared to the German model, and (2) direct external engagement in the EU political arena.[38]

(1) National route—the national route, i.e. the contribution to the preparation of the national position in EU decision-making fora, is based on the following channels: *A)* participation of the Regions in national consultation fora (State-Regions Conference and Comitato interministeriale per gli affari europei) and, in particular, through the *B)* Regional Council (the regional parliament).

A) Participation in national consultation fora—the Italian Regions may request the submission to the State-Regions Conference (Conferenza Stato-Regioni) of any EU proposal touching upon matters falling within their legislative responsibility.[39] The State-Regions Conference is a political body bringing the national and the

---

[36] See Article 6(2) and (3) of the Statute: '(2) The Region contributes to the process of European integration and is committed to promote, in collaboration with other European regions, the full realization of the principles of autonomy, self-government and regional identities even within the European Union. (3) The Lombardia Region participates, in compliance with the Constitution and the Community legal order, in the making phase of European Union policies'. See also Article 11 of the Regional Law No. 17 of 21 November 2011: '(1) The Region, in the areas that fall within its responsibility and in the pursuance of the aims of the Statute, takes part in the programmes and projects of the European Union. (2) Furthermore the Region promotes the knowledge of the activities of the European Union among the local authorities and the other public and private bodies within the regional territory and favours their participation in the programmes and projects of the European Union'. On the participation of the Italian regions in the EU decision-making process, cf. Villamena (2011), pp. 157 ff. See also Gaeta (2 July 2014), passim.

[37] The only example of exercise of substitute powers is the suspension in 2006 by a Government Decree Law of the application of a statute of the Liguria Region. This statute was in breach of Directive 79/409/EEC of 2 April 1979 on the conservation of wild birds. On this occasion, the State intervention followed an Order of the President of the ECJ issued in the context of an infringement case against Italy (cf. Order of the President of the ECJ in the Case C-503/06). Cf. supra Chap. 2.

[38] On this summa divisio, cf. Panara and De Becker (2011), pp. 307 ff.

[39] Cf. Art. 24(4) Law of 27 November 2012.

regional governments around a table for discussion and negotiation of issues relevant to the regional level.[40] However, apart from healthcare, which is a field where the Regions are vested with important responsibilities and which has a huge impact on public expenditures, this body does not play a key role in determining the national position of Italy in the EU. Furthermore, the national government is not bound to adopt the regional position, not even in areas falling within the regional legislative remit.

A delegate nominated by the Regions takes part in the meetings of the Comitato interministeriale per gli affari europei (CIAE, Interdepartmental Committee for European Affairs) when the issues on the agenda are of interest for (i.e., do not necessarily fall within the legislative responsibility of) the Regions. This body discusses EU affairs with the aim of deciding the position of Italy on the EU level. However, like in the State-Regions Conference, the State Government is not bound to take account of the regional views, not even if it is an area of regional legislative responsibility.[41] Yet both the State-Regions Conference and CIAE can contribute legitimacy to the Italian involvement in the EU, if and to the extent that the regional voices are taken duly into account in the formulation of the Italian position in EU decision-making fora.

B) The role of the Regional Council of Lombardia[42]—full legitimacy of partic-ipation in the EU decision-making process requires that due account is taken of the prerogatives of democratically representative bodies within regions. Like for the Landtage in Germany, and particularly for Baden-Württemberg, the role of the Regional Council of Lombardia in the EU decision-making process is protected by law. The Regional Council shall pass an annual resolution by the end of January each year evaluating the annual Work Programme of the EU Commission and laying down the guidelines for the action of the Regional Executive in the EU.[43] In addition, the Regional Council can pass a resolution laying down instructions for the Regional Executive concerning the position of Lombardia in relation to a

---

[40] Cf. Constitutional Court Ruling No. 116 of 1994: '[The Conference] is the privileged forum for discussion and negotiation of policy between the State and the Regions'.

[41] Cf. Art. 2(2) Law of 27 November 2012. The work of CIAE is supported by the Comitato tecnico di valutazione degli atti dell'Unione europea (expert committee for the evaluation of EU measures). Each Region can send a representative to take part in the works of those working groups that deal with issues that are relevant to the Regions. Cf. Art. 19(5) Law of 27 November 2012.

[42] The incumbent (since 2013) President of the Regional Council, Raffaele Cattaneo, is promoting the role of the Regional Council in EU affairs and more in general of regional parliaments in the EU by promoting academic and political debate on this important issue. Cattaneo is in the Subsidiarity Working Group of CALRE, which is the only permanent working group of CALRE.

[43] The approval of this resolution shall occur in the context of the annual EU session of the Regional Council. The EU session also includes the examination of the conformity/nonconformity of regional legislation with EU law and the approval of the annual regional law implementing EU legislation in the regional territory (legge europea regionale). See Art. 3(1) of Regional Law No. 17 of 21 November 2011.

certain EU proposal. In this way, the direction of the engagement of Lombardia with the EU is put under the influence and control of the Regional Council.

The Council may even require that an EU proposal is put on the agenda of the State-Regions Conference, where this will be discussed with the aim to reach a mutually acceptable common position for Italy on the EU level.[44] In this way, the regional parliament is granted a say on the working of a body that includes only the representatives of the regional governments. However, as previously explained, the State-Regions Conference has not been able so far to play a key role in determining the Italian position in the EU.

The Regional Council carries out a scrutiny of *subsidiarity* of EU proposals relevant to the Region and can require the Regional Executive to take action accordingly in the national and EU cooperation fora open to the Region.[45] The Lombardia model emancipates the engagement of the Region with subsidiarity concerns from consultation of the Regional Council by the national Parliament. The Regional Council *itself* takes the initiative to adopt a resolution on subsidiarity and communicates the resolution to the Regional Executive, the national Parliament, the Committee of the Regions and the Conference of the Presidents of the Legislative Assemblies of the Italian Regions and of the Autonomous Provinces. In addition, the Regional Council of Lombardia, like any other regional parliament with legislative power, 'can' also be consulted by each Chamber of Parliament in the context of the early warning system.[46] However, until recently, this tool has not produced any impact on the work of the Lombardia Regional Council. The Regional Council passed the first resolution expressing subsidiarity concerns in relation to the proposal of a Regulation on organic production and labelling of organic products.[47]

The Lombardia Region also promotes the involvement of the Municipalities, of other local authorities and of other public and private entities in EU activity by informing them about Union law and policy and by facilitating their participation in

---

[44] Cf. Art. 6(2) of Regional Law No. 17 of 21 November 2011.

[45] Cf. Art. 7(1), (2) and (3) of Regional Law No. 17 of 21 November 2011.

[46] Article 8(3) of Law No. 234 of 24 December 2012 stipulates that the Chambers 'can consult' (*possono consultare*) the Councils and Assemblies of the Regions and of the Autonomous Provinces of Trento and Bolzano. See the 'foundation provision' in Article 6(1) of the Lisbon Subsidiarity Protocol.

[47] COM/2014/0180. Cf. Regional Council Session of 27 May 2014 and EU Committee (First Committee) Session No. 10 of 14 May 2014. The Italian Senate completed the subsidiarity scrutiny on 27 May 2014 with no subsidiarity/proportionality concerns (see Resolution of the Agriculture Committee of the Senate issued on 27 May 2014, Doc XVIII n. 63/17ma (IT) available, along with an English summary, from the website www.ipex.eu, accessed September 2014). The examination by the Chamber of Deputies started on 20 May and has not been completed. This episode reflects the sceptical view, shared by experts and by many staff within the Lombardia Region, that the early warning system as currently structured fails to enforce regional interests effectively.

EU programmes and projects.[48] For example, an important task of the Delegation of the Region Lombardia to the EU is to inform regional stakeholders and potential bidders from the regional territory (companies, etc.) about EU funding opportunities.

(2) Direct external engagement in the EU political arena—there are a few direct participation channels for Lombardia: A) the representation of the Region by the Delegation to Brussels, B) the appointment of regional experts to working groups of the Council and committees of the Commission and, but like for Baden-Württemberg by far less significant, C) the Committee of the Regions (CoR).

A) Regional Delegation to Brussels—since 1998, Lombardia has an office in Brussels (Delegazione). The mission of the office is to strengthen the coordination between the policies of the Region and those of the EU. The Delegation aims to represent and promote the 'System-Lombardia' on the EU level. The concept of 'System-Lombardia' is designed to mean a synergy of regional players, including the stakeholders from the regional territory, aimed to facilitate involvement in EU affairs and to build a coordinated engagement with the EU.[49] The role of the Delegation is to represent the interests stemming from the regional territory, rather than the Region as an abstract entity and to make sure that Lombardia works as a 'system'. To this purpose, the Delegation offers support to regional stakeholders in order to improve their performance in Brussels. In this context, the lobbying activity of the Delegation has to be understood as lobbying for the regional territory. For example, in relation to renewable sources of energy in Lombardia, due to the intensive agriculture and the presence of livestock in the Pianura Padana, there is an interest in investments on energy production from biomasses. The task of the office is to lobby the Commission and the other institutions to obtain the provision of some EU funding for this type of renewable energy. Another example is Horizon 2020. The delegation convened an informal discussion table in Milan inviting all the regional stakeholders. Following from that, a common position was developed, and it was played on various tables in Brussels (as a regional actor, as a private association of lobbyists, as a state, etc.). Since on many issues there are diverging views among the stakeholders, the role of the Delegation is to identify elements that are common to all of them (or at least to as a large as possible coalition) and then to find allies (companies, Member States, other regions, etc.) on the EU level.[50]

---

[48] Cf. Art. 11(2) of Regional Law No. 17 of 21 November 2011. On the involvement of these players in the annual 'EU session' of the Lombardia Regional Council, cf. Art. 3(2) of Regional Law No. 17 of 21 November 2011.

[49] The stakeholders are all grouped within the Casa della Lombardia. This is a representation of key economic and social players from the regional territory (including, for example, the Conference of the Rectors of the Universities of Lombardia; Assolombarda, which is an association of approximately 5,000 firms from Milan, Lodi, Monza and Brianza; Expo2015; the Regional Agency for the Protection of the Environment; the Regional Council of Lombardia; etc.

[50] For example, in relation to Expo2015, the common ground among the stakeholders was found in the fight on counterfeiting of grocery products. This proposal found the support of about 60 other European regions and led to the production of a petition paper for the Commission and the

The lobbying activity of the Delegation is addressed to the Commission (especially after the Treaty of Lisbon), the MEPs (especially, albeit not exclusively, those who are from Lombardia, irrespective of political allegiance[51]) and the Permanent Representation of Italy to the EU. Working with the Permanent Representation, in particular, is of key importance, given that the national government, not the sub-national players, has the right to vote in the Council. State-Regions coordination, i.e. the search for a common position to be upheld in the Council, takes place in Brussels more than in Rome. Often the State-Regions dialogue needs to involve only some Regions or even only one (for example, if the issue on the agenda concerns a particular cultivation that takes place in a few Regions, only these will be invited to the table).

B) The participation of Lombardia in the EU decision-making process takes place also through the appointment of regional experts taking part in the national delegations involved in the activity of the working groups and committees of the Council and of the Commission (Comitology).[52] The regional representative becomes a component of the Italian delegation to the EU, and in this way he can contribute to formulate the national position in EU decision-making fora. The limitation of this mechanism is that the regional expert must teamwork with the national delegation. He cannot take a separate and/or different stance in case of an irreconcilable disagreement with the national government. Working with the government and getting the government on its side are therefore essential for the Region. This is required by the need to guarantee the unitary position of the Italian Republic, which is an expression of the duty for Italy to speak with a single voice in the EU political arena.[53]

European Parliament. The entire lobbying activity in Brussels is based on variable coalitions with other territories and stakeholders.

The labelling of origin of products is one of the key issues on the agenda of the regions, and it is one of the ways in which the regions promote themselves and their economy on the EU level. To an extent, it demonstrates that the EU is really a 'Europe of regional and local territories and economies' rather than (only) of the nation-states, which are largely artificial creations.

[51] Occasionally, however, when there is a political division in the territory, this is reflected by the behaviour of the MEPs. For example, on the quality of air there was a division among stakeholders and among political parties in Lombardia, and this was reflected in the behaviour and engagement of the MEPs.

[52] Article 6(4) of the Regional Law No. 17 of 21 November 2011 stipulates: 'In the circumstances indicated by the law, the regional Executive (= the regional government) communicates to the Office of Presidency of the regional Council (= the regional parliament) the names of the experts identified by the Region who take part in the delegations of the (national) Government in the activities of the working groups and committees of the EU Council and of the Commission'. See also Article 5(1) of Law No. 131 of 5 June 2003 ('La Loggia' Law).

[53] Cf. Article 5 of the Italian Constitution, which defines the Republic as 'one and indivisible'. In the literature, see Parodi (2003), pp. 41 ff. Article 5 of Law No. 131 of 5 June 2003 ('La Loggia' Law) stipulates that when matters of exclusive legislative competence of the Regions are on the agenda of the Council, a President of a Region can be appointed head of the Italian delegation to the Council. Yet pursuant to Article 16(2) TEU, 'The Council shall consist of a representative of each Member State at ministerial level, who may commit the government of the Member State in question and cast its vote'. Therefore, the State representatives in the Council must have 'ministerial' dignity. Unlike in Germany, the Italian constitutional law does not confer ministerial status to the Presidents of the

C) CoR—despite the fact that not all the Italian Regions are entitled to a seat in the CoR, two-thirds of the 24 seats allocated to Italy are assigned to the regional authorities. Due to the political weakness of the CoR, in the past Lombardia did not ask to be represented in it and used to leave a seat available to the neighbouring Region of Piemonte (until recently almost always ruled by the same centre-right coalition). Things, however, changed with the new legislature period (2013 onwards), when the President of the Regional Council of Lombardia became Member of the CoR. Nonetheless, the CoR continues to be seen by regional policymakers from Lombardia essentially as a forum for networking and exchange of information and/or best practice rather than as an institution capable of channelling regional interests effectively, especially those of a player such as Lombardia with the size and problems comparable to a state.[54]

A key feature of the current European strategy of Lombardia is to get involved in regional networks, such as the Four Motors and especially the Alpine Macro-Region.[55] In this way, a critical mass for accessing EU funding more easily can be reached and also a critical mass to have a stronger voice in Europe and a more direct relationship with the EU.

All in all, it would appear that participation mechanisms on the national level (State-Regions Conference and CIAE) are for Lombardia less effective than direct contact with national authorities and EU policymakers. This is particularly true in relation to attracting EU funding to the regional territory, especially Horizon 2020, Euranet Plus, etc. It must be noted that EU funding has become a key issue for Lombardia during the last few years due to the fact that due to the high sovereign debt of Italy there is less funding available for the regional territory from the central government than 5–10 years ago.

Regions. In any case so far, this provision has remained on paper only, and no regional representative has ever been appointed head of the Italian delegation. Cf. Villamena (2011), p. 171.

[54] At present, Lombardia is represented in the CoR by one Member, President of the Regional Council Raffaele Cattaneo, and one Alternate, a Regional Councillor. Interestingly, whilst most other Italian Regions are represented by members of the Regional Executive, the Region Lombardia has chosen a different approach. This certainly evidences the current commitment of Lombardia to strengthen the role played by its Regional Council in the EU. At the same time, it needs to be highlighted that since 2013 Lombardia is ruled by a coalition that includes the Lega Nord of the incumbent Head of the Regional Executive, Roberto Maroni, and the Nuovo Centrodestra led by the President of the Regional Council, Raffaele Cattaneo. Membership of the CoR by the President of the Regional Council can therefore be seen also as a way to enhance the political visibility of the smaller coalition partner.

[55] The EU Strategy for the Alpine Region (EUSALP) was launched by the European Council of 19–20 December 2013. It involves five Member States (Austria, France, Germany, Italy, Slovenia) and two non-Member States (Liechtenstein and Switzerland). Lombardia also engages in transfrontier cooperation with other regions, for example in the framework of ARGE ALP, a working community of ten Alpine regions from Austria, Germany, Italy and Switzerland. Last but not least, Lombardia coordinates the Italian participation in the Alpine Space Programme and the Interregional Programme ESPON (both largely funded through the ERDF). In this capacity, it participates in the relevant international and EU fora. Cf. Session of the Regional Executive of Lombardia No. 56 of 28 March 2014.

D. Case Study 3: Integration in the EU and 'Region Building'—Liverpool City Region and the Merseyside Brussels Office (MBO)

The combined authority named Liverpool City Region was created on April 2014. It includes Liverpool City Council, four metropolitan borough councils within Merseyside (Knowsley, Sefton, St Helens and Wirral), the local enterprise partnership (Liverpool City Region Local Enterprise Partnership[56]) and the unitary authority of the adjacent Borough of Halton in Northwest of England. It is a federation of local authorities (most of which are located in Merseyside) with strategic powers over economic development, regeneration and transport, all of which are profoundly affected by EU legislation and policy. Accordingly, it is of key importance for the Combined Authority to engage properly with the EU, both in the implementation phase and in the promulgation of EU law and policy.[57]

In England, there is no formal procedure for the involvement of the local authorities in the EU lawmaking and policymaking process that is comparable to that existing for the devolved administrations of Northern Ireland, Scotland and Wales.[58] Yet a number of EU policies on transport, environment, economic matters, etc., produce a huge impact on the life of the local communities and their economy.[59] In England, like in Germany and in Italy, there is a responsibility of the sub-national level of government for European integration. This involves both 'passive' (implementation of EU law/policy) as well as 'active' dimensions (participation in the promulgation of EU law/policy). The passive dimension originates directly from EU law and the jurisprudence of the Court of Justice. All public authorities, whether national or sub-national, must comply with EU law and implement it for what is within their remit.[60] This stance is also reflected in the

---

[56] Local enterprise partnerships (LEPs) are voluntary partnerships between local authorities and businesses established in 2011 by the Department for Business, Innovation and Skills to help identify local economic priorities and promote economic growth and job creation within a certain local area. Currently (September 2014), there are 39 LEPs in operation across England.

[57] Liverpool City Region Combined Authority was established on 1 April 2014 under the Local Democracy, Economic Development and Construction Act 2009. The current (September 2014) membership of the Combined Authority is as follows: Phil Davies (Chair of the Combined Authority, Wirral), Ron Round (Vice Chair of the Combined Authority, Knowsley), Rob Polhill (Halton), Joe Anderson (Mayor of Liverpool), Barrie Grunewald (St Helens), Peter Dowd (Sefton) and Robert Hough (Liverpool City Region LEP).

[58] On these mechanisms, see the Memorandum of Understanding and Supplementary Agreements of September 2012 and in the literature Varney (2011), pp. 275 ff.

[59] Cf. Varney (2013), pp. 353–354.

[60] Cf. ECJ Case 72/81, *Commission v Belgium* [1982] ECR 183, and Joined Cases 227-230/85 *Commission v Belgium* [1988] ECR 1. See also ECJ Case 8/88 *Germany v Commission* [1990] ECR I-2321 at 2355–2366. In the literature, cf. Lenaerts and Van Nuffel (2011), pp. 629–631; Schaus (1994), p. 79. See also the Case 103/88 *Costanzo Spa v Comune di Milano* [1989] ECR 1839, according to which every administrative body must apply EU law and set aside any domestic rules conflicting with it. Cf. supra Chap. 2.

jurisprudence of UK courts.[61] Furthermore, pursuant to the Localism Act 2011, local authorities face potential responsibility for failures to comply with EU obligations, and in the Act there are mechanisms aimed to ensure compliance with EU law by local authorities (see Part 2 of the Localism Act 2011).[62]

The active dimension of the responsibility for European integration emerges principally from the nature of the English local authorities as it results from the Localism Act 2011. Section 1 of the Act, which could be considered as a part of the UK constitution, stipulates a general power of competence of the local authorities. In this way, these authorities are established as pleno jure representatives of the local community. Subject to existing limitations in the law, this wide-ranging power of the local authorities includes the right to look after all the interests stemming from the local community even beyond the mere local dimension. Many local interests may have a national or European dimension. For example, a piece of EU of legislation could have a particular impact on a certain portion of the UK territory or on the economy of a given community. In such circumstances, the local authorities are constitutionally entitled, even required, to engage with the EU to represent and defend the interests of their community. In the era of European integration, engagement with the EU can be seen as an integral part of the constitutional mission of English local authorities.

The key instrument for the engagement of Liverpool City Region (and previously of Merseyside) with the promulgation of EU law and policy is the Merseyside Brussels Office (MBO), which was established in 1996 to represent Merseyside at the heart of the EU. Following the creation of Liverpool City Region in April 2014, in the near future MBO is likely to be renamed 'Liverpool City Region Brussels Office'.[63] MBO is very small in comparison to its homologues of Baden-Württemberg and Lombardia (currently, only one staff member works at MBO). However, it is of a similar size and budget to most offices from the Northwest of England.

The Office is entirely funded through the subscriptions paid by its local partners. Currently, these include a wide spectrum of territorial authorities (Knowsley Metropolitan Borough Council), specialised agencies (Merseyside Fire and Rescue Service, Merseytravel, Merseyside Recycling and Waste Authority), higher education institutions (Liverpool University) and organisations with a broader mission (Liverpool City Region LEP, Liverpool Vision, Network for Europe). To an extent, it can be argued that the current MBO membership reflects a combination of Type I (based on territorial authorities) and Type II (based on task-specific authorities) multilevel governance arrangements. In this way, the MBO, like in particular the office of Lombardia (cf. supra Sect. C), aims to represent the 'Merseyside system',

---

[61] This can be argued in particular from the House of Lords in *Factortame Ltd v Secretary of State for Transport (No. 2)* ([1991] 1 AC 603 and from the Court of Appeal in *Thoburn v Sunderland City Council* [2002] EWHC 195 (Admin).

[62] Cf. Varney (2013), pp. 354–355.

[63] Jenkins and Sharples (no date but 2014), slide 7.

including a variety of territorial authorities, specialised agencies, research institutions and economic players.[64]

The MBO is overseen by a Strategic Board on which all MBO partners have a seat. On the Board there are officers, not elected politicians. Local politicians are involved only occasionally in the work of the MBO. As a result, the accountability of the Office and its connection to the local community (the citizen) appear to be very limited. Whilst things may change significantly following the creation of the Liverpool City Region Combined Authority, at present it is impossible to consider the Office as an accurate projection of the local community at the EU level. Also, there seems to be no effective antidote to prevent the possibility that the lobbying activity of the Office could reflect the priorities of some 'powerful' local stakeholders (the subscribers) rather than those of the wider community.[65] For example, whilst there are local working groups on specific issues (such as waste management, transport and regeneration), there is no cross-sectoral grouping or overarching policy grouping developing a democratically legitimated strategy for the Office. Admittedly, the positive results achieved by MBO in the interests of its partners generate output legitimacy for the Office. However, there seems to be no or inadequate input legitimacy from the perspective of the local community. The MBO has tried to overcome this issue by involving democratically legitimated non-partner stakeholders in the development of a Merseyside strategy on certain issues. For example, waste collection, waste prevention and disposal of waste, these are issues for which the lead authority is the Merseyside Recycling and Waste Authority, and also Liverpool City Council and other local authorities participate regularly in the activity of the relevant working group.[66]

---

[64] Type I multilevel governance, whose prototype is federalism, includes general-purpose territorial jurisdictions (states, regional and local authorities). These 'bundle together multiple functions, including a range of policy responsibilities, and in many instances, a court system and representative institutions'. In this context, 'every citizen is located in a Russian Doll set of nested jurisdictions, where there is one and only one relevant jurisdiction at any particular scale'. Type II multilevel governance embraces 'task-specific jurisdictions', such as specialised agencies and task-specific organisations that provide a certain local service, select a product standard, monitor water quality in a particular river and so forth. On the Type I–Type II distinction, see Marks and Hooghe (2004), pp. 15 ff. The quotes in the text can be retrieved, ibid. pp. 16–17. Cf. also Hooghe and Marks (2003), pp. 233 ff.; Hooghe and Marks (2010), pp. 17 ff. Cf. supra Chap. 3.

[65] Jenkins and Sharples (no date but 2014), slides 4 and 5, propose that the MBO should be included in the governance structure of the Liverpool City Region Combined Authority. Accordingly, the MBO should receive core funds on behalf of the partners of the Combined Authority. In this way, the MBO will switch from a 'subscriber-led' to a 'strategy-led' approach.

However, the problem of a 'subscriber-led' agenda for the MBO is already (before the reform of the Office) partly counterbalanced by the fact that all the current subscribers belong to the (admittedly wide category of the) public sector. Accordingly, their institutional mission and their lobbying activity in Brussels should be driven by the sectoral public interest pursued by them. Currently, only one subscriber is a democratically legitimated public authority that is a direct and democratic expression of a local community (Knowsley Metropolitan Borough Council).

[66] These arrangements do not seem to be enough to ensure the democratic and input legitimacy of the MBO. To this purpose, it seems to be required the following: (1) the creation of a clear

There are four areas of work of the MBO: (1) policy, (2) funding, (3) partnership, (4) promotion.

(1) Policy—this area of work concerns both the implementation phase (i) and the promulgation of EU law and policy (ii). (i) In relation to implementation, the role of the Office is to obtain information at an early stage of the decision-making process and to pass this information on to the local authorities. In this way, the implementation of EU law and policy at local level is significantly facilitated by MBO. (ii) In relation to the creation of EU law and policy, the role of the Office is to lobby the relevant EU policymakers in order to obtain law and policy that suit and reflect the interests of the local partners in the best possible manner. An example of successful lobbying activity is that carried out by the MBO in relation to the ERDF. In the past, ERDF Objective 1 included those regions whose GDP was below 76 % of the average EU GDP. All other regions fell in a different group. By lobbying collectively with other regional authorities, MBO succeeded in obtaining the creation of a new category, the transition regions, whose GDP is between 75 and 90 % of the average EU GDP. This is convenient to Merseyside, as its GDP falls within this group of regions.[67]

Lobbying is carried out by the Office by pursuing several channels: A) Commission, B) UK Permanent Representation to the EU (UKRep), C) European Parliament.[68] Due to its institutional role as the representative of Merseyside (i.e., of a local community) on the EU level, the MBO (like the representations of Baden-Württemberg and of Lombardia) is not a registered lobbyist.[69]

A) Commission—the Office contacts relevant policymakers working at the Commission, in particular the members of the relevant commissioner's cabinet. Like most other regional offices and lobbying organisations, sometimes the MBO organises social events and receptions during which it is easier to approach the relevant people informally and to talk about the interests of Merseyside.

B) UKRep—there are regular contacts between the MBO and members of the UKRep. For example, in relation to Regional Policy, the relevant contact person is the responsible for this policy area in the UKRep. These contacts are of key importance for the MBO because it is ultimately the national government that is entitled to cast the UK vote in the Council. However, the MBO does not always find in the UKRep an ally. For example, the UK government was against the

---

reporting line for the MBO in the context of Liverpool City Region Combined Authority and (2) greater engagement of the MBO with the local community. In this way, it would be possible to achieve closeness and openness of the EU action on the local level and democratic legitimacy of the action of the Office. Cf. Panara and Varney (2014), pp. 3 ff.

[67] On the EU Regional Policy and specifically on the ERDF, cf. Bovis (2011), pp. 90 ff.

[68] The MBO does not currently do any work with the CoR (even though occasionally in the past the MBO has used also that channel). Currently (September 2014), Merseyside has no Member or Alternate in the CoR. Potentially, though, despite the lack of decisional power of the CoR, this could be an important avenue for the promotion of the image of Merseyside on the EU level and especially for networking with other sub-national authorities.

[69] Cf. Transparency Register at http://ec.europea.eu/transparencyregister/info/homePage.do?redir=false&locale=en (accessed September 2014).

introduction of the transition regions in the context of ERDF for the 2014–2020 period. On that occasion, the MBO acted beyond the UK government (in this way setting a striking example of multilevel governance in the EU at work or of regional foreign policy[70]). In addition to the work with the UKRep, there is a regular exchange of information between the MBO and the UK government in London. Occasionally, there are also direct contacts between the MBO and policymakers from the Westminster government to discuss issues, for example, on environmental matters and transport, which are particularly key to Merseyside.

C) European Parliament—Especially since the role of the European Parliament has been enhanced by the Treaty of Amsterdam and the Treaty of Lisbon, another important channel for the MBO is the contacts with those MEPs, irrespective of nationality, who are rapporteurs or chairs of the relevant committees within the European Parliament.[71]

(2) Funding—the second area of work of the MBO is to promote awareness at local level on available EU funding and to lobby the EU policymakers during the budgeting process in order to obtain that the EU funding is shaped in the most expedient manner for Merseyside (i.e., in a way that suits the features and ability of local players). The activity of the MBO also includes receiving clarifications from EU policymakers on how funding and application processes work and on the correct meaning of the applicable legal rules. Through this set of activities, the MBO aims to maximise the chances of success for local applicants.

The MBO does not have the task of encouraging partnerships for structural funding or of encouraging applications for structural funding from the local level (these are the tasks of the national government through the National Growth Board and its local EU sub-committees). However, the MBO brings funding opportunities to the attention of potential applicants and offers support for their applications.[72]

(3) Partnership—the third area of activity of the MBO concerns the creation of networks with other players on the EU level, especially other regions of the Northwest of England.[73] This networking activity leads to the exchange of best practice, to the preparation of joint funding bids and to joint lobbying concerning policy.

(4) Promotion—the fourth and final area of activity of the MBO concerns the promotion of the image of Merseyside. For example, the MBO played a role in relation to important events, such as the Liverpool European Capital of Culture (2008) and the International Festival for Business organised by Liverpool Vision

---

[70] On the concept and legal implications of 'paradiplomacy' as a regional mini-foreign policy potentially disconnected from the foreign policy of the Member State, cf. Panara and De Becker (2011), pp. 330–331.

[71] There is no privileged contact or relationship with UK MEPs.

[72] ERDF programmes that are particularly relevant to the work of the MBO are Horizon 2020, Creative Europe and LIFE Programme for the environment.

[73] A tangible sign of the cooperation among regional players from the Northwest of England is the location itself of their Brussels offices. All these offices are currently based in the same building in Rue du Trône 4.

(Liverpool, 2014). In relation to these events, the role of the MBO consisted in advising the MBO partners on how to apply for funding and how to organise the events.

As mentioned previously, among the partners of the MBO there is Liverpool University. As a partner of the MBO, Liverpool University participates in the local groupings, and in this way it contributes to shape policy through academic know-how.[74] More specifically, Liverpool University and the MBO are jointly trying to inform the public debate locally by becoming a source of critical thinking for local public policy development. An example of this type of activity is the organisation of events on issues that are key to local policy formulation. In this way, Liverpool University and the MBO promote partnerships with local politicians who are interested in becoming aware of EU policy initiatives.[75] The MBO has also done some work in cooperation with other (currently non-MBO partner) higher education institutions based in Merseyside, such as Liverpool John Moores University (LJMU).[76] The close link between research/academia and the work of MBO can be seen as very positive because it brings the Office closer to important local players (Liverpool University and LJMU, together, have a student population of about 50,000 in addition to the staff) who are able to provide research-based non-market-driven advice (Table 5.1).

E. Concluding Remarks

In all the examined case studies, there emerges a duty, as well as a right, of the 'regions' to participate in the EU decision-making process. This 'duty' has been called 'responsibility for integration in the EU' and incorporates an obligation to work on the EU level in the interests of the local community and territory. This is a result of the nature of the 'region' as a public law entity, which is expression of a territorial community. As a result, this entity has to pursue the interests of the community both when an interest has a local dimension and when it has a supra-national (EU) dimension, i.e., it is impacted on by EU law and policy.

---

[74] An example of impact generated by Liverpool University is on the Maritime Agenda. The EU Commission has tried to increase its work on this field. Obviously, this is an area of interest for Merseyside, and Liverpool University has provided a considerable amount of knowledge.

[75] At Liverpool University, there is a research institute organising events concerning local policy issues, and the MBO often collaborates with them. Liverpool University is also a member of the European grouping of universities, where all research areas are represented, promoting public and regional engagement.

[76] For example, through the MBO, Liverpool John Moores University (LJMU) became involved in the regional research network. At present (September 2014), LJMU is studying the opportunity to become a partner of the MBO.

Table 5.1 Summary of regional involvement in EU lawmaking and policymaking in Baden-Württemberg (BW), Lombardia (L) and Merseyside (M)

	CoR	Direct participation in the Council	Work with the Member State's permanent representation	Participation in the works of Council and Commission's working groups and committees (comitology)	Brussels Office	Second chamber or other domestic fora	Work with MEPs	Associations & networks for joint lobbying and joint funding bids	Early Warning System	ECI
BW	Y	(Y)	Y	Y	Y	Y (Bundesrat)	Y	Y	(Y)	Y
L	Y	(Y)	Y	Y	Y	Y (State-Regions Conference and CIAE)	Y	Y	(Y)	(N)
M	N	N	Y	N	Y	N	Y	Y	N	(N)

A few trends were highlighted in the previous analysis. These include the tendency to represent the region as a 'system' on the EU level (for example, the 'System-Lombardia'), i.e., to use the regional contact channels with the EU as a way to defend the interests of regional stakeholders (companies, research institutions, specialised agencies, etc.). This is a result of the eclipse of a rigidly defined 'remit' of the various players in the context of EU multilevel governance. The regions do not act necessarily *only* in the areas falling within their remit as defined by the national constitution. They engage on the EU level any time this is required by the need to protect interests rooted in the local community and territory. Arguably, multilevel governance in the context of European integration has led to partly overcoming the rigid allocation of responsibilities that is traditionally adopted by national constitutional law. This tendency is exemplified also by recent legislative innovations at national level. The Localism Act 2011 introduced in the UK a general power of competence of local authorities (see Part 1, Chapter 1 of the Act). According to this, subject to existing limitations in the law, local authorities have a responsibility to take care of all the interests stemming from the local community, even if these interests have a dimension that goes beyond the mere local level, for example a European dimension. Another tendency emerging from the previous analysis is that in the case of Liverpool (and also in Lombardia), both Type 1 (the regional authority) and Type 2 multilevel governance players (specialised agencies, such as transport or waste and recycling authorities, etc.) are involved in lobbying activity on the EU level.

Another thread common to the three case studies is that direct contacts with the national government (or with the permanent representation in Brussels) and lobbying are generally perceived as more effective communication channels than national mechanisms of participation in the EU. This is especially the case in Italy, where the participation mechanisms (State-Regions Conference and CIAE) are rather weak, and in England, where there is no structured form of participation for local authorities in determining the national position in relation to the EU. The situation is more complicated in Germany, where, thanks to the Bundesrat, the participation of the Länder in EU affairs is potentially more influential. Even in Baden-Württemberg, though, it emerges that direct communication with the EU institutions or the permanent representation of Germany is typically perceived by local politicians and public officials as more effective than internal participation through the Bundesrat. This is essentially due to the fact that internal participation requires horizontal cooperation (i.e., coordination with the other Länder), in addition to vertical cooperation (i.e., coordination with the Federal Government), and this can be both difficult and time consuming.

Lobbying of the Commission, the MEPs, etc., is therefore the primary tool used by the regions to play a role in the EU political arena. However, lobbying requires appropriate resources (e.g., skilled staff, adequate budgetary provision) and particularly the ability to create alliances with other players. This explains why a key element of the strategy of all the analysed regions is to take part in regional networks both for lobbying purposes and for reaching a 'critical mass' for attracting EU funding to the regional territory.

The practical importance of lobbying alongside (or even above) domestic participation channels may raise legitimacy issues. National coordination mechanisms aimed to define the national position in the Council are typically based on the involvement of all the relevant sub-national players on an equal footing. Direct lobbying by sub-national players or networks of national players does not offer a comparable guarantee in terms of objective legitimacy of the EU decision-making process. A key issue in this context is promoting the accountability of the regional offices in Brussels to the local community, as well as making sure that the lobbying activity pursues democratically selected interests originating from the local community. The previous analysis highlights that more 'structured' regions, such as Baden-Württemberg and Lombardia, where the office is a part of the executive branch and the regional government is under the control of the regional parliament, are better equipped to subject the selection of interests to the democratic control of the local community. By contrast, the situation is more fluid and ambiguous in Merseyside, where the office is not immediately accountable to elected politicians and is not adequately linked to the wider local community.

The national participation mechanisms in place for the regional players in Germany and in Italy contribute to reshaping the role of the nation-state in certain areas of regional responsibility. In these areas, the central government should become a coordinator of regional interests. However, the system, despite its importance for legitimacy purposes, does not always hold together for two main reasons. First, because the entire 'philosophy' of the national participation system revolves around a rigid concept of 'remit' (for example, legislative remit), moving from the assumption that the simple circumstance that the regions have responsibilities in a certain field generates automatically an interest in participating in the formation of the national position in the EU. In reality, the previous analysis suggests that, irrespective of the regional remit (i.e., also outside and beyond such remit), more practical interests, for example economic activities taking place in the regional territory, are far more likely to generate an interest in participating in the EU decision-making process on the national and EU levels.

Second, the system does not hold together because it is based on the idea that the national government, i.e. the nation-state, can always coordinate successfully the interests of the regional players. The experience demonstrates that this is not always the case and that the regions are sometimes in disagreement with the national government (as well as with fellow regions from the same country). For this reason, regional players, especially those with sufficient resources to play a role on the EU level, if they cannot have the central government on their side, may choose to lobby the EU institutions directly and to take part in asymmetrical and changeable coalitions of regions, Member States, associations, etc., which push towards solutions opposed by the government of the own Member State.

Engagement of sub-national players on the EU level, along with asymmetrical and variable coalitions (alleanze a geometria variabile) among sub-national authorities and other players, is an important component of the EU atypical participatory democracy (this concept will be further developed in the next chapter).

References

C. Bovis, The role and function of structural and cohesion funds and the interaction of the EU regional policy with the internal market policies, in *The Role of the Regions in EU Governance*, ed. by C. Panara, A. De Becker (Springer, Heidelberg, 2011), pp. 81 ff

U. Fastenrath, *Kompetenzverteilung im Bereich der auswärtigen Gewalt* (C.H. Beck, München, 1986)

C. Gaeta, Scrutinizing regional governments on EU affairs: exchange about legal provisions, existing instruments and best practices. Presentation at the conference 'Strengthening the role of regional parliaments in EU affairs', CoR, Brussels, 2 July 2014, at http://cor.europa.eu/en/events/Documents/Gaeta%20CoR%202.6.2014.pdf. Accessed Sept 2014

L. Hooghe, G. Marks, Unraveling the central state, but how? Types of multi-level governance. Am. Polit. Sci. Rev. **97**(2), 233 f. (2003)

L. Hooghe, G. Marks, Types of multi-level governance, in *Handbook on Multi-Level Governance*, ed. by H. Enderlein et al. (Edward Elgar, Cheltenham, 2010), pp. 17 ff

H. Jenkins, J. Sharples, *The Merseyside Brussels Office – Update on New Supports Arrangements*, slides presentation, no date (but 2014)

W. Kluth, Die Integrationsverantwortung der Landesparlamente. Landes- und Kommunalverwaltung (LVK), (7), 289 f. (2010)

K. Lenaerts, P. Van Nuffel, *European Union Law*, 3rd edn. (Sweet & Maxwell, London, 2011)

M. Lindh et al., *Fusing Regions? Sustainable Regional Action in the Context of European Integration*, Nordic Council of Ministers Research Programme Report (2009)

G. Marks, L. Hooghe, Contrasting visions of multi-level governance, in *Multi-Level Governance*, ed. by I. Bache, M. Flinders (OUP, Oxford, 2004). pp. 15 ff

H. Meyer, *Die Föderalismusreform 2006: Konzeption, Kommentar, Kritik* (Duncker & Humblot, Berlin, 2008)

M. Nettesheim, *Die Integrationsverantwortung der Länder – Folgerungen aus dem Urteil des Bundesverfassungsgerichts vom 30. Juni 2009 ("Lissabon-Urteil")*, Tübingen, 30 July 2009

M. Nettesheim, Die Integrationsverantwortung – Vorgaben des BVerfG und gesetzgeberischen Umsetzung. Neue Juristische Wochenschrift (NJW) (4), 177 f. (2010)

C. Panara, In the name of cooperation: the external relations of the German Länder and their participation in the EU decision-making. Eur. Const. Law Rev. **6**(1), 59 f. (2010)

C. Panara, Germany: a cooperative solution to the challenge of the European integration, in *The Role of the Regions in EU Governance*, ed. by C. Panara, A. De Becker (Springer, Heidelberg, 2011). pp. 133 ff

C. Panara, A. De Becker, The role of the regions in the European Union: the "Regional Blindness" of both the EU and the Member States, in *The Role of the Regions in EU Governance*, ed. by C. Panara, A. De Becker (Springer, Heidelberg, 2011). pp. 297 ff

C. Panara, M. Varney, *Promoting 'Openness' and 'Closeness' of the EU to the Citizen: Preliminary Thoughts on How to Enhance the Role of Merseyside Brussels Office in 'Bringing Europe Home'*, research report to the Merseyside Brussels Office, 7 September 2014

G. Parodi, Interessi unitari e integrazione comunitaria negli ordinamenti decentrati. La "razionalizzazione" degli strumenti di garanzia del principio unitario, in *La definizione del principio unitario negli ordinamenti decentrati*, ed. by G. Rolla (Giappichelli, Torino, 2003), pp. 41 ff

I. Pernice, [Comment to] *Article 32 GG*, in *Grundgesetz. Kommentar*, vol. 2, 2nd edn. ed. by H. Dreier (Mohr Siebeck, Tübingen, 2006), pp. 771 ff

A. Schaus, L'exécution des traités. Revue belge de droit international **27**(1), 66 f. (1994)

R. Streinz, [Comment to] *Article 23 GG*, in *Grundgesetz. Kommentar*, ed. by M. Sachs, 4th edn. (C.H. Beck, München, 2007). pp. 895 ff

M. Varney, Devolution and European representation in the United Kingdom, in *The Role of the Regions in EU Governance*, ed. by C. Panara, A. De Becker (Springer, Heidelberg, 2011). pp. 275 ff

M. Varney, Local government in England: localism delivered? in *Local Government in Europe: The 'Fourth Level' in the EU Multi-Layered System of Governance*, ed. by C. Panara, M. Varney (Routledge, London/Oxford, 2013). pp. 330 ff

S. Villamena, State and regions vis-a-vis European integration: the "Long (and Slow) March" of the Italian regional state, in *The Role of the Regions in EU Governance*, ed. by C. Panara, A. De Becker (Springer, Heidelberg, 2011). pp. 157 ff

Chapter 6
The Constitutional Dimension of Multilevel Governance in the EU

A. The EU Polycentric System of Governance

A territorial authority is the expression of a territorial community that normally includes all the people who reside in a certain larger or smaller territory. Among the territorial authorities, the state reflects what legal scholars often indicate as 'state community', i.e., a group that may coincide with the 'nation', the 'citizens' or, more extensively, all those who, irrespective of their nationality, live in a certain territory or are anyway subject to the regulatory and coercive power of a given state.[1]

A community, however, is not the only constitutive element of a territorial authority. A territorial authority must have a territorial jurisdiction and an institutional structure, that is, it must have an organisation and rules that apply to the organisation and the members of the group (for example, the rules on the organisation of the state or of a municipality, a state law regulating certain economic activities, the building or traffic regulation of a municipality, etc.).[2]

The sub-national territorial authorities are characterised by the fact that they are 'self-governed', i.e., they enjoy some political autonomy within the framework of the nation-state and are entitled to pass democratically legitimated decisions on issues falling within their territorial and material remit.[3] In the context of a

---

[1] Cf. Crisafulli (1970), pp. 52 and 57–63. On the concept of 'community' from a sociological perspective, cf. Weber (1999 [1922]), pp. 38–40, and Tönnies (1955 [1887]), passim.

[2] This notion of 'territorial authority' is influenced by Santi Romano's theory of legal order. Cf. Romano (1951). See also Giannini (1993), pp. 96–101.

[3] The notion of self-government is laid down by Article 3 of the European Charter of Local Self-Government. The first paragraph of Article 3 sketches out the contours of political autonomy: 'Local self-government denotes the right and the ability of local authorities, within the limits of the law, to regulate and manage a substantial share of public affairs under their own responsibility and in the interests of the local population'. The second paragraph of the same Article outlines the democratic nature of local self-government: 'This right shall be exercised by councils or assemblies composed of members freely elected by secret ballot on the basis of direct, equal, universal

© Springer International Publishing Switzerland 2015
C. Panara, *The Sub-national Dimension of the EU*,
DOI 10.1007/978-3-319-14589-1_6

'multilevel polity', i.e. of a polity like the contemporary state, constituted by a plurality of levels of government (central, regional, local), no territorial authorities may exist in isolation. These coexist and interact in a number of ways with the other levels of government.

Typically, the sub-national authorities are established, and their essential elements are regulated by the state constitution (for example, in relation to their fundamental role and prerogatives). In a sense, the sub-national authorities are 'created' by the state, if not *historically* (many sub-state groups and entities pre-exist the state), at least *legally*, insofar as they derive their current authority from the state constitution. However, thanks to their autonomy, they live their own life and are subject to the state only to a limited extent. For example, they can create their own networks with other sub-state authorities nationally and internationally, including their contacts with the EU through offices in Brussels and/or European associations of sub-national authorities.

European integration places a further echelon of power above the nation-states, at supranational level. Since its foundation in 1957 and up to now, the Community (later Union) has seen its sphere of activity expanding both *territorially*, due to its progressive enlargement, and *materially*, because of the inclusion of an increased range of powers in the Treaties and because of the judicial activism of the ECJ. Accordingly, also the nature and role of the European nation-state have changed dramatically since 1957, with an increasing shift of power from the domestic to the supranational arena.[4]

The Union is able to enlarge its sphere of competence by using the procedure set in Article 352 TFEU, but this requires *unanimity* among the Member States. Also, despite the pro-integration activism of the Court of Justice, which introduced the principle of supremacy of EU law, direct effect, the doctrine of indirect effect, the principle of State liability, etc., there is a compelling argument testifying the survival of the core of state sovereignty. Even if the Union has been created for an unlimited period of time, the Member States have the right to dismantle it through a new treaty or to withdraw from the Union. In this way, they can still *theoretically* do what the units of a typical federation are not entitled to do; they can recover their original full sovereignty. Accordingly, from a strictly legal point of view, the *ultimate sovereignty* continues to belong to the Member States.[5]

---

suffrage, and which may possess executive organs responsible to them. This provision shall in no way affect recourse to assemblies of citizens, referendums or any other form of direct citizen participation where it is permitted by statute'. Cf. Panara (2013), pp. 369–375. Specifically on political autonomy, cf. Giannini (1993), pp. 307–310.

[4] Cf. Art. 5(2) TEU: 'Under the principle of conferral, the Union shall act only within the limits of the competences conferred upon it by the Member States in the Treaties to attain the objectives set out therein. Competences not conferred upon the Union in the Treaties remain with the Member States'. Partial exceptions to the requirement of an explicit legal basis for Union's action are the implied powers of the Union and the flexibility clause of Article 352 TFEU. Cf. Lenaerts and Van Nuffel (2011), pp. 120–124.

[5] Cf. Art. 50 TEU. This is, for example, quite clearly the British position. See the case *Macarthys Ltd v Smith* ([1979] ICR 785 at 789) per Lord Denning: 'If the time should come when our Parliament deliberately passes an Act – with the intention of repudiating the Treaty or any

Yet denying that the Member States have significantly diluted (or 'fused'[6]) their sovereignty within the Union would simply overlook legal and political realities. The impact of the Union on the national (and sub-national) level is much broader than one can read at first glance in the Treaty. All the traditional 'hard cores of sovereignty' have been affected by European integration. Key decisions concerning welfare and taxation, especially in the Member States belonging or aiming to join the Eurozone, are largely under the influence of the EU. The Member States remain in control of some traditional aspects of state sovereignty, such as police, foreign policy, defence, albeit even these are subject to increasing forms of coordination on the EU level through Police Cooperation and the Common Foreign and Security Policy, respectively.[7]

The greater presence of the regions on the EU level is closely linked to the constitutional evolution that has taken place in some Member States since the creation of the European Community. A considerable wave of decentralisation has swept across the Member States between the 1970s and the early years of the new century. Important milestones of this transition are the Italian Regions becoming operational in 1970,[8] the full transformation of Belgium into a federal state in 1994,[9] the progressive creation of a 'unitary decentralised state' in France since 1982,[10] the introduction of devolution in the UK in 1998[11] and the constitutional reforms in Germany in 1994 and 2006 aiming to strengthen the position of the

---

provision in it – or intentionally of acting inconsistently with it – and says so in express terms – then ... it would be the duty of our courts to follow the statute of our Parliament'. Accordingly, it would appear that the UK Parliament is still free to repudiate the Treaty and not to comply with obligations under it. See also *Thoburn v Sunderland City Council* [2003] QB 151 (per Laws LJ). On federalism and sovereignty, cf. de Vergottini (1990), pp. 837–838. On national sovereignty in the context of European integration, cf. Jakab (2006), pp. 375 ff.

[6] Cf. Wessels (1997), pp. 268 ff.

[7] Interestingly, also traditionally intergovernmental areas of Union action, such as the Common Foreign and Security Policy, are becoming increasingly supranational (i.e., increasingly subject to the scrutiny of supranational institutions such as the European Parliament and the CJEU). In the Case C-658/11 *Parliament v Council*, the European Parliament succeeded in having annulled a Council decision relating to the EU's anti-piracy operation off the coast of Somalia (a matter of CFSP) for lack of information provided to it by the Council. By failing to do so, the Council had impeded the European Parliament in exercising its 'democratic scrutiny' (cf. para. 79 of the judgment). In this way, the CJEU also showed its willingness to exercise its judicial scrutiny on certain aspects of the 'sovereignty-sensitive' field of the Common Foreign and Security Policy.

[8] Act No. 108 of 17 February 1968 and Act No. 281 of 16 May 1970.

[9] Cf. the profound modification of the Belgian Constitution, which led to the publication of a new coordinated version of the Constitution in the Belgian Official Journal on 17 February 1994. The new Article 1 of the Constitution states that Belgium is a federal state composed of Communities and Regions. Cf. also the Special Act of 16 July 1993 (which came into effect on 1 January 1994), later amended by the Special Act of 8 August 1980.

[10] Cf. Act of 2 March 1982 and Constitutional Act of 28 March 2003.

[11] Cf. Scotland Act 1998, Government of Wales Act 1998, Northern Ireland Act 1998.

Länder at home and in the EU.[12] The net result of this situation is that now the sub-state territorial communities do enjoy a much stronger role in the EU multilevel system of governance. If until approximately 1992 (Treaty of Maastricht) the EU could be plausibly described as a system of 'concentric circles' (EU, Member States, sub-state levels) with the nation-state as its fulcrum, since 1992 the situation is substantially different and the EU appears to be a more 'polycentric' system of governance in which the nation-state has handed over considerable part of its previous fulcrum role both upwards, to the Union, and downwards, to the sub-national authorities.

B. Multilevel Governance in the EU 'Constitutional Space'

A constitution is a fundamental law dictating crucial aspects of the life of a polity, such as the allocation and exercise of political power, the basic relationship between the government and the governed, the civil, political and social rights of the citizens. In the EU Member States, it would be impossible to find all the answers concerning the constitutional system *only* by looking at a single national constitution. This is due to the fact that a considerable portion of political power is vested in the EU. Accordingly, the Union is concerned with the same fundamental constitutional questions that, prior to European integration, were limited to the state. The regulation and limitation of power, checks and balances, the protection of fundamental rights and nearly every other constitutional problem all gained a crucial space on the European agenda. Constitutional language and methodology do no longer apply exclusively to the state and are increasingly used in relation to the work and structure of the European edifice. A European constitutional space has emerged consisting of the constitutional laws of the Member States and of EU law.[13]

---

[12] Cf. Constitutional Revision Act of 27 October 1994 and Constitutional Revision Act of 28 August 2006 (better known as 'Föderalismusreform', i.e. reform of the federal system). Spain and Portugal joined the European Community in 1986 as a regional state (Spain) and as a unitary regional state (Portugal), respectively. Austria joined the European Union in 1995 as a federal state. In 2001, both Belgium (Special Act of 13 July 2001 modifying the Special Act of 8 August 1980) and Italy (Constitutional Revision Act No. 3 of 18 October 2001) have significantly strengthened the position of their sub-state territorial authorities.

[13] On the concept of European legal space (*europäischer Rechtsraum*), cf. Huber (2008), pp. 442–448. The use of a constitutional language is not a new feature in EU law. Cf. Case 294/83 *Parti écologiste "Les Verts" v EP* [1986] ECR 1339, where the Court for the first time defined the EEC Treaty as the 'constitutional charter' of the Community (para. 23). Cf. also Opinion of the Court of Justice 1/91 of 14 December 1991 concerning the Agreement for the creation of the European Economic Area [1991] ECR I-6079 (para. 1); Joined Cases C-402/05 P and C-415/05 P *Kadi v Commission and Council* [2008] ECR I-6351 (para. 281). In *Kadi*, the Court also referred to the 'constitutional architecture of the pillars' (para. 202); pointed to the 'constitutional principles of the EC Treaty, which include the principle that all Community acts must respect fundamental

This feature of the European legal system is well captured by von Bogdandy's description of it as a system of 'partial' or 'complementary' constitutions (*Teilverfassungen*), both dealing with the same fundamental problem, the exercise and limits of public power.[14] In a similar way, Pernice develops his 'multilevel constitutionalism' theory, which construes the European legal system as a 'constitutional composite' (*Verfassungsverbund*) resulting from the national constitutions and the EU primary law, once again highlighting that the national constitutions do no longer cover the entire spectrum of exercise of public power within the EU sphere of influence.[15]

Multilevel governance is a product of the European legal/constitutional space. This concept is not linked *exclusively* to the national legal order *or* to the EU legal order. Its constitutive elements stem from the combined and coordinated work of the national constitutional system(s) and of the EU. Only a holistic approach, the combined analysis of the domestic system(s) and of the EU, can provide a satisfactory answer in relation to the status of the sub-national authorities in the EU or in relation to the coordination between sub-national authorities and the EU. Multilevel governance is *legally* and *methodologically* part of the complex European constitutional space. As suggested in Chap. 2, a number of elements corroborate this submission:

1) In the EU multilevel system, Treaty making/amendment is not an exclusive prerogative of the Member States. In some Member States, the sub-national authorities are involved in these processes, and in the case of Belgium each regional parliament can veto the entry into force of a new Treaty.
2) The lawmaking process in the Council is not entirely 'State dominated'. The sub-national entities enjoy participation rights that result from the combination of EU and national processes.
3) The sub-national authorities have a duty to comply with EU obligations and at the same time a right to implement EU law/policy in the areas falling within their responsibility. In a number of Member States, failure by a sub-national authority to comply with EU obligations causes a financial liability of the responsible sub-national authority and could also originate the exercise of EU-related State substitution powers. At the same time, infringement

---

rights' (para. 285); and, finally, stated that the judicial review by the Court is a 'constitutional guarantee stemming from the EC Treaty' (para. 316). Cf. also the Laeken Declaration of 15 December 2001 and the following Treaty Establishing a Constitution for Europe. The use of constitutional methodology and terminology has become quite common among legal scholars: cf., for example, Lenaerts and Van Nuffel (2005), pp. 1–7; Schütze (2012).

[14] Cf. von Bogdandy (2009), p. 24. See also von Bogdandy (2000), pp. 163 ff.

[15] Cf. Pernice (2010), pp. 102 ff. On Pernice's multilevel constitutionalism theory, cf. Pernice (2009), pp. 349 ff. Birkinshaw's notion of European Public Law entails the very same idea that the national public law [of the UK] has been radically changed by the [UK] accession to the Union. Accordingly, the full understanding of the public law [and of the legal system] in force in one Member State requires looking at both the national and the supranational dimension. Cf. Birkinshaw (2003), especially pp. 361 ff.

proceedings initiated by the Commission are not necessarily a matter regarding exclusively the Member State; the sub-national authorities in some Member States are involved in those proceedings.

4) The ECJ's jurisprudence on locus standi is rather 'State centric', insofar as the sub-national authorities are granted limited rights to challenge Union acts *directly* before Union Courts. However, a holistic analysis embracing both the EU and the Member State level reveals that in some Member States the sub-national authorities can oblige the Member State to initiate judicial proceedings on their behalf. The Treaty of Lisbon introduced the Committee of the Regions' right to bring a direct challenge before the ECJ on grounds of subsidiarity, as well as the right of each chamber of national parliament (including 'second chambers' representing the sub-national authorities) to oblige the State to bring a direct challenge before the ECJ on grounds of subsidiarity.

The status of the sub-national authorities in the EU multilevel system (i.e., the EU-related 'rights' and 'duties' of the sub-national authorities) enjoys a considerable degree of strength and stability. The legal position of these authorities is an outcome of the EU as a 'compound of constitutions' since their position is rooted in the EU primary law (the 'constitutional charter' of the Union) and in the State constitution. Accordingly, multilevel governance is not, cannot be, limited to 'politics' and 'soft law'. This submission will be further scrutinised in the next section.

C. Multilevel Governance Beyond Soft Law

The Lisbon Treaty has rearranged multilevel governance in the EU by acknowledging the role of the sub-national authorities in the architecture of the EU. The key Treaty provisions in this respect are the following:

- Article 4(2) TEU, pursuant to which the Union shall respect the national identities of the Member States 'inherent in their fundamental structures, political and constitutional, *inclusive of regional and local self-government*' (emphasis added).
- Article 5(3) TEU, according to which 'in areas which do not fall within its exclusive competence, the Union shall act only if and in so far as the objectives of the proposed action cannot be sufficiently achieved by the Member States, *either at central level or at regional and local level*, but can rather, by reason of the scale or effects of the proposed action, be better achieved at Union level' (emphasis added).
- Article 10(3) TEU, which entails the aspiration that decisions shall be taken as openly and as closely as possible to the citizen. This provision is part of Article 10 TEU, which is devoted to the democratic principle.

From the Treaty of Lisbon, it emerges that the full realisation of three key principles of EU law (protection of national identities of the Member States, subsidiarity, democracy) requires not only that the powers of the sub-national authorities are protected (protective function of multilevel governance) but especially that the sub-national authorities perform an active role in the EU (dynamic and creative function of multilevel governance). This is particularly evident in the involvement of regional parliaments with legislative powers in the early warning system (cf. Article 6(1) of the Lisbon Subsidiarity Protocol) and in the fact that, if possible, political and administrative decisions shall be taken by the level of government that is closest to the citizen (cf. Article 10(3) TEU). The Treaty of Lisbon aims to enhance significantly the role of the sub-national authorities in order to strengthen subsidiarity and democracy and to ensure the full respect of national identity. In this way, the Treaty of Lisbon makes regional and local authorities become protagonists of the strategic objectives set by the Treaty. The framework established by the Lisbon Treaty has to be translated into EU and Member State laws and practices and also into regional law and practice. The voice given to regional authorities must be reflected by an appropriate legal framing, and this must happen at EU, national and sub-national levels. The concept of regional responsibility for European integration (*Integrationsverantwortung der Länder*) addresses specifically the concern of active participation of the sub-national authorities in the EU and of their willingness and ability to perform an active role in the making phase of EU law and policy (cf. supra Chap. 5).[16]

The absolute importance of the constitutional objectives that the Treaty of Lisbon aims to achieve through and with the cooperation of the sub-national authorities (protection of local/regional self-government as a key aspect of national identity, subsidiarity, democracy) leads to the suggestion that in most national systems, mere soft law arrangements (such as white papers, non-legally binding agreements, administrative practice, etc.), despite their flexibility and potential impact, do not alone suffice for this purpose. Multilevel governance contributes legitimacy to the participation of the Member States in the EU and to the decision-making activity of the Union (cf. supra Chap. 3). This is another key constitutional objective of the Union and of the Member States, which in most national systems cannot be left solely to soft law arrangements. The achievement of these objectives requires a stability that often only hard law mechanisms can provide effectively. This submission is best understood by looking at one of the landmark EU law cases, *Commission v Netherlands* (1987), in which the Court of Justice held that 'mere administrative practices, which by their nature are alterable at will by the authorities', do not ensure an appropriate transposition of the European directives, i.e., do not ensure the achievement of the objectives established at EU level.[17] By the same

---

[16] See Nettesheim (2009), passim; Nettesheim (2010), pp. 177–178. On the 'responsibility for integration' of the parliaments of the Länder, see Kluth (2010), pp. 289 ff.

[17] Cf. Judgment of the Court of 13 October 1987, Case 236/85, *Commission v Netherlands*, ECR 1987, p. 3989. Later confirmed by Judgment of the Court of 15 March 1990, Case C-339/87,

token and mutatis mutandis (directives entail secondary objectives, whilst the Treaty lays down primary objectives), the change introduced by the Treaty of Lisbon needs to be reflected in an appropriate change in legislation and constitutional law. This conclusion does not wipe out everywhere the potential importance of soft law arrangements. The value of these mechanisms can be mostly symbolic (for example, the European Charter on multilevel governance) or even practical (see, for example, the UK memoranda of understanding binding in honour only,[18] which fit perfectly into the peculiar characteristics of the UK constitutional system). It can be concluded that hard law and soft law instruments shall work together towards the achievement of major Treaty objectives (protection of national identity, subsidiarity, democracy through closeness, legitimacy).

Multilevel governance is quite clearly a public law concept. It concerns the exercise of authoritative decision-making, and as a result it does also concern the relationship between the individual citizen and the communities of which he is a member. Multilevel governance demands the introduction at Union, state and local levels of suitable forms of participation of state and sub-state communities in the EU decision-making process and in the implementation of EU law and policy. It also requires an active engagement of the sub-state communities in the EU level. Failure to do so would undermine the achievement of some key objectives established by the Treaty of Lisbon in relation to the protection of a key feature of national identity (regional and local self-government), subsidiarity and closeness to the citizen. Due to its general suit laid down through general propositions, especially by the White Paper on multilevel governance of the Committee on the Regions,[19] and due to its lack of specificity, from a legal perspective multilevel governance can be described as a principle requiring a certain 'method of governance' rather than as a prescriptive set of specific guidelines or criteria. Failure to implement this principle on the national and sub-national levels does not lead sic et simpliciter to the intervention of the Court of Justice or to an infraction procedure. However, in case of noncompliance with the requirements of multilevel governance, for example in case of absence or inadequacy of the legal framework for regional participation in the EU decision-making process, there exists a space for forms of judicial intervention by the Court of Justice and by domestic courts (particularly by the constitutional courts of the Member States). More specifically, Union courts can play a role

1) in relation to the Treaty articles embodying the idea of multilevel governance,
2) particularly in relation to the concept of 'national identity' of Article 4(2) TEU, and

---

Commission v Netherlands, ECR 1990 I-851, and by Judgment of the Court of 17 November 1992, Case C-236/91, *Commission v Ireland*, ECR 1992 I-5933.

[18] Cf. Memorandum of Understanding and Supplementary Agreements of September 2012. This document superseded the earlier Memorandum of Understanding and Supplementary Agreements of December 2001 (Cm 5240).

[19] Cf. Committee of the Regions (2009).

3) in relation to acts of secondary law that contain reference to the concept (principle) of multilevel governance.

Domestic courts can play a role

1) for the enforcement of national multilevel governance arrangements,
2) in relation to the constitutional review of these arrangements, and
3) through the definition of key concepts, such as 'national identity', 'fundamental structures, political and constitutional' and 'regional and local self-government' (cf. Art. 4(2) TEU).[20]

D. The Multilevel Constitutional Foundation of Multilevel Governance

Multilevel governance lays down a 'method of governance' for the EU based on the involvement of sub-national authorities in the making and implementation of EU law and policy. Sub-national territorial authorities are expression of sub-national communities (cf. supra Sect. A). In the words of the Italian legal scholar Massimo Severo Giannini, territorial authorities are 'enti esponenziali' ('exponential entities' or, better, 'representative institutions') of territorial communities. Accordingly, more precisely, multilevel governance requires the introduction and the operation at Union, Member State and sub-national levels of adequate forms of participation of sub-state communities in the EU decision-making process and in the implementation of EU law and policy. Given that consultation and negotiation with the sub-national authorities can take considerable time and resources, the involvement of sub-national entities in the EU decision-making process could impair the efficiency, and particularly the rapidity, of Union decisions. However, albeit the involvement of sub-national players must be engineered in a rational manner and must be as time and cost-effective as possible, it needs to be reminded the ultimate constitutional rationale for regional and local involvement in the EU. This is the *legitimacy* of Union action and of Member States' participation in the EU (cf. supra Chap. 3). Therefore, a limited loss of efficiency and rapidity has to be seen as an acceptable price to be paid for the greater good of legitimacy of Union decisions. Mutatis mutandis, this is a similar toll to that which has to be paid to the democratic process in the context of a democratic and pluralistic society. At this stage of the study, it is required a deeper reflection on the nature and content of legitimacy in the context of multilevel governance at Union (1), national (2) and sub-national levels (3).

(1) Multilevel governance arrangements on the EU level (Committee of the Regions, early warning system, consultation with sub-national authorities and their associations through 'structured forms') aim to promote the objective (i.e., erga omnes) legitimacy of the EU decision-making process and ultimately of

---

[20] Cf. supra Chap. 3.

the EU as an organisation. The legal foundation of the involvement of the sub-national authorities in the EU primary law can be found in three key Treaty provisions: (A) Article 4(2) TEU on the protection of the local and regional self-government by the EU, (B) Article 5(3) on the principle of subsidiarity and (C) Article 10(3) on closeness to the citizen. A Union that would not recognise the role of the sub-national authorities through appropriate arrangements would be at odds with its own constitutional nature as a multilevel system that includes the sub-national authorities and relies on these for the achievement of certain key objectives (protection of national identity, subsidiarity, democracy through closeness to the citizen). Without respect for the role of the sub-national entities, the Union would be undermining the functioning of its own constitutional foundation (the Treaty). At the same time, the Union would be in an irreconcilable conflict with the constitutional laws of those Member States, which attribute crucial importance to local/regional self-government for democracy, separation of powers and good governance. Accordingly, legitimacy for the EU means essentially coherence with its *direct* (the Treaty) and *indirect* constitutional foundations (the constitutions of its 'primary components', i.e., the Member States). The aspiration of the EU is to legitimise itself and its action erga omnes through procedures that are open in principle to *all* the sub-national authorities that fit certain objective criteria (for example, participation in the early warning system is limited to 'regional parliaments with legislative powers'; cf. Article 6(1) Lisbon Subsidiarity Protocol).

The weakness of these forms of regional/local participation on the EU level is that they are not necessarily the most effective routes for single regional and local authorities aiming to obtain tangible results in the framework of the Union decision-making process. For example, the early warning system, for how it is structured, can only exceptionally modify the course of action of the Union, whilst the Committee of the Regions is a merely consultative body despite the increasingly persuasive value of its positions. This situation pushes the sub-national authorities to seek direct contact with the Commission or with MEPs or to use participation channels prompted at national level (for example, the Bundesrat in Germany and other forms of internal coordination at national level).

(2) The participation mechanisms created at national level aim to align the national system of local/regional self-government with the requirements of European integration. If these mechanisms are inclusive and effective, they allow the attainment of two important constitutional aims: the achievement of key Treaty objectives concerning the protection of national identity, subsidiarity and closeness/democracy and also and especially the protection of the Member State constitutional system of local and regional self-government (constitutional identity of the Member State). In this way, national mechanisms (or sub-national mechanisms, when the involvement of local government authorities takes place on the regional level) ensure the legitimacy of the Member States' participation in the EU.

   The participation channels created at national level to promote regional participation in the Council respond to a logic of objective legitimacy and involve all the authorities belonging to the same level of government (for example, all the regions). The inclusiveness of the national participation routes is not always seen by single authorities (especially those that are more powerful and active in the European arena) as the most effective way to protect their interests. Again, like for participation channels on the EU level, the preference of local and regional players often goes to direct contact with the EU or with the national government.[21]

(3) The principal route at regional/local level for participation on the EU level is the creation of regional offices in Brussels with the mission of lobbying the Commission and the MEPs on behalf of the regional/local community. Whilst this participation route is often seen as the most effective by regional/local authorities, because it allows for a direct relationship between the local/regional level and the EU, from a more general perspective lobbying does not appear capable of generating objective legitimacy of Union action. This is due to the fact that politically and economically stronger sub-national players, thanks to greater and better staffed offices in Brussels, are likely to obtain more from their lobbying activity than smaller and weaker players. Also, lobbying is not subjected to procedural rules ensuring an equal weight to all those involved in the negotiation. Yet engagement of the sub-national authorities with the EU is constitutionally required for two reasons: first, because the sub-national authorities, being 'enti esponenziali', have the responsibility of pursuing the interests stemming from the local community at any level, be it local, national or supranational, and, second, because these authorities, like any other national authority or body, have to collaborate for the achievement of all the Union objectives, including the Treaty objectives that command additional sub-national participation in the EU ('responsibility for European integration', cf. supra Chap. 5).

   It is absolutely crucial that the regional offices are accountable to the local community. Only in this way could it be said that the EU has been brought as closely as possible to the citizen (cf. Art. 10(3) TEU) and that the local community is involved in the work of the EU. The Brussels offices of the German Länder and of the Italian Regions are departments of the Land or regional executive branch, and as such they report to the Land or regional minister, who, in turn, is accountable to the Land or regional parliament (cf. supra Chap. 5). Things are more complicated for English local authorities, where often the offices are not an institutional part of the local government (like in Merseyside until the recent creation of the Liverpool City

---

[21] This is particularly the case in Spain, where certain Autonomous Communities, such as Catalonia and the Basque Country, prefer to have a direct communication channel with the Spanish Government and with the EU, rather than participating through the ordinary channels involving all the other Autonomous Communities. Cf. Chicharro Lázaro (2011), pp. 185 ff.; Beltrán García (2012), pp. 423 ff.

Region combined authority on April 2014). They are created by local partners and accountable to a board of managers appointed partly by democratically representative bodies (local authority councils) and partly by non-elected organisations (local service providers, police authority,[22] academic institutions and even local enterprises). The closeness credo of the EU requires that accountability is established towards democratically elected local assemblies. At the same time, openness (which is coupled with 'closeness' pursuant to Article 10(3) TEU, 'as openly as possible to the citizen') requires that the action of the offices is also communicated to the wider community through meetings with the public and any other appropriate channel (local newspapers, radio, TV, Internet, etc.).

E. Multilevel Governance v Federalism and Regionalism

Federal or regional states and the EU based on multilevel governance are all multilevel systems.[23] All of them are constituted by a plurality of mutually interacting levels of government, and from this point of view all of them belong to the same wider family. However, there are some major legal differences between federalism and regionalism, on one hand, and multilevel governance, on the other[24]:

(1) The first and obvious difference concerns the allocation of sovereignty. According to the traditional construction, in regional and federal systems the sovereignty belongs to the central government (called 'state' or 'federation'). Responsibilities are allocated to the different tiers of government by the state or federation (typically by the state or federal constitution). State or federal courts (typically the state or federal constitutional court) adjudicate on the disputes concerning the distribution of powers. In the EU, things work in a different manner. Despite the loss of considerable shares of power, the core of state sovereignty still belongs to the Member States, not the Union. The responsibilities are allocated to the Union by the Member States through the Treaties. The Court of Justice adjudicates disputes concerning the distribution of powers between the Member States and the Union, even though some Member State

---

[22] Although, of course, the police authorities and fire and rescue authorities are indirectly elected as the boards are constituted of local councillors from the local authorities in the relevant areas.

[23] Gary Marks and Liesbet Hooghe argue that the intellectual foundation of what they call Type 1 multilevel governance is federalism. Cf. Marks and Hooghe (2004), p. 17. On the concept of 'multilevel system', cf. Benz (2009), pp. 21 ff.

[24] In the context of this study, it is accepted the opinion that at least in Europe federal and regional states are in fact sub-types belonging to the same typology defined as 'decentralized state' (Volpi) or 'autonomic state' (Reposo). The difference between federal state and regional state is historical and quantitative (e.g., scope of sub-state powers) rather than qualitative. Cf. Volpi (1995), pp. 367 ff.; Reposo (2005).

courts claim to be entitled to annul or to set aside European acts that go beyond the Union's remit.[25]

(2) The second difference is that, unlike federalism/regionalism, multilevel governance in the EU is not a two-level game between a central government (the Union in the case of the EU) and the federated or regional authorities (the Member States' governments in the EU). The two-level game is exactly the 'error' that multilevel governance theory aims to overcome in European studies. The main claim of multilevel governance is that in the EU there are *many* political players at *many* different levels and that the political game within the EU is not merely a Member States' governments'-Union institutions' game. Accordingly, multilevel governance goes beyond federalism, which is largely a two-level game, to include the layers of government at sub-national level (i.e., also the sub-national authorities *within* the Member States).

The concept of 'autonomic state' or the similar concept of 'decentralized state' could be of use for the EU insofar as they embrace all the different layers of government including the local government (i.e. the sub-regional level of government). However, these concepts have been developed in the traditional context of the state, and the EU is not a state but a sui generis polity. Accordingly, the 'autonomic state' or 'decentralized state' framework is not suitable for the EU.[26] Like the European Union, which is a totally unique polity, also multilevel governance in the EU is a unique concept. The EU based on multilevel governance shares many features with other multilevel systems (e.g., federal and regional systems), but it is not entirely traceable back to typical/classical federalism or regionalism.

Multilevel governance in the EU defines the mutual relationship and interaction between layers of government, and in this way it lays down the 'method of governance' of the EU in relation to the role of the different territorial authorities in the European polity. Unlike federalism or regionalism, which is established and regulated primarily by state constitutional law, multilevel governance depends equally upon the contribution of EU primary law and state constitutional law. It

---

[25] See the decision of the Czech Constitutional Court of 31 January 2012 concerning the Slovak Pensions in which the Court declared a judgment of the CJEU ultra vires. See also the recent judgment of the German Federal Constitutional Court (7 February 2014) on the Outright Monetary Transactions (OMT), where the German Court referred the matter to the CJEU for a preliminary ruling. This case (still pending before the CJEU at the time of writing) raises serious concerns. The German Federal Constitutional Court considers giving an ultra vires ruling regarding a decision by the Governing Council of the European Central Bank (ECB) concerning OMT unless the CJEU announces that that decision is partially incompatible with primary law or restricts its scope. See also German Federal Constitutional Court, Ruling 12 October 1993 on the Maastricht Treaty, and Ruling 30 June 2009 on the Lisbon Treaty.

[26] On the concept of 'autonomic state', cf. Reposo (2005), passim. The expression 'autonomic state' is the literal translation of the Italian phrase 'stato autonomico' and echoes the Spanish expression 'Estado de las Autonomías'. On the concept of 'decentralized state', cf. Volpi (1995), pp. 367 ff.

is a typical product of the European constitutional composite (i.e., of multilevel constitutionalism).[27]

F. Multilevel Governance and European Constitutionalism

Constitutionalism is a notion that has been extensively studied and to which a plurality of meanings can be ascribed. In the context of this study, constitutionalism shall be understood in accordance with Article 16 of the Declaration of the Rights of Man and of the Citizen of 1789: 'Toute Société dans laquelle la garantie des Droits n'est pas assurée, ni la séparation des Pouvoirs déterminée, n'a point de Constitution' (A society in which the observance of the rights is not assured, nor the separation of powers defined, has no constitution at all). Within the understanding of this definition, a legal order can be deemed as having a 'constitution' only if it embodies certain guarantees relating to the protection of the rights of subjects and to the limitation of state power.[28]

Multilevel governance in the EU leads to variable, wider and cut-crossing coalitions (*geometrie variabili*[29]) at European and national levels along (asymmetrical) territorial and cultural cleavages. National governments and majority coalitions, as well as Union institutions, are limited in their prerogatives due to the domestic and EU arrangements concerning multilevel governance. Multilevel governance brings to the fore and gives voice to multiple political arenas and players *within* the Member States. In the words of Gary Marks, multilevel governance is 'a system of continuous negotiation among nested governments at several territorial tiers' as a result of 'a broad process of institutional creation and decisional reallocation that had pulled some previously centralized functions of the state' up and down.[30] Such political complexity, with its array of negotiations, agreements and also substantive restrictions, plays a role in contributing to the key mission of constitutionalism of regulating, tying, limiting the exercise of power.

Multilevel governance contributes to constitutionalism in the European constitutional space by limiting the exercise of public power by the Union and the Member States (1) and by expanding the role of the sub-national communities beyond the sub-national and national dimension (2).

---

[27] On the concept of 'form of government' (or 'type of state') in relation to the territorial division of powers in the framework of the state, cf. De Vergottini (2007), pp. 119 ff. and 372 ff.; Pinelli (2007), pp. 194 ff.

[28] Cf. Matteucci (2010 [1964]); Crisafulli (1970), pp. 86–89; Spadaro (2006), p. 2369; Fioravanti (2009). On the history of Anglo-American constitutionalism, cf. the classic McIlwain (1947).

[29] In the Italian political jargon, the phrase 'geometrie variabili' indicates that parliamentary and party political majorities and coalitions may vary in relation to the different issues on the agenda.

[30] Cf. Marks (1993), p. 392. See also Stephenson (2013), p. 820.

(1) More specifically, multilevel governance limits power in two ways:

A) By obliging Union institutions and domestic authorities to comply with a certain procedure (i.e., by determining *how* a majority or a public power has to adopt a certain decision)—in this way, the Union incorporates (albeit it does not necessarily have to take it on board) the point of view of the sub-national authorities in relation to certain policy issues. Examples of procedural requirements are the compulsory (albeit non-binding) opinions of the Committee of the Regions and the need for a national government to discuss and sometimes negotiate the national position in the Council on a certain policy issue with the sub-national authorities.

It needs to be emphasised that this position reflects a direction, a fundamental aspiration, rather than an actual state of the art already in place. This confirms the nature of multilevel governance as a principle and also highlights its dynamic potential for the future development of the Union. Indeed, some procedural arrangements are rather weak due to their limited ability to determine the final outcome of the EU decision-making process. This is the case, for example, of the 'early warning system' and of the consultative activity of the Committee of the Regions (which in its current form has difficulties in representing the whole complexity of the sub-national level within the EU). Other arrangements are stronger to the extent that the decision-making process can be (at least *partly*) (co-)determined by the sub-national authorities. This is the case of some participation mechanisms on the national level, in particular those in place in federal Member States such as Belgium and Germany, which allow the sub-national authorities to decide the national position in the Council when an issue on the agenda encroaches on key regional responsibilities or interests.

B) By determining the substance of the action of Union institutions and of national authorities (i.e., by delimiting *what* a majority or public power can or cannot do)—multilevel governance is essentially a procedural principle (it lays down a method of governance for the EU multilevel polity). However, the procedural requirements of multilevel governance presuppose substantive limitations too. In this way, the action of the Union or of a national majority is also substantively (*inhaltlich*) limited. Examples of substantive limitations are the requirement of no ultra vires action by the Union (which protects the autonomy of national and regional authorities) and the obligation for the EU and the national governments to respect the sub-national entities' right (and duty) to be the first to implement EU law within their remit (precedence right/duty).

Table 6.1 summarises the procedural and substantive limits to power arising from multilevel governance arrangements at domestic and at EU levels:

Table 6.1 Limits to power stemming from multilevel governance

	Procedure	Substance
Domestic level	– Domestic processes for regional/local involvement in EU lawmaking and policymaking – Domestic processes to ensure compliance with EU obligations (e.g., substitute powers that need to comply with a certain procedure) – Regional involvement in the early warning system	– Constitutional constraints on national governments (e.g., regional/local autonomy, subsidiarity) – Implementation of EU law to be respectful of internal division of powers (except for substitute powers) – Member States must set up adequate forms of regional/local involvement in EU lawmaking/policymaking as required by and compatible with national constitutional system
EU level	– Committee of the Regions' compulsory opinions – Duty for the Commission to consult widely before making legislative proposals – Early warning system – EU Regional Policy	– Art. 4(2) TEU – Subsidiarity/proportionality – To an extent/de facto: yellow/orange card in the early warning system – Prohibition of ultra vires action by the Union

(2) Multilevel governance breaks the traditional state monopoly on external relations by granting participation rights to the sub-national entities in the EU lawmaking and policymaking process.[31] By so doing, multilevel governance introduces a limit to the power of the national government in the external arena. This limit concerns both the normal EU legislative process (secondary law) and (but only in some Member States such as Belgium and Germany) the Treaty-making process (cf. supra Chap. 2).

G. Multilevel Governance and Democracy

The democratic deficit of the EU is a recurring Leitmotiv in European studies. Whilst the Union regulates important sectors of public life (consumers' protection, environment, EU citizenship, etc.), the general political direction of the Union is not an immediate expression of the will of the majority of the European people manifested in a general European election. The political direction is determined through negotiations and compromises between a number of players at national and European levels, which are sometimes unintelligible to the lay European citizen.

---

[31] Cf. Panara (2013), pp. 408–412. Cf. also Panara (2010), pp. 82–83.

This is a consequence of the institutional architecture of the Union, which often fosters a feeling of democratic deficit among the European public.[32]

Even though the European Parliament plays a role in the formation phase of the Commission and may oblige the Commission to resign, the Commission is not fully equivalent to an elected government derived from a majority party or coalition within the European Parliament. The 'kingmakers' of the Commission are the national governments, which choose the President of the Commission and propose the Commissioners. Despite the increase in its political weight in the Lisbon Treaty, the European Parliament is not yet comparable to a national parliament in terms of role and powers. The Council, which is the principal lawmaking institution, is only *indirectly* democratically legitimated since the national governments are accountable to the respective national parliaments. In a similar way, also the European Council is only *indirectly* democratically legitimated. The ideological cleavages (left/right, socialist/popular, progressive/conservative, etc.) that are the typical and traditional political divides in the Member States are only *partly* reflected in the European Parliament, where there are different and alternative political groups but there is no clear-cut majority/opposition distinction.[33]

The question is whether multilevel governance has a role to play in enhancing the democratic life of the EU. The rationale for the introduction of multilevel governance is not, at least *directly*, to address the democratic deficit as previously described (institutional architecture, majority/opposition dynamics, etc.). Multilevel governance arises from the need for participation of sub-national entities in the European arena. In this way, it generates a sui generis form of participatory democracy in the EU. In the context of this study, 'participatory democracy' includes any arrangement, other than traditional representative and direct democracy, through which the citizen is enabled to input to the public life of his community.[34] The duty of the Commission to consult *widely* before proposing legislation (cf. Article 2 Protocol on Subsidiarity and Proportionality), the consultation of the Committee of the Regions during the lawmaking process (cf. Article

---

[32] On the democratic deficit in the EU, see Bellamy (2010), pp. 2 ff.; Dahl (1999), pp. 19 and 31; Lord (2001), pp. 641 ff.; Majone (1998), pp. 5 ff.; Moravcsik (2002), pp. 603 ff.; Wimmel (2009), pp. 181 ff.; Representation and Democracy in the EU: Does one come at the expense of the other? (2013).

On the need and requirements for transforming the EU into a parliamentary system, see Jakab (2012), passim.

[33] In the aftermath of the economic crisis, it is emerging a fundamental cleavage between pro-integration (and pro-common currency) and anti-European (and especially anti-common currency) groups. However, it has to be noted that both the first and the second camps include political parties and movements with very different identity, history and tradition. For example, the pro-European camp includes both socialist and popular parties (with the notable exception of the UK Conservative Party), whilst the anti-European camp includes far right or nationalist groups (like the National Front in France), as well as democratic forces (like the Movimento 5 Stelle in Italy) and leftist movements.

[34] On the concept of participatory democracy, cf. Pateman (1970) and Barber (2003). The concept of participatory democracy is harshly criticised by Sartori (2007), pp. 78 ff.

307 TFEU), the 'structured dialogue' between the Commission and the associations of territorial authorities, the involvement of sub-state authorities by the Member States in the formulation of the national position in EU fora can all be considered atypical forms of participatory democracy. It is 'atypical' because the participants are not individuals but sub-state authorities with democratic representative character. More specifically, it is possible to identify the following patterns of participatory democracy:

(i) Consultation, which can be compulsory (e.g., consultation of the Committee of the Regions on certain topics established by the Treaty) or non-compulsory (e.g., generic obligation for the Commission to consult widely)—it can take place on the EU level (e.g., 'structured dialogue' between the Commission and the associations of territorial authorities) or on the national level (e.g., domestic consultation with the regions before determining the position of the Member State in the Council).[35]

(ii) Co-determination by the sub-national authorities of the national position in the EU—co-determination is articulated in different ways in the different Member States (e.g., direct participation in the Council in Germany and Belgium, agreement of the national position with the regions in Austria and Spain, etc.).[36]

The outlined participatory democracy mechanisms contribute to enhance democracy within the Union. Unlike corporations and other private, non-democratically legitimated entities, the sub-national authorities are democratically legitimated organisations that constitute an essential part of the democratic life of their countries. This submission materialises in the Swedish Instrument of Government, whose first chapter stipulates that 'Swedish democracy is founded on the free formation of opinion and on universal and equal suffrage. It shall be realised through a representative and parliamentary polity and through local self-government' (Chapter 1, Section 1, paragraph 2, Instrument of Government). From this constitutional provision, it emerges that local self-government has a prominent role for Swedish democracy.[37] The position is similar in other Member States. The democratic nature of local and regional self-government gives local/regional entities additional authority on the EU level. When their representatives speak in EU lawmaking or other fora, often they speak on behalf of a community that democratically elected them. The added value of their contribution lies in the fact that they act on behalf of a democratically legitimated authority, give voice to a local community/territory and can be held accountable by a local or regional assembly. By granting them a say or by listening to their voice, the Union is actually granting a

---

[35] On the 'dialogue' between Commission and regional/local authorities, see the Commission's Communication (2003). On the structured (or systematic) dialogue, cf. Ricci (2011), p. 122.

[36] Cf. supra Table 2.1. On the involvement of the sub-state entities as a form of participatory democracy, cf. Panara (2013), pp. 411–412; Mangiameli (2006), pp. 460–462, 475–476, 480–481. See also the European Parliament resolution of 14 January 2003 on the role of regional and local authorities in European integration (2002/2141(INI)), at Point 4.

[37] On the local government in Sweden, cf. Persson (2013), pp. 305 ff.

say or listening to a body legitimated to speak on behalf of a community. Admittedly, there are scenarios in which the local or regional representatives represent an entire Member State (e.g., Land Minister sitting in the Council on behalf of Germany) or, at least in theory, an entire sub-national level of government within a Member State rather than an individual community (this is the case of the members of a national delegation to the Committee of the Regions).

Despite its contribution to the democratic life of the Union, multilevel governance gives rise to some short circuits and unresolved issues in relation to certain aspects of democracy:

A) The democratic deficit is not directly addressed by multilevel governance. Multilevel governance does not establish a European democracy based on the majority principle. On the contrary, the atypical participatory democracy created or encouraged by multilevel governance introduces further limits to the powers of the parliamentary majority at domestic level (see, for example, internal cooperation leading to the formation of the national position in the Council) and on the EU level (see, for example, the early warning system, the advisory role of the Committee of the Regions, the wide consultation by the Commission before proposing legislation).

B) The democratic idea is inevitably linked to the equality principle. The different resources (e.g., funding, qualified personnel, equipment, information, technology) afforded by each sub-national authority are likely to allow each player to perform differently in the EU decision-making process. An authority that is able to spend significant resources in lobbying, networking, research, etc., is likely to make its voice heard in Brussels better than smaller or weaker players. To an extent, differences are inevitable in an EU 'united in diversity' and that is a 'constitutional composite' characterised by asymmetry. However, the basic principle of equality, translated into the formula 'one man, one vote', is one of the founding principles of democracy. By bringing multilevel governance into a legal framework, it becomes possible to address the equality concern especially at national level, through the creation of appropriate participation mechanisms that facilitate the involvement of *all* the authorities concerned. The Union too should identify and develop adequate and non-discriminatory communication channels with the sub-national authorities (for example, by selecting sufficiently representative regional or local associations whose internal democratic life is indisputable). The local and regional authorities should develop effective ways to input to the Union's decision-making activity and, more in general, take responsibility to input to the life of the Union (for example, by creating offices in Brussels staffed with highly qualified personnel and also through the appointment of personnel with appropriate qualifications in EU law and policy working in offices at home).

C) Multilevel governance may promote awareness of European integration, its processes and impact on the local level, if local politicians are accountable to local elective assemblies and, more profoundly, to the local public opinion (the local community) for their action on the EU level. This aspect concerns particularly the work of the regional offices in Brussels, whose activity must be reported to local elective assemblies in order to ensure democratic control on it and at the same to bring the EU 'as close as possible to the citizen' as commanded by Article 10(3) TEU.

H. Concluding Remarks

Traditionally, national governments are the domini of the external relations of the nation-state. Things work in a different manner for the Member States of the European Union. Indeed, on the EU level, multilevel governance breaks the state monopoly of external relations by creating a new system of governance. This method of governance is a product of the European constitutional space, i.e., of the combined action of the national and Union constitutional systems. In this way, it is an important example of multilevel constitutionalism at work.[38] Despite many analogies with federalism and regionalism (multilevel polity, cooperation among levels of government, etc.), multilevel governance has an own conceptual autonomy in that it creates a unique multilevel game among supranational, national and sub-national players in the context of the EU. At the same time, the constitutional requirement of participation of the regional and local authorities in EU governance establishes a strong similarity between multilevel governance and the concept of cooperative federalism. It is not a case that some scholars describe the multilevel participation that is typical of multilevel governance as 'double political entanglement' (doppelte Politikverflechtung).[39]

Multilevel governance is essentially a procedural concept laying down a method of governance for the EU. It is linked to the achievement of substantive key objectives of the Union. These are the protection of regional/local self-government as an integral part of the national identity (cf. Article 4(2) TEU), the principle of subsidiarity (cf. Article 5(3) TEU), the principle of openness and closeness to the citizen (cf. Article 10(3) TEU).

Multilevel governance also contributes to constitutionalism in the EU (1) by limiting the exercise of authoritative decision-making power by the Union and by the Member States and (2) by expanding the role of the sub-national communities beyond the sub-national and national dimension. Finally, multilevel governance, even if it does not address directly the democratic deficit of the EU, contributes positively to democracy in the EU through the establishment of an atypical form of participatory democracy. It is 'atypical' because it is based on the participation and involvement of democratically representative territorial authorities in the EU decision-making process.

---

[38] Cf. Pernice (2010), pp. 102 ff.; Pernice (2009), pp. 349 ff.

[39] Cf. Hrbek (1986), pp. 17 ff. The concept of 'political entanglement' (Politikverflechtung) was created by Fritz Scharpf during the 1970s to describe the German federal system. Cf. Scharpf et al. (1976).

References

B.R. Barber, *Strong Democracy Participatory Politics for a New Age*, 2nd edn. (University of California Press, Berkeley, 2003)

R. Bellamy, Democracy without democracy? Can the EU's democratic 'outputs' be separated from the democratic 'inputs' provided by competitive parties and majority rule? J. Eur. Public Policy **17**(1), 2 f. (2010)

S. Beltrán García, Is there a real model in Spain for autonomous communities to participate in the council of the European Union or is it only a mirage? J. Contemp. Eur. Stud. **20**(4), 423 f. (2012)

A. Benz, *Politik in Mehrebenensystemen* (Verlag für Sozialwissenschaften, Wiesbaden, 2009)

P. Birkinshaw, *European Public Law* (Butterworths, London, 2003)

A. Chicharro Lázaro, The Spanish Autonomous Communities in the EU: "The Evolution from the Competitive Regionalism to a Cooperative System", in *The Role of the Regions in EU Governance*, ed. by C. Panara, A. De Becker (Springer, Berlin/Heidelberg, 2011). pp. 185 ff

Commission of the European Union, Communication, *Dialogue with Associations of Regional and Local Authorities on the Formulation on European Policy*, COM(2003) 811, 19 December 2003

Committee of the Regions, *White Paper on Multilevel Governance*, CdR 89/2009, 17–18 June 2009

V. Crisafulli, *Lezioni di diritto costituzionale*, vol. I, 2nd edn. (CEDAM, Padova, 1970)

R. Dahl, Can international organizations be democratic? A skeptic's view, in *Democracy's Edges*, ed. by I. Shapiro, C. Hacker-Cordón (CUP, Cambridge, 1999). pp. 19 ff

G. De Vergottini, *Stato federale*. Enciclopedia del diritto, vol. XLIII (Giuffrè, Milano, 1990)

G. De Vergottini, *Diritto costituzionale comparato*, vol. I, 7th edn. (CEDAM, Padova, 2007)

European Parliament, Resolution of 14 January 2003 on the role of regional and local authorities in European integration (2002/2141(INI))

M. Fioravanti, *Costituzionalismo. Percorsi della storia e tendenze attuali* (Laterza, Bari, 2009)

M.S. Giannini, *Diritto amministrativo*, vol. I, 3rd edn. (Giuffrè, Milano, 1993)

R. Hrbek, Doppelte Politikverflechtung: Deutscher Föderalismus und Europäische Integration. Die deutschen Länder im EG-Entscheidungsprozeß, in *Die Deutschen Länder und die Europäischen Gemeinschaften*, ed. by R. Hrbek, U. Thaysen (Nomos, Baden-Baden, 1986). pp. 17 ff

P.M. Huber, Offene Staatlichkeit: Vergleich, in *Handbuch Ius Publicum Europaeum*, ed. by A. von Bogdandy et al. (C.F. Müller, Heidelberg, 2008), pp. 403 ff

A. Jakab, Compromise strategies in constitutional argumentations before European integration and since. Eur. Const. Law Rev. **2**(3), 375 f. (2006)

A. Jakab, *Full Parliamentarisation of the EU Without Changing the Treaties. Why We Should Aim for It and How Easily It Can be Achieved*, Jean Monnet Working Papers 3, 1–33 (2012)

Representation and democracy in the EU: does one come at the expense of the other? J. Eur. Integr. **35**(5) (2013 Special Issue)

W. Kluth, Die Integrationsverantwortung der Landesparlamente. Landes- und Kommunal- verwaltung (LVK), **7**, 289 f. (2010)

K. Lenaerts, P. Van Nuffel, *Constitutional Law of the European Union* (Sweet & Maxwell, London, 2005)

K. Lenaerts, P. Van Nuffel, *European Union Law*, 3rd edn. (Sweet & Maxwell, London, 2011)

C. Lord, Assessing democracy in a contested polity. J. Common Mark. Stud. **39**(4), 641 f. (2001)

G. Majone, Europe's democratic deficit. The question of standards. Eur. Law J. **4**(1), 5 f. (1998)

S. Mangiameli, The role of regional and local government in European governance, in *Governing Europe Under a Constitution*, ed. by H.-J. Blanke, S. Mangiameli (Springer, Berlin/Heidelberg, 2006). pp. 457 ff

G. Marks, Structural policy and multi-level governance in the EU, in *The State of the European Community: The Maastricht Debate and Beyond*, ed. by A. Cafruny, G. Rosenthal (Lynne Rienner, Boulder, 1993). pp. 391 ff

G. Marks, L. Hooghe, Contrasting visions of multi-level governance, in *Multi-Level Governance*, ed. by I. Bache, M. Flinders (OUP, Oxford, 2004). pp. 15 ff

N. Matteucci, *Breve storia del costituzionalismo* (Morcelliana, Brescia, 2010) [originally published in 1964]

C.H. McIlwain, *Constitutionalism. Ancient & Modern* (Great Seal Books, Ithaca, 1947) (revised edition)

A. Moravcsik, In defence of the 'Democratic Deficit': reassessing legitimacy in the European Union. J. Common Mark. Stud. **40**(4), 603 f. (2002)

M. Nettesheim, *Die Integrationsverantwortung der Länder – Folgerungen aus dem Urteil des Bundesverfassungsgerichts vom 30. Juni 2009 ("Lissabon-Urteil")*, Tübingen, 30 July 2009

M. Nettesheim, Die Integrationsverantwortung – Vorgaben des BVerfG und gesetzgeberischen Umsetzung. Neue Juristische Wochenschrift (NJW) **4**, 177 f. (2010)

C. Panara, In the Name of Cooperation: the external relations of the German Länder and their participation in the EU decision-making. Eur. Const. Law Rev. **6**(1), 59 f. (2010)

C. Panara, The contribution of local self-government to constitutionalism in the Member States and in the EU multilayered system of governance, in *Local Government in Europe: The 'Fourth Level' in the EU Multilayered System of Governance*, ed. by C. Panara, M. Varney (Routledge, Oxford, 2013). pp. 368 ff

C. Pateman, *Participation and Democratic Theory* (Cambridge University Press, Cambridge, 1970)

I. Pernice, The Treaty of Lisbon: multilevel constitutionalism in action. Columbia J. Eur. Law **15**(3), 349 f. (2009)

I. Pernice, Verfassungsverbund, in *Strukturfragen der Europäischen Union*, ed. by C. Franzius (Nomos, Baden-Baden, 2010). pp. 102 ff

V. Persson, Sweden – local government in Sweden: flexibility and independence in a unitary state, in *Local Government in Europe: The 'Fourth Level' in the EU Multilayered System of Governance*, ed. by C. Panara, M. Varney (Routledge, Oxford, 2013). pp. 305 ff

C. Pinelli, *Forme di stato e forme di governo* (Jovene, Napoli, 2007)

A. Reposo, *Profili dello Stato autonomico*, 2nd edn. (Giappichelli, Torino, 2005)

S. Ricci, The Committee of the Regions and the challenge of European governance, in *The Role of the Regions in EU Governance*, ed. by C. Panara, A. De Becker (Springer, Berlin/Heidelberg, 2011). pp. 109 ff

S. Romano, *L'ordinamento giuridico* (Sansoni, Firenze, 1951) (reprint of the 2nd ed. 1946)

G. Sartori, *Democrazia. Cosa è*, 2nd edn. (Rizzoli, Milano, 2007)

F.W. Scharpf et al., *Politikverflechtung: Theorie und Empirie des kooperativen Foederalismus in der Bundesrepublik* (Kronberg et al., Scriptor, 1976)

R. Schütze, *European Constitutional Law* (CUP, Cambridge, 2012)

A. Spadaro, Costituzionalismo, in *Enciclopedia filosofica*, vol. III (Bompiani, Milano, 2006), p. 2369

P. Stephenson, Twenty years of multilevel governance: 'Where Does It Come From? What Is It? Where Is It Going?'. J. Eur. Public Policy **20**(6), 817 f. (2013)

F. Tönnies, *Community and Association* (Routledge, London, 1955) [English translation of *Gemeinschaft und Gesellschaft*, 1887]

M. Volpi, Stato federale e stato regionale: due modelli a confronto. Quaderni Costituzionali **15**(3), 367 f. (1995)

A. von Bogdandy, Zweierlei Verfassungsrecht. Europäisierung als Gefährdung des gesellschaftlichen Grundkonsenses? Der Staat **39**(2), 163 f. (2000)

A. von Bogdandy, Founding principles, in *Principles of European Constitutional Law*, ed. by A. von Bogdandy, J. Bast, 2nd edn. (Hart, Oxford, 2009). pp. 11 ff

M. Weber, *Economia e società*, vol. I (Comunità, Milano, 1999) [Italian translation of *Wirtschaft und Gesellschaft*, Economy and Society, 1922]

W. Wessels, An ever closer fusion? A dynamic macropolitical view on integration processes. J. Common Mark. Stud. **35**(2), 268 f. (1997)

A. Wimmel, Theorizing the democratic legitimacy of European governance: a Labyrinth with no exit? J. Eur. Integr. **31**(2), 181 f. (2009)

Chapter 7
Summary Thoughts and Agenda for Future Research

A

Sub-national authorities are an integral part of the European edifice and enjoy rights and duties in accordance with the asymmetric constitutional mosaic resulting from the combination of EU and domestic constitutional laws (multilevel constitutionalism theory). A number of elements corroborate this submission:

1) In the EU multilevel system, Treaty making/amendment is not an exclusive prerogative of the Member States. In some Member States, the sub-national authorities are involved in these processes, and in the case of Belgium each regional parliament can veto the entry into force of a new Treaty.
2) The lawmaking process in the Council is not entirely 'State dominated'. The sub-national entities enjoy participation rights that result from the combination of EU and national processes.
3) Sub-national authorities have a duty to comply with EU obligations and at the same time a right to implement EU law and policy in the areas falling within their responsibility. In a number of Member States, failure by a sub-national authority to comply with EU obligations causes a financial liability of the responsible sub-national authority and could also originate the exercise of State substitution powers. At the same time, infringement proceedings initiated by the Commission are not necessarily a matter concerning exclusively the Member State; the sub-national authorities in some Member States are involved in those proceedings.
4) The ECJ's jurisprudence on locus standi is rather 'State centric', insofar as the sub-national authorities are granted limited rights to challenge Union acts *directly* before Union Courts. However, a holistic analysis embracing both the EU and the Member State levels reveals that in some Member States the sub-national authorities can oblige the Member State to initiate judicial proceedings on their behalf. The Treaty of Lisbon introduced the Committee of the Regions' right to bring a direct challenge before the ECJ on grounds of

© Springer International Publishing Switzerland 2015
C. Panara, *The Sub-national Dimension of the EU*,
DOI 10.1007/978-3-319-14589-1_7

subsidiarity, as well as the right of each chamber of national parliament (including second chambers representing the sub-national authorities) to oblige the State to bring a direct challenge before the ECJ on grounds of subsidiarity.

The status of the sub-national authorities in the EU multilevel system (i.e., the EU-related rights and duties of the sub-national authorities) enjoys a considerable degree of strength and stability. The legal position of these authorities is an outcome of the EU as a 'compound of constitutions' (*Verfassungsverbund*[1]) since their position is rooted in the EU primary law (the 'constitutional charter' of the Union) and in the State constitution. Accordingly, in addition to its 'political' dimension (descriptive), multilevel governance, to be intended as the way the various levels of governance shall be linked and work with each other, also has a 'legal' dimension (prescriptive). This legal dimension shall be reflected into hard law (as well as soft law arrangements) at national and Union levels. Soft law arrangements, alone, do not necessarily provide the stability that is required for the achievement of the strategic Treaty objectives linked to multilevel governance in the EU.

B

Multilevel governance is a principle resulting from the EU constitutional composite and, more precisely, a 'procedural' principle commanding a 'method of governance'. It is linked to the achievement of substantive key objectives of the Union. These are the protection of regional/local self-government as an integral part of the national identity (cf. Article 4(2) TEU), the principle of subsidiarity (cf. Article 5 (3) TEU), the principle of openness and closeness to the citizen (cf. Article 10 (3) TEU). According to the Committee of the Regions' White Paper of 2009 and to the European Charter of 2014, multilevel governance commands participation and involvement of the sub-national authorities in EU lawmaking and policymaking and in the implementation phase of EU law and policy.[2] The previous analysis has demonstrated that this involvement is required by the Member States' constitutions in order to protect regional and local autonomy as an essential feature of their constitutional identity. It is also required by EU primary law since the Union must

---

[1] Cf. Pernice (2010), pp. 102 ff. On multilevel constitutionalism theory, see Pernice (2009), pp. 349 ff.

[2] Committee of the Regions (2009), at front page. The same notion is adopted in the European Charter of Multilevel Governance (cf. Preamble): 'We stand for a multilevel-governance Europe "based on coordinated action by the European Union, the Member States and regional and local authorities according to the principles of subsidiarity, proportionality and partnership, taking the form of operational and institutional cooperation in the drawing up and implementation of the European Union's policies"'. In the literature, cf. Warleigh (1999), pp. 6–7.

respect the 'national identity' of the Member States, to be understood as their 'constitutional identity' (cf. Article 4(2) TEU).

C

Despite a number of analogies with some traditional forms of government such as federalism and regionalism, multilevel governance has an own conceptual autonomy in that it creates a unique multilevel game among supranational, national and sub-national players in the context of the EU multilevel system. At the same time, the constitutional requirement of participation of the regional and local authorities in EU governance creates a strong similarity between multilevel governance and cooperative federalism. It is not a case that some scholars describe the multilevel participation that is typical of multilevel governance in the EU as 'double political entanglement' (*doppelte Politikverflechtung*). In this way, they establish a parallel between multilevel governance and the German model of cooperative federalism.[3]

D

The raison d'être of multilevel governance is to contribute *legitimacy* to the participation of the Member States in the EU and to the EU decision-making activity. Legitimacy (objective 'input legitimacy' erga omnes) can be conveyed only by structured participation procedures at national and EU levels, provided that these meet certain criteria (openness, equality and effectiveness). Mere lobbying by single regions or their associations can be fruitful for these regions and lead to subjective 'output legitimacy', but it does not achieve full and objective legitimacy.[4] The implementation of multilevel governance is required for legitimacy of Member States' participation in the EU and, as a result, for the legitimacy of the EU lawmaking and policymaking and of the Union as a supranational organisation. The core idea of multilevel governance is similar to the concept of 'participation to compensate the loss of autonomy', which characterises the German federal system. In Germany, the Länder have suffered over the years an erosion of their statehood,

---

[3] Cf. Hrbek (1986), pp. 17 ff. The concept of 'political entanglement' (*Politikverflechtung*) was created by Fritz Scharpf during the 1970s to describe the German federal system. Cf. Scharpf et al. (1976).

[4] See Table 3.1. Respect for 'national identity' by the EU (cf. Art. 4(2) TEU) and therefore 'legitimacy' is ensured *not only* by participation in multilevel governance but also by the recognition of the role of regional/local authorities in other sectors, such as 'locus standi' ex Article 263 TFEU, adequate defence/participation mechanisms in case of substitution powers of the State and of infraction proceedings, appropriate involvement in the implementation of EU law/policy (cf. supra Chap. 2).

due in particular to the increasing concentration of legislative power in the hands of the Federation.[5] However, at the same time, the Länder obtained important rights of participation in the exercise of federal powers through the Bundesrat, the chamber representing the Länder on the federal level. In the EU, which embraces both Member States and infra-state units (EU atypical multilevel system), some participation rights must be granted also to the infra-state entities. The EU multilevel system is asymmetrical, and the participation rights of the sub-state entities depend *largely* on the role assigned to each tier of government in the constitutional system of each Member State. The Union shall prompt tools that the Member States and their sub-national entities have the right to use. For example, the Union allows for the participation of regional ministers in the Council (cf. Article 16(2) TEU); the Union also features an ad hoc body, the Committee of the Regions, representing a (hypothetical) 'third level'; last but not least, the Union has created instruments promoting sub-national involvement in the EU decision-making process and/or in the implementation of EU law and policy (for example, the 'structured dialogue' and the tripartite contracts). All these mechanisms follow the logic of multilevel governance, whose aim is to reconcile the constitutional standing of the infra-state units and supranational integration in the EU. In this way, multilevel governance arrangements can legitimise the European system of governance through an effective involvement of the sub-national entities in the making and in the implementation phases of EU law and policy.

E

As an all-embracing principle commanding a 'method of governance' for the EU, multilevel governance is expected to have an impact on other cornerstone principles of the EU such as subsidiarity. This is a fundamental constitutional principle in the EU, Germany and Italy. In all these systems, subsidiarity aims primarily to protect the *autonomy* of the lower echelons of government by favouring proximity of power to the citizen. Multilevel governance is based on 'coexistence and interaction', i.e., autonomy of and coordinated action/cooperation between different layers of government. By contrast, subsidiarity embodies the idea of 'exception', i.e., that only exceptionally powers shall be exercised by higher layers of government, the rule being proximity of governance to the citizen.[6] Subsidiarity became a judicially enforceable principle both in Germany and in Italy, even though, more often, courts have upheld the 'exception' (i.e., action by the central authority), rather than protecting proximity. Subsidiarity typically became a tool justifying intervention by the central authority. The key role of multilevel governance in relation to

---

[5] Cf. Erbguth (1995), pp. 549 ff.; Hesse (1962).

[6] Swaine (2000), pp. 53–54, even suggests that the principle of subsidiarity entails a presumption of competence in favour of the Member States.

subsidiarity is to promote a shift of focus from the negative (exceptionality of the intervention by the central authority) to the positive, inclusive, aspect of subsidiarity, i.e., that all the layers of government must contribute, in areas of their responsibility, to the achievement of the Union's objectives. In the multilevel systems analysed (Germany, Italy and EU), the appropriate locus for the enforcement of subsidiarity is not the courtroom but participation in the lawmaking and policymaking processes in accordance with partnership and loyal cooperation. Judicial enforcement plays a role only if there is a clear or evident abuse, i.e., where the attribution of a certain power to the central authority is illogical or untenable. Multilevel governance requires 'co-governance' by a plurality of levels of government of a field in which a power is exercised by a central authority but in which essential interests of the other levels are also at stake. In this way, cooperation also addresses the issue of *legitimacy* of authoritative decision-making. This is a fundamental feature of the early warning system, whose proper functioning requires the involvement of national parliaments and of regional parliaments with legislative powers. The early warning system, despite the difficulties of its functioning, 'proceduralises' the principle of subsidiarity, insofar as it creates a two-way communication channel between the institutions and the parliaments and promotes multilevel dialogue. This implies that the role of the CJEU for the enforcement of subsidiarity, apart from extreme and unlikely events of clear or evident abuse of power by the EU, could be confined to the enforcement of a procedure of political negotiation.[7]

F

In all the examined regional case studies (Baden-Württemberg, Lombardia, Liverpool City Region), a constitutional duty emerges, as well as a right, of the 'regions' to participate in the EU decision-making process. This 'duty' has been called 'responsibility for integration in the EU' and incorporates an obligation to work on the EU level in the interest of the local community and territory.[8] This is a result of the nature of the 'region' as a public law entity that is the expression of a territorial community. As a result, this entity has to pursue the interests of the community both when an interest has a local dimension and when it has a supranational (EU) dimension, i.e., it is impacted on by EU law and policy.

A few trends were highlighted in the previous analysis. These include the tendency to represent the region as a 'system' on the EU level (for example, the

---

[7] Nettesheim has recently proposed the oxymoronic notion of 'politisches Recht' (political law), indicating those legal provisions that are only or principally enforceable through forms of political coordination (*politische Koordination*). The role of the courts in this field is limited to the enforcement of the procedures of political coordination. Cf. Nettesheim (2014a, b).

[8] See Nettesheim (30 July 2009), paragraph 3; Nettesheim (2010), pp. 177–178.

'System-Lombardia'), i.e., to use the regional contact channels with the EU as a way to defend the interests of regional stakeholders (companies, research institutions, specialised agencies, etc.). This is a result of the eclipse of a rigidly defined 'remit' of the various players in the context of EU multilevel governance. The regions do not act necessarily *only* in the areas falling within their remit as defined by the national constitution. They engage on the EU level any time this is required by the need to protect interests rooted in the local community and territory. Arguably, multilevel governance in the context of European integration has led to partly overcoming the rigid allocation of responsibilities that is traditionally adopted by national constitutional law. This tendency is exemplified also by recent legislative innovations at national level. The Localism Act 2011 introduced in the UK a general power of competence of local authorities (see Part 1, Chapter 1 of the Act). According to this, subject to existing limitations in the law, local authorities have a responsibility to take care of all the interests stemming from the local community, even if these interests have a dimension that goes beyond the mere local level, for example a European dimension. Another tendency emerging from the previous analysis is that in the case of Liverpool (and also in Lombardia), both Type 1 (the regional authority) and Type 2 multilevel governance players (specialised agencies, such as transport or waste and recycling authorities, etc.) are involved in lobbying activity on the EU level.

Another thread common to the three regional case studies is that direct contacts with the national government (or with the permanent representation in Brussels) and lobbying are generally perceived as more effective communication channels than national mechanisms of participation in the EU. This is especially the case in Italy, where the participation mechanisms (State–Regions Conference and CIAE) are rather weak, and in England, where there is no structured form of participation of the local authorities in determining the national position in the EU. The situation is more complicated in Germany, where, thanks to the Bundesrat, the participation of the Länder in EU affairs is potentially more influential. Even in Baden-Württemberg, though, it emerges that direct communication with the EU institutions or the permanent representation of Germany is typically perceived by local politicians and public officials as more effective than internal participation through the Bundesrat. This is essentially due to the fact that internal participation requires horizontal cooperation (i.e., coordination with the other Länder), in addition to vertical cooperation (i.e., coordination with the Federal Government), and this can be both difficult and time consuming.

Lobbying of the Commission, the MEPs, etc., is therefore the primary tool used by the regions to play a role in the EU political arena. However, lobbying requires appropriate resources (e.g., skilled staff, adequate budgetary provision) and particularly the ability to create alliances with other players. This explains why a key element of the strategy of all the analysed regions is to take part in regional networks both for lobbying purposes and for reaching a 'critical mass' for attracting EU funding to the regional territory.

The practical importance of lobbying alongside (or even above) domestic participation channels may raise legitimacy issues. National coordination mechanisms aimed to define the national position in the Council are typically based on the involvement of all the relevant sub-national players on an equal footing. Direct lobbying by sub-national players or networks of national players does not offer a comparable guarantee in terms of objective legitimacy of the EU decision-making process. A key issue in this context is promoting the accountability of the regional offices in Brussels to the local community, as well as making sure that the lobbying activity pursues democratically selected interests originating from the local community. The previous analysis highlights that more 'structured' regions, such as Baden-Württemberg and Lombardia, where the office is a part of the executive branch and the regional government is under the control of the regional parliament, are better equipped to subject the selection of interests to the democratic control of the local community. By contrast, the situation is more fluid and ambiguous in Merseyside, where the office is not immediately accountable to elected politicians and is not adequately linked to the wider local community.

The national participation mechanisms in place for the regional players in Germany and in Italy contribute to reshaping the role of the nation-state in certain areas of regional responsibility. In these areas, the central government should become a coordinator of regional interests. However, the system, despite its importance for legitimacy purposes, does not always hold together for two main reasons. First, because the entire 'philosophy' of the national participation system revolves around a rigid concept of 'remit' (for example, legislative remit), moving from the assumption that the simple circumstance that the regions have responsibilities in a certain field generates automatically an interest in participating in the formation of the national position in the EU. In reality, the previous analysis suggests that, irrespective of the regional remit (i.e., also outside and beyond such remit), more practical interests, for example economic activities taking place in the regional territory, are far more likely to generate an interest in participating in the EU decision-making process on the national and EU levels.

Second and more importantly, the system does not hold together because it is based on the idea that the national government, i.e. the nation-state, can always coordinate successfully the interests of the regional players. The experience demonstrates that this is not always the case and that the regions are sometimes in disagreement with the national government (as well as with fellow regions from the same country). For this reason, regional players, especially those with sufficient resources to play a role on the EU level, if they cannot have the central government on their side, may choose to lobby the EU institutions directly and to take part in asymmetrical and changeable coalitions of regions, Member States, associations, etc., which push towards solutions opposed by the government of the own Member State.

G

Multilevel governance contributes to constitutionalism in the EU both by limiting the exercise of authoritative decision-making power by the Union and by the Member States and by expanding the role of the sub-national communities beyond the sub-national and national dimension, i.e., by projecting them onto the EU level.

Multilevel governance does not address directly the democratic deficit of the EU; however, it contributes positively to democracy in the EU through the establishment of an atypical form of participatory democracy. It is 'atypical' because it is based on the participation and involvement of democratically representative territorial authorities in the EU decision-making process. Engagement of sub-national players on the EU level, along with asymmetrical and variable coalitions (alleanze a geometria variabile) among sub-national authorities and other players, are an important component of the EU atypical participatory democracy.

H

Like any piece of research, also this book, whilst answering some questions, inevitably raises others that were not planned for or anticipated. Far from being a defeat, this should be seen in an optimistic light and help sketch out a possible research agenda for the future. In particular, there are two main questions that have been raised by the previous analysis and that are a gap in the current knowledge on multilevel governance in the EU. The first question concerns the choice between participation mechanisms at national level and direct contact with the EU institutions (lobbying through the regional offices). It is to be expected that different regional actors would behave differently, with more reliance on participation mechanisms at national level by smaller and poorer regional authorities and a preference for direct contact on the EU level by bigger and richer players. This hypothesis will be tested through a comparative analysis of the behaviour of four Italian Regions and four German Länder.[9]

The second question concerns specifically the role of the regional offices in Brussels. The work of these offices is key to bringing the Union closer to the citizen,

---

[9] The research will focus on the following:
  Lombardia (big and rich),
  Valle d'Aosta (small and rich),
  Sicilia (big and poor), and
  Basilicata (small and poor)
  and on
  Baden-Württemberg (big and rich),
  Bremen (small and rich),
  Sachsen (big and poor), and
  Saarland (small and poor).

as envisaged by Article 10(3) TEU. To this purpose, the offices need to be closely linked to the local community; their work needs to undergo the scrutiny by local democratically elected assemblies, whilst transparency and openness have to become a fundamental feature of this work. Only in this way would the office be a projection of the local community on the EU level. Therefore, the task of future research should be investigating how regional offices can fulfil these criteria and envisage appropriate solutions for this problem.[10] These research ideas will be implemented in the next few months and will be published in the form of journal articles or book chapters.

References

Committee of the Regions, *White Paper on Multilevel Governance*, 17–18 June 2009

W. Erbguth, Erosion der Ländereigenstaatlichkeit. Art. 30 GG und unitarische Entwicklungen national- wie gemeinschafsrechtlichen Ursprungs, in *Verfassungsrecht im Wandel*, ed. by J. Ipsen (Carl Heymanns, Köln, 1995), pp. 549 ff

K. Hesse, *Der unitarische Bundesstaat* (C.F. Müller, Karlsruhe, 1962)

R. Hrbek, Doppelte Politikverflechtung: Deutscher Föderalismus und Europäische Integration. Die deutschen Länder im EG-Entscheidungsprozeß, in *Die Deutschen Länder und die Europäischen Gemeinschaften*, ed. by R. Hrbek, U. Thaysen (Nomos, Baden-Baden, 1986), pp. 17 ff

M. Nettesheim, *Die Integrationsverantwortung der Länder – Folgerungen aus dem Urteil des Bundesverfassungsgerichts vom 30. Juni 2009 ("Lissabon-Urteil")*, Tübingen, 30 July 2009

M. Nettesheim, Die Integrationsverantwortung – Vorgaben des BVerfG und gesetzgeberischen Umsetzung. Neue Juristische Wochenschrift (NJW) **4**, 177 f. (2010)

M. Nettesheim, *Subsidiarität durch politische Koordination*, paper presented at the symposium "Grenzen Europäischer Normgebung – EU-Kompetenzen und Europäische Grundrechte", Frankfurt am Main, 19 March 2014a

M. Nettesheim, Subsidiarität durch politische Verhandlung – Art. 5 Abs. 3 EUV als entmaterialisierte Verfahrensnorm, in *Grenzen europäischer Normgebung*, ed. by D. König, D. Uwer (Bucerius Law School Press, Hamburg, 2014b)

I. Pernice, The Treaty of Lisbon: multilevel constitutionalism in action. Columbia J. Eur. Law **15** (3), 349 f. (2009)

I. Pernice, Verfassungsverbund, in *Strukturfragen der Europäischen Union*, ed. by C. Franzius (Nomos, Baden-Baden, 2010). pp. 102 ff

F.W. Scharpf et al., *Politikverflechtung: Theorie und Empirie des kooperativen Foederalismus in der Bundesrepublik* (Kronberg et al., Scriptor, 1976)

E.T. Swaine, Subsidiarity and self-interest: federalism at the European Court of Justice. Harv. Int. Law J. **41**(1), 1 f. (2000)

A. Warleigh, *The Committee of the Regions: Institutionalising Multi-Level Governance?* (Kogan Page, London, 1999)

---

[10] The intention of the author of this book is to delve into this issue with specific reference to the regional offices of UK local authorities.

Appendix: Charter for Multilevel Governance in Europe

Preamble

Given that many competences and responsibilities are shared between the various levels of governance in the European Union, we recognise the need **TO WORK TOGETHER IN PARTNERSHIP** to achieve greater economic, social and territorial cohesion in Europe. No single level can deal with the challenges we face alone. We can solve citizens' problems on the ground by **COOPERATING** better and running **JOINT PROJECTS** to tackle the common challenges ahead of us.

We stand for a multilevel-governance Europe **"based on coordinated action by the European Union, the Member States and regional and local authorities according to the principles of subsidiarity, proportionality and partnership, taking the form of operational and institutional cooperation in the drawing up and implementation of the European Union's policies"**. In this endeavour, we fully respect the equal legitimacy and accountability of each level within their respective competences and the principle of loyal cooperation.

Aware of our **INTERDEPENDENCE** and ever seeking greater **EFFICIENCY**, we believe that great opportunities exist to further strengthen innovative and efficient political and administrative cooperation between our authorities based on their respective competences and responsibilities. The objective of this Charter, drawn up by the Committee of the Regions of the European Union, is to **connect regions and cities across Europe**, whilst promoting **MULTI-ACTORSHIP** with societal actors such as the social partners, universities, NGOs and representative civil society groupings.

In line with the **SUBSIDIARITY** principle which places decisions at the most effective level and as close as possible to the citizens, we attach great importance to co-creating policy solutions that reflect the needs of citizens.

It is precisely through our commitment to the fundamental **VALUES, PRINCIPLES** and **PROCESSES** underpinning multilevel governance that we believe new modes of **DIALOGUE** and partnership will emerge across public authorities

© Springer International Publishing Switzerland 2015
C. Panara, *The Sub-national Dimension of the EU*,
DOI 10.1007/978-3-319-14589-1

in the European Union and beyond. Multilevel governance strengthens openness, participation, **COORDINATION** and **JOINT COMMITMENT** to delivering targeted solutions.

It allows us to harness Europe's diversity as a driver for capitalising on the assets of our local areas. Making full use of digital solutions, we are committed to increasing **TRANSPARENCY** and offering quality public services easily accessible to the citizens we represent.

MULTILEVEL GOVERNANCE helps us to learn from each other, experiment with innovative policy solutions, **SHARE BEST PRACTICES** and further develop **PARTICIPATORY DEMOCRACY**, bringing the European Union closer to the citizens. We believe that embracing multilevel governance contributes to deeper EU integration by further strengthening the ties between our territories, and overcoming the administrative hurdles in regulation and policy implementation and the geographical frontiers that separate us.

Title 1: Fundamental Principles

We commit ourselves to respecting the fundamental processes that shape multilevel governance practices in Europe by:

1.1. developing a **TRANSPARENT, OPEN** and **INCLUSIVE** policy-making process;
1.2. promoting **PARTICIPATION** and **PARTNERSHIP** involving relevant public and private stakeholders throughout the policy-making process, including through appropriate digital tools, whilst respecting the rights of all institutional partners;
1.3. fostering **POLICY EFFICIENCY, POLICY COHERENCE** and promoting **BUDGET SYNERGIES** between all levels of governance;
1.4. respecting **SUBSIDIARITY** and **PROPORTIONALITY** in policy making;
1.5. ensuring maximum **FUNDAMENTAL RIGHTS PROTECTION** at all levels of governance.

Title 2: Implementation and Delivery

We commit ourselves to making multilevel governance a reality in day-to-day policy-making and delivery, including through innovative and digital solutions. To this end, we should:

2.1. **PROMOTE CITIZEN PARTICIPATION** in the policy cycle;
2.2. **COOPERATE** closely with other public authorities by thinking beyond traditional administrative borders, procedures and hurdles;

2.3. **FOSTER A EUROPEAN MIND-SET** within our political bodies and administrations;

2.4. **STRENGTHEN INSTITUTIONAL CAPACITY BUILDING** and invest in policy learning amongst all levels of governance;

2.5. **CREATE NETWORKS** between our political bodies and administrations from the local to the European levels and vice-versa, whilst strengthening transnational cooperation.